7 Day

University of Plymouth Library

Subject to status this item may be renewed
via your Voyager account

http://voyager.plymouth.ac.uk

Exeter tel: (01392) 475049
Exmouth tel: (01395) 255331
Plymouth tel: (01752) 232323

ISLAM IN EUROPE

For my parents

Islam in Europe

Integration or Marginalization?

ROBERT J. PAULY, JR.
Midlands Technical College/Norwich University

ASHGATE

Published by
Ashgate Publishing Limited
Gower House
Croft Road
Aldershot
Hants GU11 3HR
England

Ashgate Publishing Company
Suite 420
101 Cherry Street
Burlington, VT 05401-4405
USA

Ashgate website: http://www.ashgate.com

British Library Cataloguing in Publication Data
Pauly, Robert J.
  Islam in Europe : integration or marginalization?
  1. Islam - Europe 2. Muslims - Europe - Social conditions
  3. Muslims - Civil rights - Europe 4. Assimilation
  (Sociology) 5. Marginality, Social - Europe - Religious
  aspects - Islam
  I. Title
  305.6'97104

Library of Congress Cataloging-in-Publication Data
Pauly, Robert J., 1967-
  Islam in Europe : integration or marginalization? / Robert J. Pauly, Jr.
    p. cm.
  Includes bibliographical references and index.
  ISBN 0-7546-4100-7
    1. Islam--Europe. 2. Muslims--Europe--Social conditions. 3. Europe-Ethnic relations.
  I. Title.

D1056.2.M87P38 2004
305.6'97'094--dc22   2003063540

ISBN 0 7546 4100 7

Printed and bound in Great Britain by MPG Books Ltd, Bodmin, Cornwall

Contents

Acknowledgments

This book would not have been possible without the assistance and support of a wide range of colleagues, family members and friends. In particular, I would like to express my gratitude to the following individuals for their roles in helping me to bring the project to fruition: my editor, Kirstin Howgate, for her encouragement and support throughout the editorial process; Irene Poulton for her assistance during the review and editorial processes; Maureen Mansell-Ward, for her diligent checking of the text; Tom Lansford for his friendship and encouragement; Simon Serfaty for his advice and guidance in this project and throughout my academic and professional careers; Peter Schulman and Xiushi Yang for their guidance in the project; Regina Karp for her guidance and support during my graduate school career; Carl Boyd for his friendship, encouragement and professional guidance; Scott Brunstetter, Jim Medler, Eric Miller and Octavius Pinkard for their friendship and camaraderie during my graduate school days; the late Bob Waive for his friendship and love of life; Markus Schmidbauer for his friendship and hospitality; Ambriel Nance for her friendship, kindness and ubiquitous smile; Kelly Whitlock and her staff at Kelly's Deli & Pub for providing me with an occasional break from the rigors of the research, writing and revision processes; and to Peggy, Bob, Mark, Chris, Sami, John and Missy Pauly for their perpetual love and support in all of my personal and professional endeavors.

Chapter 1

Introduction

Islam in Europe: Manifestations of Marginalization

In January 1989, Muslim activists staged a demonstration in the city of Bradford in north-central England, the culmination of which was the burning of a copy of British author Salman Rushdie's *The Satanic Verses*. Organized by the Bradford Council of Mosques (BCM) in response to what it perceived as a derogatory portrayal of Islam in general and the prophet Muhammad specifically in the novel, the event received extensive local, national and international media coverage. It followed an unsuccessful request by the United Kingdom Action Committee on Islamic Affairs three months earlier for the British government to ban the release of Rushdie's work for public perusal. Subsequently, Iranian cleric Ayatollah Khomeini issued an Islamic decree (*fatwa*) demanding Rushdie's execution, a measure that garnered the support of the BCM and served to heighten Muslim-Christian tensions across the United Kingdom.[1] As British journalist Adam LeBor notes, the "scars on both sides still run deep, still shaping perceptions, strengthening stereotypes and entrenching mutual acrimony."[2]

Eight months after the onset of the imbroglio in Bradford, three female students of North African ethnic extraction attempted to wear their traditional Islamic head scarves (*foulards*) while attending classes at the Gabriel Havez Secondary School in Creil, a small town just north of Paris. School officials excluded the girls from classes on the premise that their *foulards* were a form of religious expression and thus in violation of the French government's 1905 law separating church and state affairs. Ultimately, national officials backed the Creil decision, albeit through an ambiguous ruling suggesting that future disputes of that nature be handled on a case-by-case basis at the local level.[3] The *foulard* affair sparked a vigorous national debate that focused both on the particulars of the Creil episode and the broader standing of Muslims in French society, the most significant result of which to date was the National Assembly's February 2004 passage of a law specifically banning all prominent religious symbols from public schools.

Nearly a decade following the eruption of the *foulard* affair, a similarly divisive series of developments highlighted broadly similar ethnic, religious, social and political tensions in Germany. In January 1999, the government of the southeastern German *Länd* of Bavaria deported a 14-year-old boy of Turkish descent to Istanbul on the pretext of a series of minor criminal infractions. The youth—identified generically in media accounts as Mehmet—was born in Munich to Turkish immigrant parents and had lived there throughout his life. However, he did not possess German citizenship, a circumstance that enabled Bavarian authorities to enact deportation proceedings.[4]

Furthermore, Mehmet's deportation was carried out concurrent with the development of a heated national debate over a proposal by the ruling Social Democratic Party (SPD) government to reform a 1913 law mandating that only those of purely German ethnicity receive citizenship.[5]

Though separated by time, space and contextual distinctions, these three sets of developments are related in that they reflect a fundamental societal divide between the Christian and Muslim segments of the population of a given state in contemporary Western Europe. Such divisions, in turn, have grown out of religious as well as ethnic, racial and socio-economic differences pitting native-born majorities against non-European minority groups within nation-states across the region over the past half-century.

The exclusion of Muslims of myriad ethnic backgrounds from the economic, political and social benefits afforded to the majority populations of European Union member states generally and those situated in France, Germany and the United Kingdom specifically is a modern manifestation of this long contentious relationship. The marginalization of Muslims in these states is driven in large part by widespread Western misperceptions of Islam as a monolithic faith whose adherents possess a universal penchant for the proliferation of radical religious fundamentalism, irrespective of their variegated ethnic and national backgrounds. The fact that Islam permeates both public and private life in often highly visible manners—the wearing of headscarves or full veils by women and calls to prayer over loudspeakers, for example—fuels such misjudgments in societies within which these types of behavior are not the norm.[6] As John Esposito notes, the "modern notion of religion as a system of personal belief makes an Islam that is comprehensive in scope, in which Islam is integral to policy and society, 'abnormal' in so far as it departs from an accepted 'modern' secular norm. Thus, Islam becomes incomprehensible, irrational, extremist, threatening."[7]

In Western Europe, where governments advocate and most citizens accept the tempered practice of Christian faiths such as Protestantism and Catholicism in the context of overtly secular societies, strict adherence to the tenets of Islam appears out of place. However, the permanent exclusion of Muslims from the mainstream is not an acceptable solution. Rather, it is essential that members of the majority and minority attempt to develop an inclusive society with room for a European brand of Islam that will serve the spiritual needs of second, third and fourth generation Muslims born and raised on the continent. Tariq Ramadan, a second generation European Muslim of Egyptian descent, has proposed precisely such an approach. According to Ramadan, "[w]e need to separate Islamic principles from their cultures of origin and anchor them in the cultural reality of Western Europe. I can incorporate everything that's not opposed to my religion into my identity and that's a revolution."[8] If pursued in a balanced manner, such an integration process is likely to enhance rather than detract from the respective identities of the majorities and minorities involved. As Ramadan argues, "[i]nstead of thinking in cold, formal terms of a passive integration of Muslims, we should be looking enthusiastically to make a positive contribution in building a new

Europe. Their presence is a source of richness: it contributes to reflection on the place of spirituality in secularized societies and on the egalitarian promotion of religious and cultural pluralism."[9]

The issue of Islam in Europe is relevant at present primarily because of the increasing prevalence of Muslims both regionally in the context of the EU and nationally in its most economically and politically influential states—France, Germany and the United Kingdom. Currently, there are approximately four to six million Muslims residing in France,[10] 2.8-3.24 million in Germany[11] and 1.6-1.8 million in the United Kingdom.[12] The communities in which they live are composed primarily of Algerians, Moroccans and Tunisians in the French case, Turks, Kurds and Bosnians in the German case, and Pakistanis, Bangladeshis and Indians in the British case. At the broader regional level, there are approximately 12-15 million Muslims living in EU member states, with that total expected to climb to 23 million by 2015.[13] Put simply, such demographic projections suggest that the need to integrate Western Europe's Muslims will only grow more pronounced in the future.

Research Questions

With the aforementioned anecdotal and statistical evidence providing a necessary contextual foundation, this book will address the following research questions:

- First, what causal factors have engendered the development of waves of Muslim migrants and subsequent establishment and entrenchment of Islamic communities in France, Germany and the United Kingdom since the end of World War II? To what extent are these factors related?
- Second, at present, what cultural, economic, ethnic, linguistic, political, religious and social characteristics distinguish Muslims from the societal majorities in France, Germany and the United Kingdom?
- Third, to what extent have such characteristics served to exclude Muslims from acceptance by the majority populations of France, Germany and the United Kingdom and the accompanying economic, political and social benefits?
- Fourth, how effectively have the French, German and British governments facilitated the integration of Muslims—individually and communally—within their respective societies over the past two decades?
- Fifth, at what level of government—local, regional, national or supranational—are policies fashioned to fully integrate Muslims in France, Germany and the United Kingdom likely to prove most effective?
- Sixth, what benchmarks are likely to prove most useful in judging the extent of integration of Muslim minorities within the French, German and British societies?
- Seventh, what domestic and international consequences have the failure to fully integrate Muslims in France, Germany and the United Kingdom entailed over the past two decades? How are the roles of Muslims most likely to change vis-à-vis

the political processes in those states in the future?
- Eighth, to what extent can the EU assist France, Germany and the United Kingdom in developing more inclusive policies with regard to their respective Muslim communities over both the short and long terms?
- Ninth, what is the most likely course for interaction among ethnically and religiously distinctive Muslims and Christians in the contexts of Western Europe generally and France, Germany and the United Kingdom specifically in the future?

Theses

In addressing these research questions, the book will present and discuss the following interconnected theses:

- First, the growth of Islamic communities concurrent with the aging of the majority populations of France, Germany and the United Kingdom over the past half-century has created an as yet unmet need to fully integrate Muslims of variegated ethnic backgrounds within the societies of those states. That need is certain to grow more pronounced as the proportion of Muslims residing therein increases.
- Second, the failure to fully integrate Muslims within the societies of France, Germany and the United Kingdom has the potential to foster social and political instability in those states over both the short and long terms.
- Third, the construction of an effective framework to fully integrate Muslims within the French, German and British societies—and, ultimately, in the broader Western European context—over the long term will necessarily entail interactive policy formulation, coordination and implementation at the local, regional, national and supranational levels. However, given the prevalence of Islamic communities in particular localities and the resultant higher degree of interaction among Muslims and governmental authorities in those environs as opposed to the limited dispersion of Muslims regionally and nationally in France, Germany and the United Kingdom, a local-level approach is more desirable in the short term.
- Fourth, once the full integration of Muslim minorities—or at least positive progress toward the achievement of that objective—is realized within given municipalities in France, Germany or the United Kingdom, wider-ranging regional, national and supranational level projects are likely to prove more feasible in light of insights drawn from the local level.

Structure of the Book

The book addresses the research questions and theses through the presentation of six related chapters. Collectively, these chapters both examine past contributions and present original ideas on Islam in Europe generally and the integration of Muslims within France, Germany and the United Kingdom specifically. In particular, the forthcoming chapter lineup includes:

- A review of the relevant literature and placement of the book within and beyond those contributions, followed by a brief presentation of the methodology utilized.
- A case study of Islam in France.
- A case study of Islam in Germany.
- A case study of Islam in the United Kingdom.
- A case study of the broader Western European regional level with the EU as the focal point.
- A concluding section drawing linkages among the case studies, and explaining the overarching significance of the book's findings.

A general summary of these chapters appears below, in the context of which the French, German and British case studies are addressed in the same sub-section.

Literature Review

This chapter consists of two sections, the first of which necessarily dwarfs the second. The first section reviews the relevant literature on the issues of international migration, Islam and the West, and the construction of individual, communal and national identities and the pertinence of these issues vis-à-vis the integration of minority groups within given states in three parts. First, it divides the international migration literature into sections on fundamental and hybrid explanatory theories before discussing which frameworks are most useful in the Western European context. Second, it divides the Islam and the West literature into subsections on general and Western European regional approaches, placing emphases on those most applicable to France, Germany and the United Kingdom. Third, it also divides the literature on identity and minority integration into general and Western European subsections, with the latter directed primarily toward the country and regional case studies. The second section explains the significance of the book in the context of the literature discussed in the first section.

Case Studies of Islam in France, Germany and the United Kingdom

These chapters are all structured in the same manner in order to provide a clear framework to analyze the distinct evidence associated with each national context. The eight-section structure is as follows:

- An anecdotal introduction to set the scene.
- An examination of the causal process resulting in the development, establishment and entrenchment of Muslim minorities in a given country.
- An evaluation of the present level of inclusion or exclusion of those minorities

through the use of demographic, economic, socio-religious and political indicators.

- A comparison of the similarities and differences in the prevailing Muslim communal and majority national—and, where applicable—local and regional identities in that country.
- An examination of the integration models utilized by the government vis-à-vis Muslim minorities in that country, stressing both the strengths and weaknesses of those approaches.
- An evaluation of the implications of the successes and failures—sub-divided into economic, social, security and political categories—associated with the integration models employed by those countries.
- The development of a framework to improve the integration of Muslim communities in that country, with an emphasis placed on the requisite articulation of a set of uniform benchmarks for progress.
- A set of conclusions.

Case Study of Islam in Western Europe

This chapter consists of four sections. The first section discusses the contentious history of Muslim-Christian relations as pertains to Western Europe. The second section describes the transformation of Western European identity in the aftermath of World War II. The third section examines the evolving role of the EU in facilitating improvements in the integration of minority groups generally and Muslims specifically in the societies of its member states. The fourth section evaluates the potential for the development of a hybrid Euro-Islamic identity in the twenty-first century and beyond.

Conclusions

This chapter consists of six sections. The first section explains how the chapter fits into the structure of the book—in short as an analytical means to develop an effective framework to integrate Muslims into Western European societies by comparing and contrasting the four case studies. The second section examines domestic level similarities and differences in the case studies with respect to Muslim communities. The third section distinguishes domestic level similarities and differences in the case studies from the perspectives of the French, German and British governments. The fourth section denotes similarities and differences between the domestic and Western European regional case studies. The fifth section discusses the potential for the cultivation of a more ethnically and religiously inclusive Western Europe over the long term through a synthesis of linkages among the case studies. The sixth section evaluates the theses in light of the evidence presented in the case studies, and concludes by explaining incisively the significance of the study as relates to the development of a deeper understanding of the issue of Islam in contemporary Western Europe.

Methodology

This topic was chosen for three fundamental reasons. First, the growing presence of Islam has had a considerable impact on the governance of societies across Western European generally and those of France, Germany and the United Kingdom in particular over the past half-century. Yet, it has been neglected by scholars relative to the attention given to more high profile issues such as transatlantic cooperation, European integration, and national and supranational politics and leadership. This book endeavors to fill at least part of that void in research and interpretation. Second, examining the integration of Muslims in the French, German and British societies also affords one an opportunity to gain a deeper understanding of related issue areas—most notably domestic and international economics, politics and security. Third, the increasing relevance of Islam in each of the above national constructs has affected the wider EU deepening and widening processes. As a result, it is essential to address supranational as well as national trends and developments germane to the evolving relationship between Islam and Christianity within and beyond the continent.

Although by no means exhaustive, the domestic and Western European regional case studies explain in a reasonably comprehensive manner how Muslim communities have had an impact upon and been affected by governments, citizens and institutions across the region. The domestic case studies draw on past research and recent statistical data in order to provide credible descriptions of the similarities and differences in the characteristics of Muslims living in France, Germany and the United Kingdom and the roles they have played in those societies. The regional case book addresses the broader implications of the presence of Islam on the continent in terms of the evolution of the definition of European identity and the extent to which that definition will become inclusive enough to accommodate Muslims as well as Christians in the future. Articulating explicitly the many linkages between the case studies, in turn, allows for the presentation of insights that might otherwise be overlooked.

The selection of countries to feature in the case studies was not difficult. France, Germany and the United Kingdom possess the largest communities of Muslims in Western Europe and are also the most economically powerful and politically influential states in that region. While challenging in terms of the scope of the research undertaken, the inclusion of all three states is necessary in order to fully address the impact of Islam in the region. The structural similarity of the domestic case studies provides a common link from one chapter to the next. The potential for repetition this format entails—while a valid concern—is by no means insurmountable if handled through explicit explanation in sections that draw on the same general evidence (the description, for instance, of the five pillars of Islam). The European regional chapter, on the other hand, avoids repetition by focusing on many of the historical elements of the relationship between Islam and Christianity on the continent and intergovernmental and supranational issues that are not addressed in the domestic case studies.

The order in which the chapters are presented is designed to facilitate a smooth progression from discussions of the specificity of the integration of Muslims in particular domestic contexts to an examination of the broader regional implications of the presence of Islam in Europe over the long term. Similarly, the chapter comparing and contrasting the domestic and regional cases links the arguments made in each and—in so doing—highlights the study's distinctive scholarly contributions overall. The concluding section, although necessarily repetitive because of the need to revisit the theses, emphasizes the extent to which the evidence presented in the case studies validates those theses.

The book uses a variety of primary and secondary sources to support its arguments. The fact that the secondary sources exceed the primary sources markedly is a reflection of the relatively limited scope of available primary source materials on the Muslims of Western Europe. Those primary sources that were consulted and utilized are particularly germane to the descriptions of Muslim communities in the domestic case studies and the articulation of the EU's treaty-related contributions to the handling of the issues of immigration and minority integration in the regional chapter. These sources are qualitative as well as quantitative in nature and include government censuses and other data collected by national statistics offices, treaties and reports published by European supranational institutions, media accounts, polls and studies conducted by non-governmental organizations. The evidence drawn from these sources has both strengths and weaknesses, with the former naturally outweighing the latter. The book, for example, lacks a single database upon which to rely and thus loses uniformity across case studies. As a result, it does not rely on the use of elaborate statistical tests, the reliability of which typically demands such uniformity. However, by consulting a range of national and supranational governmental, non-governmental and Muslim communal sources, it gives credence to the viewpoints of a variety of actors affected by the issue of Islam in Europe.

Notes

1.   Philip Lewis, *Islamic Britain: Religion, Politics and Identity Among British Muslims— Bradford in the 1990s* (London: I.B. Tauris, 1994), 1-2; Adam LeBor, *A Heart Turned East: Among the Muslims of Europe and America* (New York: St. Martin's Press, 1998), 148-50.
2.   LeBor, *A Heart Turned East*, 149.
3.   Maxim Silverman, *Deconstructing the Nation: Immigration, Race and Citizenship in Modern France* (New York: Routledge, 1992), 1; Cynthia DeBula Baines, "L'Affaire des Foulards: Discrimination and the Price of a Secular Public Education System," *Vanderbilt Journal of Transnational Law* 29-1 (1996); Gilles Kepel, *Allah in the West: Islamic Movements in America and Europe*, trans. Susan Milner (Stanford: Stanford University Press, 1997), 180-90.
4.   "Turkish Germans," *Economist* [London] (9 January 1999); Paul Geitner, "14-year-old

Boy Finds Himself at Center of German Storm," *Associated Press* (23 September 1998).

5. "Turkish Germans." Only 160,000 of the 2.1 million Turks residing in Germany had German citizenship when the proposal was made following the September 1998 national election.

6. Nazih N. Ayuh, *Political Islam: Religion and Politics in the Third World* (New York: Routledge, 1991), 35. Ayuh notes that "Islam is indeed very much a social religion, seeking to organize the practices of social life, and above all the minute details of family life. This purpose, moreover, is not regarded as a personal pursuit, but as a social (collective) one."

7. John L. Esposito, *The Islamic Threat: Myth or Reality* (New York: Oxford University Press, 1995), 231.

8. Quoted in Nicholas Le Quesne, "Trying to Bridge a Great Divide," *Time* (11 December 2000).

9. Tariq Ramadan, "Immigration, Integration and Cooperation Policies: Europe's Muslims Find a Place for Themselves," *Le Monde Diplomatique*, 3-4 (1998).

10. Jean-Paul Gourévitch, *La France africaine: Islam, intégration, insécurité: infos et intox* (Paris: Le Pré aux Clercs, 2000), 189-90; "Islam: France's Second Religion," *Time International* (10 June 2000); Christopher Caldwell, "The Crescent and the Tricolor," *Atlantic Monthly* 287-11 (2000): 22.

11. Central Islam Institute Archives, *Muslims in Germany* (Soesen, Germany: Central Institute Islam Archives, 2001; German National Office of Statistics, *Foreign Population from a Choice of Islamic Countries in Germany* (Berlin: German National Office of Statistics, 2000); "Turkish Germans."

12. British Office for National Statistics, *Census 2001: Ethnicity and Religion* (London: British Office for National Statistics, 2002); General Register Office, Scotland, *Census 2001: Ethnicity and Religion* (Edinburgh: General Register Office, Scotland, 2002); "A Map of Muslim Britain," *Guardian* [London] (17 June 2002); "How Many British Muslims?," *Muslim Council of Britain* (2001).

13. Omer Taspinar, "Europe's Muslim Street," *Foreign Policy* 135-2 (2003); "How Restive are Europe's Muslims?," *Economist* (18 October 2001); M. Ali Kettani, "Challenges to the Organization of Muslim Communities in Western Europe," in *Political Participation and Identities of Muslims in Non-Muslim States*, ed. W.A.R. Shadid and P.S. Van Konigsveld (Kampen, Netherlands: KOK Pharos Publishing House, 1996), 33-34; Tariq Ramadan, *To Be a European Muslim* (Leicester, UK: Islamic Foundation, 1999), 120.

Chapter 2

Literature Review

Introduction

The topic of this study—the impact of Muslim immigration on society and governance in Western Europe in general and France, Germany and the United Kingdom in particular—bridges multiple academic disciplines. Most significantly, it is associated with the fields of economics, history, political science, psychology and sociology. Therefore, a review of the literature relevant to the topic must touch upon a variety of related but by no means identical theoretical frameworks. In order to address these themes incisively, this chapter employs an interdisciplinary approach categorized into three issue areas: (a) international migration, (b) Islam and the West and (c) identity/integration of minorities. After summarizing the literature germane to the topic in each of these areas, the chapter compares and contrasts the arguments made therein to those put forth in this book.

For the benefit of the reader, a summary of the chapter's format is instructive at this juncture. The chapter consists of the following four sections:

Review of Relevant Literature on International Migration

This section has two parts. The first part summarizes seven theories—the macroeconomic, microeconomic, new economics, dual labor market, world systems, networks and institutional models, respectively—that seek to explain international migration processes. The second part examines the theories among those presented in the first part that are most applicable to the Western European context and the reasons why.

Review of Relevant Literature on Islam and the West

This section is divided into two parts. The first part examines the prevailing global level theoretical approaches to the relationship between the Western and Islamic worlds—confrontational, cooperative and ambivalent. The second part focuses on the aspects of those approaches that are most germane to the Western European context generally and those of France, Germany and the United Kingdom specifically.

Review of Relevant Literature on Identity and Integration

This section also has two parts. The first part stresses the primacy of domestic over systemic level theories with respect to identity formation and the integration of minority groups in general terms. Additionally, it evaluates the utility of constructivism as an explanatory tool in this respect. The second part places an emphasis on domestic level integrative models applicable in the contexts of France, Germany and the United Kingdom in light of the distinctive identities of the majority and minority populations in these states.

Book's Contributions to the Existing Literature

This section makes three points regarding the book's contributions to the existing literature on the impact of Muslim immigration on society and governance in Western Europe generally and in France, Germany and the United Kingdom specifically. First, it emphasizes the need to draw linkages among the French, German, British and broader Western European regional case studies. Second, it develops a four-tiered integrative framework by way of a bottom-up approach proceeding from the local to the regional to the national and then to the supranational levels as a means to fully integrate Muslim minorities into the French, German, British societies. Third, it places an emphasis on Christian-Muslim relations as one of the defining issues of the twenty-first century as pertains to the completion of an inclusive, united Europe.

Review of Relevant Literature on International Migration

The field of international migration includes a variety of theoretical approaches to explain the movement of peoples from one state or region of the world to another, none of which is, in itself, wholly sufficient. As one renowned group of scholars in the field explain, present "patterns and trends in immigration . . . suggest that a full understanding of contemporary migratory processes will not be achieved by relying on the tools of one discipline alone. . . . [Because] theories conceptualize causal processes at different levels of analysis—the individual, the household, the national and the international—they cannot be assumed, a priori, to be inherently incompatible."[1] For the purposes of this review, such theories are best addressed first in terms of seven general models, those associated with macroeconomics, microeconomics, new economics, dual labor markets, world systems, migration networks and institutions.

The macroeconomic model is one of the oldest and most well known explanatory approaches to international migration studies. Put simply, it attributes migration flows from one state or region to another to structural differences in the supply and demand for labor in those contexts. Such exchanges of labor usually prove beneficial on both ends of the transaction, with respect to the markets if not always the individual workers involved. Proponents of this model, which emerged concurrent with and partially in response to the increased demand for unskilled labor in Western Europe following the conclusion of World War II, include W. Arthur Lewis, Gustav Ranis, J.C.H. Fei, J.R.

Harris and Michael P. Todaro.[2]

The macroeconomic approach served as the basis for the development of a series of related propositions, as described by Douglas S. Massey, Joaquin Arango, Graeme Hugo, Ali Kouaouci, Adela Pellegrino and J. Edward Taylor. First, differences in wage rates between states trigger international migration. Second, the elimination of wage differentials causes such labor-induced population transfers to cease. Third, international flows of skilled workers respond to fluctuations in the rate of return on human capital, which differs at times from wage rates and thus may yield patterns of migration opposite to that associated with unskilled labor. Fourth, labor markets are the principal mechanisms producing international migration. Fifth, it follows that the manipulation of labor markets by governmental bodies is a useful means to control migration flows.[3]

As opposed to the macroeconomic framework, the microeconomic model of international migration emphasizes individual choice in the movement of workers from one state to another. It suggests that rather than responding exclusively to periodic fluctuations in the demand for labor, workers conduct short- and long-term cost-benefit calculations and elect to migrate only if they discern a positive economic return, whether reflected in terms of wages or quality of life. For example, workers from the developing world would not likely choose to relocate unless they expected to acquire jobs carrying improvements in the standard of living relative to that existing in their native countries. Advocates of this model include Todaro, Larry A. Sjaastad, Lydia Maruszko and George Borjas.[4]

The multiple factors involved in the decision-making process described in the microeconomic model lead to several additional conclusions that differ from those related to the macroeconomic approach. First, international migration is a product of differentials in both earnings and employment rates and thus will not occur in the absence of such disparities. Second, individual characteristics in terms of skill level with respect to labor categories (skilled vs. unskilled) result in differing rates of migration among particular social classes in given states. Third, the size of the differential in returns determines the level of the flow of migrants between states. Fourth, attractive living conditions in a particular state have the potential to draw migrants even without the guarantee of considerable wage increases in that context. Fifth, governments control migration primarily through the manipulation of wage rates and restrictive immigration policies rather than the manipulation of supply and demand in labor markets.[5]

In the 1980s and 1990s, scholars including Taylor, Oded Stark, D. Levhari, E. Katz and Jennifer Lauby advanced a "new economics" model of international migration that distinguished itself from the aforementioned neoclassical macro and microeconomic models by focusing on family units rather than individual or state-level actors. While similar to the macroeconomic model, the new economics approach places a greater emphasize on selectivity in migrant decision-making at the household level. It explains that as opposed to the involuntary dispersal of all males to occupy unskilled jobs in foreign lands, families often gain more collective benefits by selectively sending some members to work abroad while others pursue employment in their country of origin contingent upon demand for their respective labor skills.[6]

The new economics model was the basis for the following set of theses, which altered appreciably the research agenda for international migration given the almost exclusive previous reliance upon the neoclassical models of the 1950s, 1960s and 1970s. First, families, households or other culturally defined entities are the most useful units for analysis with respect to migration flows. Second, there are strong incentives for households to engage in both international migration and local activities in pursuit of economic prosperity. Third, incentives for transnational movements will not always cease once overall wage differentials between states no longer persist; instead, family members may migrate to capitalize on a sector of the market that does not exist in their native country. Fourth, households' expected gains from migration are contingent upon their placement in the income distribution in a particular state. Fifth, governments can influence migration rates not only by manipulating labor markets but also through policies that shape insurance, capital and futures markets in manners that alter income distributions among families.[7]

While the neoclassical and new economics models are limited in scope to the decision-making of individuals and households, dual labor market theory focuses on the broader state and regional levels in explaining the causes of migration flows. Initially developed by Michael J. Piore, the dual labor market approach contends that immigration is the result of pull factors in receiving states rather than push factors in the sending states from which migrants originate.[8] In short, demand for unskilled labor in industrialized societies draws workers from the developing world. Factors fueling that demand in receiver states include structural inflation, lack of motivation in the domestic labor force and the inherent dualism between labor and capital.[9]

Although the dual labor market model shares some similarities with the neoclassical economics, it also features four corollaries that differ from those associated with the micro-level decision-making approaches. First, international migration is based largely on a demand for labor that is met by the recruitment of foreign workers by governments and private corporations. Second, international wage differentials are not an indispensable element in the migration process; instead, the demand for labor emanates from structural economic needs and is expressed through recruitment practices. Third, low-level wages in receiving states do not rise in response to a dearth of immigrant workers; rather they are held constant through social and institutional mechanisms that do not respond to supply and demand. Fourth, because immigrants fill a demand for labor structurally built into modern economies, influencing this demand entails major organizational alterations in a given economy.[10]

On the other hand, rather than limit themselves to the characteristics of labor markets in particular domestic societies, Immanuel Wallerstein, Alejandro Portes, John Walton, Elizabeth M. Petras, Manuel Castells, Saskia Sassen and Ewa Morawska attribute international migration flows to the capitalist penetration of non-capitalist economies.[11] Known as the world systems model, this theory suggests that modern industrial states have triggered increased migration flows by consolidating land under foreign ownership, extracting raw materials, shifting labor markets to the detriment of distinct social classes and shifting population centers from rural to urban areas in the developing world.[12] Examples include the past European colonization of Africa, Asia and Latin America and the modern expansion of multinational corporations in those regions.

World systems theorists' advocacy of the premise that international migration stems from the political and economic organization of the expanding global economy is articulated more explicitly in four corollaries to their general stance. First, labor flows out of developing states as capitalist investment foments changes that create mobile populations with growing affinities for the material benefits perceived as available on a larger scale in the core states of the developed world. Second, international migration is considerably more likely between past imperial powers and former colonies in light of their deeply ingrained cultural, linguistic, administrative, investment, transportation and communication links. Third, since migration waves are a result of the globalization of the market economy, governments can best influence those waves through the regulation of overseas investment by transnational corporations. Fourth, the failure of governments to protect investments via political and military intervention in the developing world, produce unwanted movements of refugees that foster political and social problems at home.[13]

Each of the above theoretical approaches offers useful explanations for the genesis of particular international migration waves. Alternatively, the networks model emphasizes the potential for interpersonal linkages among immigrants and family members and other acquaintances in their states of origin to lower the risks and increase the perceived long-term benefits associated with international migration. According to Hugo, Massey, Taylor, Felipe Garcia Espana, Douglas T. Gurak and Fe Caces, these connections cause the probability of migration to rise over time, which results in the establishment and eventual entrenchment of immigrant communities in receiving states.[14]

The networks approach provides a theoretical foundation for five general rules related to the examination of migration processes over time, particularly when limited to distinct regional contexts. First, international migration will increase until the network connections have diffused to such an extent within a given sending state that all who wish to emigrate from that state can easily do so. Second, the effects—if any—of wage differentials and employment rates on the promotion or discouragement of migration will diminish progressively as the falling costs and risks of population waves accompanying the development of migrant networks between states decrease. Third, as networks expand, migration waves become gradually more representative of the society of the sending state. Fourth, receiving states will have less success in stemming migration waves over the long term because the process of network formation lies largely outside governmental control. Family reunification programs undertaken by governments, for example, tend to strengthen rather than weaken migration networks.[15]

One offshoot of the networks model is the institutional theory of international migration promulgated by Massey, Arango, Hugo, Kouaouci, Pellegrino and Taylor. This approach, which focuses on the development of public and private advocacy groups to safeguard the rights of migrants, has two related elements. First, international migration tides will become increasingly institutionalized concurrent with the proliferation of organizations designed to support, sustain and promote international movement. Second, given the difficulties modern states have experienced in managing the growth and subsequent expansion of the powers of international and non-governmental institutions, whether at the global or regional level, governments will find it more and more difficult to control migration in the future.[16]

Scholars have responded to the growing complexity of international migration processes by developing hybrid explanatory models that utilize a range of theoretical approaches that transcend multiple disciplines. Take the cumulative causation model originally proposed by Gunnar Myrdal and subsequently refined by scholars such as Massey, Taylor, Stark and Shlomo Yitzhaki.[17] It has three related tenets. First, social, economic and cultural changes fostered by international migration tides between sending and receiving states instill a powerful momentum to the movement of populations over borders, one that is not easily influenced by governments. Second, by recruiting migrant workers to offset domestic labor shortages, governments render those jobs less desirable to natives. Third, as a result, even when the domestic labor supply increases, natives are unlikely to occupy those jobs filled in the past by immigrants, ultimately creating a demand for the recruitment of more migrants in the future.[18]

The migration systems model, advocated by scholars such as James T. Fawcett and Hania Zlotnick, is comparable to the cumulative causation approach in its overarching scope.[19] However, it is more effective as a means to synthesize the most significant elements of world systems, networks and institutions constructs into a broad theoretical framework. This model is built around four precepts. First, migration systems are not conditioned by geographic proximity, given that population waves therein relate primarily to political and economic relationships rather than physical ones. Second, multipolar migration systems, through which a set of dispersed core states receives immigrants from a group of overlapping sending states, are possible if not probable. Third, multiple membership in migrations systems is more common among sending than receiving states. Fourth, stability does not imply a fixed structure in a particular migration system. Thus, as a system changes in accordance with the prevailing political and economic conditions, states may join or drop out.[20]

While these theories are applicable to a variety of geographical contexts. However, not all are equally germane to Western Europe generally or France, Germany and the United Kingdom specifically. Four of the aforementioned and described theoretical constructs are particularly instructive as relates to these contexts: the dual labor market, new economics, networks, and cumulative causation models. The reasons why are discussed on a model-by-model basis below.

Dual Labor Market Model

This approach is an ideal means to explain the initial development of Muslim communities in France, Germany and the United Kingdom in the aftermath of World War II. These states lacked the requisite unskilled labor supply for physical and economic reconstruction in the 1950s and 1960s because of the reductions in their respective working-age populations. As a result, they recruited foreign workers, many of whom were Muslims, to satisfy a short-term labor demand. These projects were orchestrated by the governments of France and Germany and private businesses in the United Kingdom, drawing migrants from North Africa, Turkey and the Indian subcontinent.

New Economics Model

This framework is useful in explaining both the initial establishment and subsequent growth of Islamic communities throughout Western Europe. Young males in households in the developing world, whether North Africa, Turkey or the Indian sub-continent, took advantage of the French, German and British guest worker programs in order to boost their incomes, then sent the money to family members still residing in their countries of origin. Once the low-wage jobs filled by immigrants dried up concurrent with the economic stagnation that gripped Western Europe after the 1973-74 oil crisis, guest worker remittances decreased. Rather than remain separated, workers and their families reunited in their new homes in France, Germany and the United Kingdom, resulting in the long-term entrenchment of Muslim enclaves in those countries.

Networks Model

This approach is similar to the new economics model in its emphasis on the importance of the interpersonal linkages among migrants in Western Europe and their families and acquaintances abroad. Primarily because of such linkages, as Muslim immigrants reunited with family members, the character of the communities they established in France, Germany and the United Kingdom shifted from one characterized by cultural ambivalence to one featuring more of the ethnic and religious traditions associated with their respective homelands. While Western European governments enacted policies to stem the flow of new labor migrants in the mid-1970s, they also permitted family reunifications, which only strengthened the networks established and cultivated since the 1950s.

Cumulative Causation Model

This approach is particularly helpful in explaining both the allure of Western Europe to migrants from developing countries and the backlashes against those individuals following periodic economic downturns in that region. The perception that they will achieve higher standards of living in Western Europe leads to increases in the number of migrants flowing into states such as France, Germany and the United Kingdom. Unfortunately, upon arrival, they find there is a dearth of jobs. The majority populations of those states, in turn, often mistakenly attribute rising unemployment levels to minority Muslims occupying jobs that natives would otherwise fill. However, in part because unskilled jobs are associated with immigrants, most members of the majorities express little interest in such occupations even when openings do exist.

Review of Relevant Literature on Islam and the West

The entrenchment and growth of Muslim communities in France, Germany and the United Kingdom over the past 25 years has engendered vigorous national debates over the place of Islam within and outside of Western Europe. While distinct in many ways, these discussions have transpired in the context of a broader international debate among academics and policymakers over the evolving relationship between Islam and the West.

During the Cold War, scholars and practitioners of international relations viewed the world primarily through a bipolar lens. The globe was split into Western and Eastern segments, with the United States and Soviet Union acting as the principal players in the former and latter contexts, respectively. Each side pursued a set of interests conditioned largely by disparate ideologies, which it either shared with or imposed upon the states situated within its sphere of influence. While the United States defined its interests in democratic political and capitalist economic terms, the Soviet Union adhered to and attempted to advance totalitarian political and communist economic philosophies. Given their geopolitical predominance, the United States and Soviet Union drove interactions among states throughout the system. Events were interpreted primarily on the basis of relations between the superpowers.

When the Cold War ended through the collapse of communist regimes across Central and Eastern Europe in the fall and winter of 1989-90, the unification of Germany in October 1990 and the dissolution of the Soviet Union in December 1991, academics set to work developing new theoretical constructs to explain interactions among states in the international system. Few such approaches are as novel as that offered by Samuel P. Huntington in his provocative 1996 work *The Clash of Civilizations and the Remaking of World Order*.[21] In contrast to the Cold War era, which featured states struggling for power on the basis of disparate political and economic philosophies, Huntington contends that contemporary international relations are increasingly conditioned by common cultural identities transcending state boundaries in regions across the globe. He asserts that "culture and cultural identities, which at the broadest level are civilizational identities, are shaping the patterns of cohesion, disintegration and conflict in the post-Cold War world," noting that individuals residing within these civilizations define themselves in terms of "ancestry, religion, language, history, values, customs and institutions," identifying culturally with "tribes, ethnic groups, religious communities, nations and, at the broader level, civilizations."[22]

Huntington describes the emerging civilizational system as one divided between groups of Western and non-Western states, which are categorized into eight major civilizations—Western, Sinic, Islamic, Orthodox, Japanese, Hindu, Buddhist and Latin American. He acknowledges that states will remain the central actors in international affairs, but also contends that interactions among those states are "increasingly shaped by civilizational factors."[23] The major civilizational players in the new system are those defined as Western, Sinic and Islamic, with the United States and China heading the first two and the third lacking any one predominant state actor. In particular, his approach vis-à-vis the Islamic civilization has attracted widespread public interest since the 11 September 2001 terrorist attacks carried out by Al Qaeda on the World Trade Center in New York and the Pentagon on the outskirts of Washington, D.C.

Huntington developed his paradigm as a means to synthesize four general post-Cold War models of order he classifies as *One World: Euphorias and Harmonies, Two Worlds: Us and Them, 184 States* and *Sheer Chaos.*[24] The first model, of which Francis Fukuyama is the principal advocate, suggests a diminution of if not an end to conflict as a byproduct of the victory of the American-led West over the Soviet-sponsored East in the Cold War.[25] The second mirrors the Cold War system but replaces the ideological confrontation pitting the United States against the Soviet Union with cleavages rooted in religious, economic and cultural differences, which divide the world between North and South, Christianity and Islam, and Orient and Occident. The third reflects the self-help world of neo-realists such as Kenneth Waltz and John Mearsheimer, with states striving to advance their interests unilaterally in an anarchical international environment.[26] The fourth, proposed by Zbigniew Brzezinski and Robert Kaplan among others, focuses on the intensification of ethnic conflict manifested in a proliferation of failed states in regions as geographically diverse as Central Africa and the former Yugoslavia.[27]

Huntington contends that his civilizational model serves as a useful lens through which to synthesize the most relevant aspects of each of the above approaches. He points out, for example, that "[v]iewing the world in terms of seven or eight civilizations . . . does not sacrifice reality to parsimony as do the one- and two-world paradigms; yet it also does not sacrifice parsimony to reality as the statist and chaos paradigms do."[28] Huntington's model has both strengths and weaknesses, the collective identification of which serves as an effective means to review the literature on Islam and the West in both the global and Western European contexts. The following discussion does so in four parts, those related to the shifting balance of civilizations, the emerging order of civilizations, clashes of civilizations and the future of civilizations.

While the world standard of living was highest among Western states during the twentieth century, Huntington suggests that overall power levels are presently shifting in favor of the Sinic and Islamic civilizations, with both entities demonstrating an ability to modernize without abandoning their distinctive cultural and religious identities.[29] With respect to Islam in particular, he cites Maxine Rodinson's contention that "there is nothing to indicate in a compelling way that the Muslim religion [has] prevented the Muslim world from developing along the road to modern capitalism."[30] Additionally, Huntington argues that Western primacy is likely to diminish as the relative demographic, economic, military and political power of the Sinic and Islamic civilizations increase over the long term.[31]

In comparing the relative power resources of the Western and Islamic civilizations, Huntington points both to rising population levels throughout the Islamic world and increases in the number of Muslims residing in the West (most notably in the United States and Europe). He cites, for example, statistical estimates indicating that the percentage of the global population adhering to Islamic religious precepts rose from 12.4 in 1900 to nearly 20 percent at present,[32] increases that have enabled Islam to establish itself as the second most practiced religion in the world behind Christianity with approximately 1.2 billion followers.[33] In light of these demographic trends and the increasing emphasis on distinctive cultural characteristics in the post-Cold War era, Huntington asserts that the potential for clashes among the most powerful civilizations is in a perpetual state of growth, predicting that future clashes are most likely to occur between the American-led West and the Sinic or Islamic civilizations—if not both— arising from a volatile "interaction of Western arrogance, Islamic intolerance and Sinic assertiveness."[34] Furthermore, Huntington contends that the "Islamic and Sinic societies which see the West as their antagonist, have reason to cooperate with each other against the West," particularly with respect to issues areas such as human rights, economics and the development of weapons of mass destruction.[35]

Huntington is correct to acknowledge that American power has declined in relative terms over the past half-century. However, he underestimates the extent to which the United States remains a largely peerless power by virtue of its collective economic strength, military capabilities, political influence and global commercial outreach. Although qualifying his arguments with the caveat that the reduction of Western power vis-à-vis that of the Islamic and Sinic civilizations is a long-term trend, Huntington indirectly and unjustly downplays the short-term renewal manifested in the growth of the American economy over the past decade.

Similarly, in focusing on the rising popularity of political Islam from the late 1970s into the early 1990s, he fails to acknowledge explicitly the possibility that such dynamism was a transitory phenomenon rather than the harbinger of a permanent reconstitution of politico-religious philosophy. His approach in this context is somewhat ignorant of the complexity of change—past, present and future—in the Islamic world. For example, as John Esposito argues, the "history of contemporary Islam is a story of challenge and response, tension and conflict, atavism and creativity or renaissance, retreat and advancement, religious and intellectual retrenchment, reformation and revolution."[36] Similarly, Shireen Hunter notes that "Islamic civilization is a hybrid and a syncretic phenomenon that developed from early Islamic encounters with other regions and civilizations in the course of its historical expansion; the notion of Islamic civilization as a unique and coherent phenomenon does not reflect reality. Like all civilizations, Islamic civilization is a living, evolving organism, constantly responding to new realities and circumstances."[37]

Notwithstanding the growth in popularity and political strength of fundamentalist movements such as the Egyptian Muslim Brotherhood and Algerian Islamic Salvation Front—particularly among the lower classes—in the 1990s, Huntington exaggerates these groups' present potential to challenge state authority in the Greater Middle East. More balanced scholarly approaches provide a clearer picture of the relationship between governance and political Islam in the contemporary Muslim world. As Hunter explains, "Islam's role is directly linked with struggles for power, influence and legitimacy within Muslim societies and in the context of their interaction with the outside world; thus Islam is used by various groups to acquire and maintain power and to legitimize and delegitimize existing power structures."[38] Similarly, as Olivier Roy notes, the "socioeconomic realities that sustained the Islamist wave are still here and are not going to change. . . . The Islamic revolution, the Islamic state, the Islamic economy are myths, but we have not heard the last of Islamic protestation."[39]

More specifically, scholars often clash over the relevance of the state in modern Muslim societies. Bernard Lewis and Bassam Tibi, for example, emphasize an augmentation and a diminution, respectively, of the power of states in the Middle East, North Africa, Central Asia and other Islamically oriented regions. Lewis contends that "present-day states in the Islamic world, even those claiming to be progressive and democratic, are—in their domestic affairs, at least—vastly stronger than the so-called tyrannies of the past."[40] By contrast, Tibi argues that "resurgent Islamic fundamentalism" is serving to undermine state power in the Greater Middle East and thus exacerbating the instability of the region."[41]

Huntington's suggestion that in the aftermath of the Cold War, the United States lacked clearly defined threats on the basis of which to prioritize its interests and develop policies to further those interests accordingly is reasonable and his identification of China as the leader of the Sinic civilization generally credible. However, his references to Iran and Turkey as candidates to develop roles as core states of the Islamic civilization are problematic. Iran is a majority Shiite state and would likely have difficulty mobilizing support among the Sunni Muslims who compose the vast majority of the population of the Muslim world. Turkey, on the other hand, is secular in political orientation and has greater potential to serve as a bridge between Islam and the West than as a leader of an emerging Islamic civilization, as evidenced by its membership in the North Atlantic Treaty Organization, aspirations to join the European Union and cooperative military relationship with Israel.

Huntington's forecast of an impending clash between the Western and Islamic civilizations is his least credible assertion. Selective cooperation among states in the Western and Islamic worlds is possible if not probable in the present and future contexts. As Esposito argues, "Islamic neo-modernists do not reject the West in its entirety; rather, they choose to be selective in approach. They wish to appropriate the best of science, technology, medicine and intellectual thought but to resist acculturation or the assimilation of Western culture and mores, from secularism and radical individualism to the breakdown of the family and sexual permissiveness."[42]

The 1990-91 Persian Gulf War, for example, demonstrated that most Muslim-majority states define their security primarily in traditional realist—as opposed to nascent civilizational—terms and act on that basis. Rather than side with Iraq against the American-led coalition in the Gulf War a diverse array of Middle Eastern states including Egypt, Saudi Arabia aligned themselves with the West, assisting in the expulsion of Iraqi President Saddam Hussein's forces from Kuwait. And while Kuwait was the only Arab state to offer overt support for a US-led coalition's liquidation of Saddam's regime in 2003, regional opposition was muted, particularly at the inter-governmental level.

While Huntington acknowledges correctly the need for a deeper American and Western European understanding of non-Western cultures, he misperceives the nature of the threat Islam poses to the West. As Lewis explains, "Islam is a powerful but still an undirected force in politics. As a possible factor in international politics, the present prognosis is not favorable. There have been many attempts at a pan-Islamic policy, none of which have made much progress."[43] Instead, Muslim-Christian friction is more likely to emanate from interactions among Islamic communities and governments in the Western world—Western Europe in particular—than through civilizational relationships. Put simply, Huntington issues a warning as to the potential for instability rooted in a clash between the Western and Islamic civilizations that is actually more likely to develop as a product of rising ethnic and religious Muslim-Christian tensions in the West.

A common Western mistake is to link all Muslims, irrespective of geographic origin and characteristics of religious practice, with transnational terrorist organizations such as Al Qaeda, which perpetrate acts of terrorism both within and beyond the Greater Middle East. Understandably, these misperceptions have grown even more pronounced since the events of 9/11. Tibi's description of the modern Muslim world as "a great variety of local cultures more or less embedded in a single great civilization," pursuing the "vision of a worldwide order based on Islam," for one, evokes Western images of the development of a threatening rather than cooperative or ambivalent Islamic civilization.[44] Unfortunately, the credence given to interpretations such as Tibi's in the West broadly and Western Europe specifically is at times buttressed by the adversarial nature of Christian-Muslim relations in the past. The first widespread interactions among individuals from the Islamic and Western Christian worlds unfolded in medieval Europe with the invasion of the Iberian Peninsula by the Umayyad Caliphate in the eighth century. Regrettably, the nature of the relationships among adherents of these rival monotheisms has remained generally adversarial in the European geographical context ever since.

Fundamentally, Islamic-Christian tensions are rooted in the universal aspirations that believers of the two faiths have professed from the outset of their respective histories. While Muslims and Christians acknowledge and profess allegiance to the same God, each group adheres to a different set of rules promulgated by a unique prophet—Muhammad in the former case and Jesus Christ in the latter. Each faith claims its *own* interpretation of the word of the *same* God as absolute. As Lewis explains, "[s]peaking in the same language at least in the figurative sense, using the same methods of argument and reasoning and adhering to identical or similar notions of what religion is about, Islam and Christendom could disagree meaningfully. When Christians and Muslims called each other infidels, each understood what the other meant, and both meant more or less the same thing."[45]

Historically, Muslims and Christians have often lived in empires and states ruled by members of the other faith. Understandably, interpretations of the degree of freedom under those respective religions are often determined by the faith to which a given individual professes allegiance. As Daniel Pipes contends, "Muslims proudly point to their record of tolerance and contrast it with the attacks on their lands by the Crusaders, modern European imperialists and Zionists. Islam's critics emphasize the lack of equal rights for non-Muslims under Muslim rule and the persecution, insecurity and humiliation they must endure."[46]

Muslims and Christians have long sought to gain deeper understandings of their counterparts' worldviews. However, scholars residing in states in the Islamic and Christian worlds and adhering to the cultural and religious precepts predominant within those contexts often approach the study of the outside world from ethnocentric perspectives that cloud their interpretation of concepts alien to one society and indispensable to another. Perhaps the greatest shortcoming of Western scholarship on regions and states dominated by Muslims is that it is often generated in response to a rising fear of as opposed to a desire to understand and accept Islam. As Lewis asserts, "[s]ince its earliest recorded history, Europe has been looking at its neighbors in the East, sometimes with fear, sometimes with greed, sometimes with curiosity and sometimes with disquiet. For centuries, indeed for millennia, relations between the two have shown a pattern of conquest and reconquest, attack and counterattack."[47]

Yet, the backdrop for Christian-Muslim encounters have changed markedly over time. In the past, they met as adversaries vying for territory, whether in Europe, Africa, the Middle East or South Asia. Over the past half-century, on the other hand, they have interacted as neighbors in Western European societies as a result of influxes of Muslim migrants from regions such as North Africa and South Asia. It is in domestic contexts such as those of France, Germany and the United Kingdom that challenges of inter-faith understanding must be met, most notably through the development of effective means to facilitate the full integration of Muslim communities in the future.

Review of Relevant Literature on Identity Formation and Integration

An evaluation of the integration of Muslim communities into the societies of France, Germany and the United Kingdom requires a review of the relevant theoretical literature on the related topics of identity formation and domestic integration. In order to distinguish clearly the similarities and differences relating to states and communities of peoples within any region of the world or state situated therein, it is first necessary to define the term identity. Fundamentally, identity is a means through which human actors of disparate backgrounds decide and subsequently express who they are. The resultant definition a person constructs is based on factors ranging from blood to social class to religion to culture to political or economic ideology. In turn, the significance assigned to each factor is contingent upon the proclivities of individuals, which thus requires that scholars employ flexible approaches when attempting to draw distinctions among nations, states and communities in distinctive regional environments.

Lewis views the phenomenon of identity construction in a bifurcated manner. In historical terms, he emphasizes two relevant clusters of factors in the development of an individual's identity, which are associated with birth and allegiance to leadership, respectively. The first cluster includes blood, place and religious community. Those three elements are then subdivided, with blood determined by family, clan, tribe and ethnic nation, place by village, neighborhood, district, province and country, and religious community by a combination of local and immediate bonds. The second cluster features loyalty to a head of state, governor of a province, administrator of a district and headman of a village.[48] According to Lewis, these related clusters have grown closer over time, in large part through the ongoing globalization process. As he explains, in "modern times, under the influence of the West, a new kind [of identity] is evolving between the two—the freely chosen cohesion and loyalty of voluntary associations, combining to form what is nowadays known as civil society."[49]

Huntington stresses the significance of a return to the past in the formation of identities in the post-Cold War era. Rather than economics, ideology or politics, he contends that individuals now define themselves more in terms of cultural background. Additionally, he emphasizes the importance of differences as opposed to similarities vis-à-vis cultural orientation, noting that individuals "define themselves in terms of ancestry, religion, language, history, values, customs and institutions. They identify with cultural groups or tribes, ethnic groups, religious communities, nations, and, at the broadest level, civilizations. People use politics not just to advance their interests but to define their identity. We know who we are only when we know who we are not and definitely when we know whom we are against."[50]

Ernest Gellner takes a more general stance, but one that favors Lewis' emphasis on the changeable nature of identity in the modern era rather than Huntington's return to age-old cultural characteristics. At a time when modern technology has increased contact among individuals in disparate regions of the developed and developing worlds, Gellner views the accumulation and interpretation of knowledge—and thus the way in which people view their surroundings—as increasingly transitory processes. As he explains, in "a stable, traditional world, men had identities, linked to their social roles, and confirmed by their overall vision of nature and society. Instability and rapid change both in knowledge and in society has deprived such self-images of their erstwhile feel of reliability. Identities are perhaps more ironic and conditional than they once were."[51]

Occupying the proverbial middle ground is Craig Calhoun, who argues that

individual identities are more likely to develop through shared group experiences at
the local level than as a result of opposition to outside entities at larger regional,
national or civilizational levels.[52]   In short, he stresses that inside and outside
influences are useful in creating particular individual and group identities, and, thus,
over-reliance on either of these elements is counterproductive noting that

> [t]ension between identity—putatively singular, unitary and integral—and identities—
> plural, crosscutting and divided—is inescapable at both the individual and collective levels.
> Individuals face the challenge of knitting together the different phases of their existence,
> their different social relationships and roles.   Groups never wholly supercede the
> individuals who make them up any more than individuals exist altogether apart from groups
> and social relations.[53]

The formation of identities occurs not just at the individual level but also at the
state level. As opposed to neo-realists of Waltz's and Mearsheimer's ilk,
constructivists such as Alexander Wendt emphasize the relevance of myriad
individual, local, regional, national and international factors in driving the behavior of
states. Wendt, for example, stresses three critical elements of constructivist theory
with respect to the identities of states. First, "states are the principal units of analysis
for international political theory." Second, the "key structures in the states system are
intersubjective, rather than material." Third, "state identities and interests are in part
constructed by these social structures, rather than given exogenously to the system by
human nature or domestic politics."[54]

Similarly, Ted Hopf articulates the particulars of constructivism in terms of six
elements common to the conventional and critical theoretical strands of that approach.
First, the "aim to denaturalize the social world by empirically discovering and
revealing how the institutions, practices and identities people take as given are actually
the product of social construction."[55] Second, the "belief that intersubjective reality
and meanings are critical data for understanding the social world."[56] Third, the
"insistence that all data must be . . . related to and situated within a social environment
in which they were gathered in order to fully understand their meaning."[57] Fourth, the
acceptance of the existence of a "nexus between power and knowledge" that takes the
form of the "power of practice in its disciplinary, meaning-producing mode."[58] Fifth,
the acceptance of the "restoration of agency to human individuals."[59] Sixth, an
emphasis on the "reflexity of self and society—mutual constitution of actor and
structure."[60]

The establishment of communities of minorities in states often results in clashes of
identities. In the French, German and British cases under consideration here, for
example, such clashes are rooted in both religious and more overarching cultural
differences between the societal majorities and communities of Muslims of various
ethnic backgrounds. Integration, which is also described by terms that include
assimilation, absorption and incorporation, is one means to bridge these majority-
minority identity gaps. A review of several general integrative frameworks is useful as
a precursor to in-depth discussions of the integrative strategies of the French, German

and British governments in the ensuing case studies.

Gary Freeman views the integration of minorities as part of a broader migration paradigm. His four-point theoretical construct functions as follows. First, it traces the development of the migration process, emphasizing the source of and impetus behind the original flow of individuals and families from sending to receiving states. Second, it focuses on the characteristics of the migrants. Third, it addresses the policies of a receiving state regarding its regulation of migration and treatment of immigrants. Fourth, it examines cultural, economic, social and political interactions among migrants and the indigenous population of the receiving state.[61]

Building on the latter two of Freeman's points, Myron Weiner lists three critical factors that affect relationships between governments and the minority group over which they preside. First, the extent to which a society "is willing to absorb migrants and, therefore, puts in place policies that grant migrants and their children the same legal status as that of the native population." Second, the "willingness of the migrants themselves to accept membership, both in the legal sense and by adopting a new identity." Third, the "structure of the labor market which enables the migrants to find a niche in the economy, one that frees them from excessive dependence upon the country's social services."[62]

More specifically, Weiner denotes five interactive "categories" that define governmental-immigrant relationships. First, the extent to which immigrants engender social and economic problems for a given receiving state. Second, the ways they threaten the cultural identity of that state. Third, the manners in which they complicate relations between the sending and receiving states by opposing the government of the former. Fourth, the degree to which they threaten the political stability and internal security of the receiving state.[63] Given these factors, he concludes that considering "how complex and often divided are the political forces in most countries to choose policies that can promote integration . . . we can appreciate why the integration of immigrants in most countries remains so problematic and, especially in the short term, so conflictual."[64]

The multicultural approach advocated by John Rex provides a contrast to Weiner's model in that it strikes a somewhat more optimistic tone. According to Rex, before grappling with the concept of the integration of minority groups, a government must accept as valid three principles, which will help to increase the tolerance of cultural diversity. First, "there are cultural values which separate groups regard as worth pursuing, and which do not threaten either the culture of other groups or the shared public political culture."[65] Second, "under conditions of the modern market economy individuals . . . seek the psychological and moral support of a group intermediate between the individual family and the state."[66] Third, "in order to fight for equality of their members, ethnic groups, like classes before them, rely upon ethnic solidarity as a valuable resource."[67]

While Rex acknowledges the importance of the accommodation of the concerns of minority communities in a multicultural society, he also stresses that the individuals of which those communities are composed must accept the following set of rules vis-à-vis interaction with the government and societal majority at large. First, recognition of the state's criminal and civil laws so long as those strictures are subject to reform in accordance with particular religious and cultural beliefs over the long term. Second, acceptance of a set of government institutions as binding within a state of residence, whether or not one feels a deep sense of loyalty or emotional attachment to that state. Third, acquisition and then use of the state's native language when interacting in the public sphere. Fourth, recognition that the practice of a particular religious faith is a private matter, albeit one that has the potential to spill over into the public arena regarding issues such as education, and government and military service.[68]

Similarly, Alejandro Portes and Ruben Rumbaut approach minority integration through the presentation of a three-part construct focusing on the policies of the government of a receiving state, the forms of social reception experienced by immigrants in that state and the characteristics of the co-ethnic community that develops subsequently in that context. With respect to the first two of the segments of this construct, government policies are classified as receptive, indifferent or hostile, and the forms of social reception the migrants encounter are denoted as prejudiced or nonprejudiced.[69]

Complementary to the aforementioned general theories, Yasemin Soysal and Tariq Ramadan offer models applicable to the Western European region in particular. Soysal's "regimes of incorporation" typology, for example, is subdivided philosophically and rationally. She describes four such regimes: corporatist [Sweden and the Netherlands], individualist [Switzerland and the United Kingdom], state-centralized [France] and mixed statist-corporatist [Germany].[70] This is a useful framework in that it allows for comparisons and contrasts among policies developed and pursued by the states—France, Germany and the United Kingdom—under consideration here.

Ramadan approaches the issue of integration from an alternate but equally effective perspective, that of Muslims residing in Western Europe. In arguing that Muslims can help to speed up minority integration processes in member states across the European Union, he offers five related observations. First, a "Muslim should see himself as involved in a contract, both moral and social, with the country in which he lives, and should respect that country's laws." Second, while secular in nature, European legislation allows Muslims to practice the fundamental tenets of their religion. Third, interpretations of the Koran that portray Europe as a *dar al harb* or anti-Islamic land of war are outdated and perceived as such by most French, German and British Muslims, who are continually offering ways to view the presence of Islamic communities on the continent in more positive terms. Fourth, Muslims "should see themselves as citizens in the fullest sense of the term and should participate (while at the same time seeking respect for their own values) in the social, organizational, economic and political life of the countries in which they live." Fifth, in "European legislation as a whole, there is nothing to prevent Muslims or any other citizens, from making choices that accord with their religion."[71]

Book's Contributions to the Existing Literature

The literature review is best viewed as a general foundation, upon which the forthcoming case studies build. The four theses presented in the introductory chapter of the book both relate to and proceed beyond particular arguments advanced in past contributions to the issue areas delineated as international migration, Islam and the West and identity construction and minority integration. This section explains briefly the similarities and differences between the existing literature and those theses.

With respect to the literature on international migration, four theoretical frameworks are relevant here—the dual labor market, new economics, networks and cumulative causation models. Collectively, these approaches provide a hybrid construct within which to examine the causative factors for the initial development and eventual entrenchment of Muslim communities in France, Germany and the United Kingdom. The study draws on segments of each of the four models in order to explain these processes. The first accounts for the initial flow of Muslim migrants to Western Europe through the guest worker programs of the 1950s and 1960s. The latter three explain the entrenchment of Muslim communities via family reunification programs in the context of the establishment of migrant networks over the long term. Ultimately, the book's assertions complement the existing literature by linking the approaches germane both to the regional and domestic environments (Western Europe generally and France, Germany and the United Kingdom specifically) and time periods (the 1980s-2000s primarily and 1950s-1970s secondarily) under consideration.

The literature on Islam and the West is subdivided into strains that emphasize confrontation, cooperation and ambivalence, respectively, vis-à-vis relationships among Muslims and Christians, whether at the individual, local, state or international levels. Philosophically, the book fits in the middle ground between the cooperative and ambivalent approaches. It stresses the need to foster inter-faith cooperation in order to preclude inter-state conflict at the international level and ensure domestic stability in the Western European regional and French, German and British national contexts. However, it also acknowledges the changing nature of the challenges governments and individuals face in finding the common ground necessary to serve as a foundation for Christian-Muslim reconciliation.

Most notably, the study puts a unique spin on Huntington's clash of civilizations paradigm. It stresses that while Huntington is correct in noting the increasing potential for conflict between members of the Islamic and Christian faiths, that threat is greater with respect to interactions among adherents of these religions who reside in Western Europe than is the case regarding state- or civilizational-level relationships internationally. It is thus prudent to give primacy to the development of policies to more fully integrate communities of Muslims within Western societies in general and those in France, Germany and the United Kingdom to prevent increases in domestic instability across Western Europe this century.

Similarly, the arguments advanced here focus on the individual and domestic levels as opposed to the international systemic context. The work of scholars such as

Freeman, Rex and Ramadan is instructive in this respect for two reasons. First, collectively, they point to the need for the consideration of a variety of factors—whether class, cultural, economic, ethnic, linguistic, political or religious in orientation—in order to explain the process of identity construction in a particular case. Second, as a result, they also emphasize the need to bridge the gaps between groups in these issue areas to facilitate the equitable integration of a minority community in a given society. The case studies presented here contribute to these approaches by stressing the importance of first identifying and developing models to redress differences between minorities and majorities at the local level before addressing those issues at the broader regional, national and international levels.

Ultimately, the book enhances present interpretations of the related issues of international migration and Islam in the West by applying its latter two theses to each of the case studies. First, the construction of an effective framework to fully integrate Muslim minorities in Western European societies over the long term necessarily entails interactive policy formulation, coordination and implementation at the local, regional, national and supranational levels. However, because of the prevalence of Islamic communities in particular localities and the resultant higher degree of interaction among Muslims and governmental authorities in those contexts as opposed to the limited dispersion of Muslims regionally and nationally in France, Germany and the United Kingdom, a local-level approach is more desirable in the short term. Second, once the full integration of Muslim minorities—or at least positive progress toward the realization of that objective—occurs in particular localities, wider-ranging regional, national and supranational level projects are likely to prove more feasible in light of insights drawn from the local level.

Notes

1. Douglas S. Massey, Joaquin Arango, Graeme Hugo, Ali Kouaouci, Adela Pellegrino and J. Edward Taylor, "Theories of International Migration: A Review and Appraisal," *Population and Development Review* 19-3 (1993): 432-33.
2. W. Arthur Lewis, "Economic Development with Unlimited Supplies of Labor," *Manchester School of Economic and Social Studies* 22 (1954): 139-91; Gustav Ranis and J.C.H. Fei, "A Theory of Economic Development," *American Economic Review* 51 (1961): 533-65; J.R. Harris and Michael P. Todaro, "Migration, Unemployment and Development: A Two-Sector Analysis," *American Economic Review* 60 (1970): 126-42; Michael P. Todaro, *Internal Migration in Developing Countries* (Geneva: International Labor Office, 1976). References made in Massey et al., "Theories of International Migration," 433.
3. Massey et al., "Theories of International Migration," 434.
4. Larry A. Sjaastad, "The Costs and Returns of Human Migration," *Journal of Political Economy* 70-5 (1962): 80-93; Michael P. Todaro and Lydia Maruszko, "Illegal Migration and U.S. Immigration Reform: A Conceptual Framework," *Population and Development Review* 13 (1987): 101-14; George Borjas, *Friends or Strangers: The Impact of*

Immigration on the U.S. Economy (New York: Basic Books, 1990). References made in Massey et al., "Theories of International Migration," 434.

5. Massey et al., "Theories of International Migration," 435-36.

6. Oded Stark and David Levhari, "On Migration and Risk in LDCs," *Economic Development and Cultural Change* 31 (1982): 191-96; Oded Stark, "Migration Decision Making: A Review Article," *Journal of Development Economics* 14 (1984): 251-59; Eliakim Katz and Oded Stark, "Labor Migration and Risk Aversion in Less Developed Countries," *Journal of Labor Economics* 4 (1986): 131-49; Jennifer Lauby and Oded Stark, "Individual Migration as a Family Strategy: Young Women in the Philippines," *Population Studies* 42 (1988): 473-86; J. Edward Taylor, "Differential Migration, Networks, Information and Risk," in Oded Stark, ed., *Research in Human Capital and Development: Migration, Human Capital and Development*, vol. 4 (Greenwich, Conn.: JAI Press, 1986), 147-71; Oded Stark, *The Migration of Labor* (Cambridge, UK: Blackwell, 1991). References made in Massey et al., "Theories of International Migration," 436.

7. Massey et al., "Theories of International Migration," 439-40.

8. Michael J. Piore, *Birds of Passage: Migrant Labor in Industrial Societies* (Cambridge: Cambridge University Press, 1979). Reference made in Massey et al., "Theories of International Migration," 440.

9. Massey et al., "Theories of International Migration," 440-41.

10. Ibid, 444.

11. Immanuel Wallerstein, *The Modern World System: Capitalist Agriculture and the Origins of the European World Economy in the Sixteenth Century* (New York: Academic Press, 1974); Alejandro Portes and John Walton, *Labor, Class and the International System* (New York: Academic Press, 1981); Elizabeth M. Petras, "The Global Labor Market in the Modern World Economy," in *Global Trends in Migration: Theory and Research on International Population Movements*, ed. Mary M. Kritz, Charles B. Keely and Silvano M. Tomasi (Staten Island, NY: Center for Migration Studies, 1981), 44-63. References made in Massey et al., "Theories of International Migration," 444.

12. Massey et al., "Theories of International Migration," 444-47.

13. Ibid, 447-48.

14. Graeme Hugo, "Village-Community Ties, Village Norms and Ethical and Social Networks: A Review of Evidence from the Third World," in *Migration Decision Making: Multidisciplinary Approaches to Microlevel Studies in Developed and Developing Countries*, ed. Gordon F. Dejong and Robert W. Gardner (New York: Pergamon Press, 1981), 186-225; J. Edward Taylor, "Differential Migration, Networks, Information and Risk," 147-71; Douglas Massey and Felipe Garcia Espana, "The Social Process of International Migration," *Science* 237 (1987): 733-38; Douglas T. Gurak and Fe Caces, "Migration Networks and the Shaping of Migration Systems," in *International Migration Systems: A Global Approach*, ed. Mary M. Kritz, Lin Lean Lim and Hania Zlotnick (Oxford: Clarendon Press, 1992), 150-76. References made in Massey et al., "Theories of International Migration," 448-49.

15. Massey et al., "Theories of International Migration," 449-50.

16. Ibid., 450-51.

17. Gunnar Myrdal, *Rich Lands and Poor* (New York: Harper and Row, 1957); Douglas Massey, "Social Structure, Household Strategies and the Cumulative Causation of Migration," *Population Index* 56 (1990): 3-26; Oded Stark, J. Edward Taylor and Shlomo Yitzhaki, "Migration, Remittances and Inequality: A Sensitivity Analysis using the Extended Gini Index," *Journal of Development Economics* 28 (1988): 309-22; J. Edward Taylor, "Remittances and Inequality Reconsidered: Direct, Indirect and Intertemporal Effects," *Journal of Policy Modeling* 14 (1992): 187-208. References made in Massey et al., "Theories of International Migration," 451.

18. Massey et al., "Theories of International Migration," 453-54.

19. James T. Fawcett, "Networks, Linkages and Migration Systems," *International Migration Review* 23 (1989): 671-80; Hania Zlotnick, "Empirical Identification of International Migration Systems," in *International Migration Systems*, ed. Mary M. Kritz, Lin Lean Lim and Hania Zlotnick (Oxford: Clarendon Press, 1992), 19-40. References made in Massey et al., "Theories of International Migration," 454.

20. Massey et al., "Theories of International Migration," 454.

21. Samuel P. Huntington, *The Clash of Civilizations and the Remaking of World Order* (New York: Schocken Books, 1996).

22. Ibid., 20-21.

23. Ibid., 36.

24. Ibid.

25. Francis Fukuyama, *The End of History and the Last Man* (New York: Avon Books, 1992).

26. Kenneth N. Waltz, "The Emerging Structure of International Politics," *International Security* 18-3 (1993); John J. Mearsheimer, "Back to the Future: Instability in Europe after the Cold War," *International Security* 15-2 (1990).

27. Zbigniew Brzezinski, *Out of Control: Global Turmoil on the Eve of the Twenty-first Century* (New York: Touchstone Books, 1993); Robert D. Kaplan, "The Coming Anarchy," *Atlantic Monthly* 281-2 (1994).

28. Huntington, *Clash of Civilizations*, 36.

29. Ibid., 78.

30. Quoted in Daniel Pipes, *In the Path of God: Islam and Political Power* (New York: Basic Books, 1983), 107.

31. Huntington, *Clash of Civilizations*, 83-84.

32. David B. Barrett, ed., *World Christian Encyclopedia: A Comparative Study of Churches and Religions in the Modern World* (New York: Oxford University Press, 1992).

33. John L. Esposito, ed., *Oxford History of Islam* (New York: Oxford University Press, 1999), xi.

34. Huntington, *Clash of Civilizations*, 184.

35. Ibid., 184-85.

36. Esposito, *Oxford History of Islam*, 652.

37. Shireen T. Hunter, *The Future of Islam and the West: Clash of Civilizations or Peaceful Coexistence?* (Westport, Conn.: Praeger, 1998), 166.

38. Ibid., 168.

39. Olivier Roy, *The Failure of Political Islam* (Cambridge: Harvard University Press, 1994), 27.

40. Bernard Lewis, *The Multiple Identities of the Middle East* (New York: Schocken Books, 1998), 99.

41. Bassam Tibi, *The Challenge of Fundamentalism: Political Islam and the New World Disorder* (Berkeley: University of California Press, 1993), 6.

42. Esposito, *Oxford History of Islam*, 683.

43. Lewis, *Islam and the West* (New York: Oxford University Press, 1993), 154.

44. Tibi, *Challenge of Fundamentalism*, 10.

45. Lewis, *Islam and the West*, 6.

46. Pipes, *In The Path of God*, 107.

47. Lewis, *Islam and the West*, 101-02.

48. Lewis, *Multiple Identities of the Middle East*, 6-7.

49. Ibid., 7.

50. Huntington, *Clash of Civilizations*, 21.

51. Ernest Gellner, *Reason and Culture: The Historic Role of Rationality and Rationalism* (Oxford: Blackwell, 1992), 182.

52. Craig Calhoun, *Critical Social Theory* (Oxford: Blackwell, 1995), 213-21.

53. Ibid., 221.

54. Alexander Wendt, "Collective Identity Formation and the International State," *American Political Science Review* 88-2 (1994); 385.

55. Mark Hoffman, "Critical Theory and the Inter-Paradigm Debate," *Millennium Journal of International Studies* 16-2 (1987): 233-36. Reference made in Ted Hopf, "The Promise of Constructivism in International Relations Theory," *International Security* 23-2 (1998): 177.

56. Richard K. Ashley, "The Geopolitics of Geopolitical Space: Toward a Critical Social Theory of International Politics," *Alternatives* 13-4 (1987): 403. Reference made in Hopf, "Promise of Constructivism," 403.

57. Hopf, "Promise of Constructivism," 177-78.

58. Charles Taylor, "Interpretation and the Science of Man," in *Interpretive Social Science: A Second Look*, ed. Paul Rabinow and William M. Sullivan (Berkeley: University of California Press, 1987), 4. Reference made in Hopf, "Promise of Constructivism," 178.

59. Hopf, "Promise of Constructivism," 178.

60. R.B.J. Walker, "World Politics and Western Reason: Universalism, Pluralism, Hegemony," in *Culture, Ideology and World Order*, ed. R.B.J. Walker (Boulder, Co.: Westview Press, 1984), 195. Reference made in Hopf, "Promise of Constructivism," 178.

61. Gary P. Freeman, "Immigration as a Source of Political Discontent and Frustration in Western Democracies," *Studies in Comparative International Development* 10-3 (1997): 43.

62. Myron Weiner, "Determinants of Immigrant Integration: An International Comparative Analysis," in *Immigration and Integration in Post-Industrial Societies: Theoretical Analysis and Policy-Related Research*, ed. Naomi Carmon (Warwick, UK: Centre for Research in Ethnic Relations, 1996), 47-48.

63. Weiner, ed., *International Migration and Security* (Boulder, Co.: Westview Press, 1993), 11.
64. Ibid., 60.
65. John Rex, *Ethnic Minorities*, 135.
66. Emile Durkheim, *The Division of Labour in Society* (Glencoe, Il.: The Free Press, 1933). Reference made in Rex, *Ethnic Minorities*, 135.
67. Rex, *Ethnic Minorities*, 135.
68. Ibid., 136-39.
69. Alejandro Portes and Ruben Rumbaut, *Immigrant America: A Portrait*, 2nd Edition (Berkeley: University of California Press, 1996).
70. Yasemine N. Soysal, *Limits of Citizenship: Migrants and Postnational Membership in Europe* (Chicago: University of Chicago Press, 1994).
71. Ramadan, "Immigration, Integration and Cooperation Policies," 2-3.

Chapter 3

Islam in France

Introduction

In October 1989, three female students of Moroccan ethnic extraction attempted to wear their traditional Islamic headscarves (*foulards*) while attending a French public school in Creil, a small town just north of Paris. Contending that these *foulards* violated the French government's 1905 law separating church and state institutions and activities, school administrators excluded the students from classes. Ultimately, national officials backed the decision taken at Gabriel Havez Secondary School in Creil, albeit through an ambiguous ruling suggesting that the settlement of future disputes of that nature proceed on a case-by-case basis at the local level.[1] The *foulard* affair sparked a vigorous national debate that focused both on the particulars of the Creil episode and the issue of Islam in France. Its most profound result to date came in February 2004 with the French National Assembly's passage of a law banning all ostentatious religious symbols from public schools.

In April 2000, a French policeman killed a Muslim teenager of North African descent in Lille, a heavy industry-based city northeast of Paris. The incident sparked two days of rioting undertaken primarily by youths from the city's Islamic community, which is composed predominantly of individuals whose forebears migrated to France from the *Maghreb* region of North Africa that encompasses present-day Morocco, Tunisia and Algeria. Similar to the *foulard* affair, these events were in part the product of the deep-rooted ethnic and religious tensions prevalent in France, where most Muslims—both those holding and bereft of citizenship—are denied the economic, political and social benefits that accompany full acceptance by the societal majority.[2]

The marginalization of minority groups is a troubling and potentially destabilizing phenomenon in any society. It is of even greater significance in the French context for two reasons. First, the philosophical cleavage between Muslims and French government officials—whether genuine, perceived or a hybrid of those characterizations—is particularly difficult to bridge in a country that has traditionally placed considerable emphasis on the unilateral loyalty of citizens to the state. As journalist Adam LeBor explains, "Islam is an obsession for France, an obsession stoked up by politicians and headline hungry reporters who feed off each other, creating a climate of intolerance and hysteria—it is no exaggeration to describe it as such—that I found nowhere else in Europe or America."[3] Second, the four to six million Muslims presently residing in France constitute that state's largest and most rapidly expanding minority group.[4] As Dalil Boubakeur, director of the Paris Mosque stresses, "Islam in part of its life in France is like a patient who has suffered and needs a convalescence, in its spiritual life, in its practice and its way of understanding with general society. The Islamic population has grown too fast in a country which was not prepared to receive such a great community in such a short time, but Islam has roots, [as well as] legitimacy in France for a long time."[5]

With these related observations as a point of departure, this chapter discusses the issue of Islam in France through the presentation of seven sections, which unfold in the following manner:

Development of Muslim Presence

This section describes the genesis, and subsequent growth of Muslim communities in France over the latter half of the twentieth century in three parts. The first part addresses the initial development of waves of Muslim migrants to France from North Africa through related pull and push factors in the 1950s and 1960s. The second part discusses the change in composition and character undertaken by these communities as a result of the family reunifications that followed the abrogation of labor migration programs in the aftermath of the 1973-74 international oil crisis. The third part examines the entrenchment of Islamic communities in urban centers such as Paris, Marseille and Lyon concurrent with the development of French-born second and third generations of Muslims in those contexts.

Characteristics of Muslim Communities

This section offers quantitative and qualitative descriptions of the Muslims of France in the 1990s and 2000s. Its four related parts focus on demographic, economic, socio-religious and political indicators, respectively.

Clashes of Identity

This section discusses the philosophical and practical issues that separate Muslims from the societal mainstream in France in three parts. The first part examines briefly the historical and contemporary elements of the French national identity in both political and social terms. The second part discusses the principal elements of Islamic identity—both generally and in the French context. The third part addresses the evolving identities of the Muslims of France, with an emphasis on the extent to which members of the younger generations are likely to forge the synthesis necessary to create a modern Franco-European variant of Islam.

Examination of French Integration Process

This section focuses on the French government's efforts to integrate Muslim minorities into society in two parts. The first part describes the principal elements of the models utilized by the French government in attempting to fully integrate Muslims. It stresses the applications of those models to the second and third generations given the emphasis the book places on the past 20 rather than 50 years. The second part evaluates the strengths and weaknesses of those models.

Implications of Integrative Shortcomings

This section discusses the implications of the government's inability to fully integrate Muslim communities into French society over the past two decades, particularly with respect to the younger generations. It does so in three related parts, which address in turn these implications as they pertain to socio-economic stratification, domestic politics and security, and international politics and security.

Measurement of Integrative Progress

This section proposes a model for use in achieving the eventual full integration of Muslims within France on a bottom-up basis. It has three parts. The first part stresses the need to cultivate the middle ground between the government and Muslim communities in order to accommodate both sides' concerns. The second part denotes a set of benchmarks to indicate the extent to which a given minority group is making positive progress in the direction of full societal integration. The third part applies those benchmarks to the French context.

Conclusions

This section determines the extent to and speed at which the integration of Muslim minorities is likely to proceed in the twenty-first century and the potential consequences.

Development of Muslim Presence

French immigration is an issue defined primarily by composition rather than quantity. Coupled with a rising demand for unskilled labor in Western Europe in the aftermath of World War II, the end of French colonial rule in Tunisia and Morocco in 1956, and in Algeria in 1962, triggered immigration waves that fundamentally altered the composition of communities of foreigners residing in France. Previously overwhelmingly European and Christian in ethnicity and faith, respectively, the French immigrant population rapidly acquired Arab and Islamic characteristics. The proportion of Muslims in that context has risen steadily in the decades since, initially through the chain migration of workers and family reunification programs and subsequently via the appearance and subsequent growth of second and third generations.

The percentage of immigrants in the French population has not changed dramatically in the past century and not at all in the last 26 years—it stood at 7.4 percent in 1975 and remains the same today.[6] However, the composition of that segment of the population has changed markedly. During that period, foreigners have migrated to France in three waves. The initial wave, which satisfied a demand for inexpensive, unskilled labor, was composed largely of 329,000 Italians and Belgians, who emigrated from their native states between 1876 and 1910.[7] The second, an inflow of 576,000 Italians, Poles and Czechs from 1920-25, helped replenish a working-age population decimated by the ravages of World War I.[8] The third, triggered by the decolonization of North Africa (1956-62) and the Algerian Civil War (1962-65), included flows of 846,000 Algerians, 270,000 Moroccans and 150,000 Tunisians to France from 1962-73.[9] In combination with concurrent increases in the supply of Portuguese and Spanish immigrants, the *Maghrebian* influx helped provide the requisite labor force to fuel vigorous French industrial growth in the 1960s.[10]

A sense of reciprocity transcended these developments. In all three cases, France lacked the requisite unskilled labor force to fuel appreciable economic growth. This was particularly true as the French joined their Western European allies in the development of an integrated regional economy through the establishment of the European Coal and Steel Community in April 1951 and European Economic Community (EEC) in June 1957. The immigrants, for their part, sought employment abroad because of a dearth of available jobs at home. The resulting transaction was essentially a marriage of convenience, one that—at least initially—featured an implicit agreement to separate on favorable terms once both sides had achieved their respective short-term economic objectives. Cheap foreign labor drove the French industrial engine when rapid growth was indispensable; francs from government coffers enabled immigrants to raise funds in anticipation of more prosperous futures in their countries of origin.

When economic growth in France and at the broader Western European level slowed in the early 1970s and stagnated in the aftermath of the October 1973 Organization of Petroleum Exporting Countries (OPEC)–induced oil crisis, the demand for labor receded sharply. As a result, the French government suspended foreign labor immigration in July 1974.[11] However, it continued to permit—albeit in a somewhat restrictive fashion—the family members of foreign workers to rejoin their husbands and fathers in France.[12] While stemming the flow of immigration stabilized the ethnically foreign population of France—those individuals with and without citizenship—at 7.4 percent at the end of 1975, it did not freeze the proportion of Muslims in that total.

Over the first 60 years of the twentieth century, more than 80 percent of French immigrants were of Central and Western European ethnic extraction, 32 percent of whom were born in Italy.[13] Most shared a common Catholic religious heritage with the French and were thus not difficult to integrate. By 1975, on the other hand, Europeans accounted for 50 percent and North Africans 24.7 percent of the immigrants in France. By 1990, increases in the number of second and third generation *Maghrebians* had boosted the proportion of North Africans to 28.1 percent as opposed to 37 percent for Europeans in the French population.[14] As Catherine Wihtol de Wenden notes, the unanticipated result of the government's halt to labor migration from North Africa was the "settlement of formerly temporary or 'turnover' migrants and the massive arrival of families, which raised new issues of multiculturalism and 'the right to be different.' "[15]

Building on these observations, Wihtol de Wenden stresses three distinct changes in the demographics of the North African presence in France since 1975, each of which has altered the nature of interactions among Muslim communities and the societal majority—locally, regionally and nationally. First, family reunifications increased markedly, as a result of fears among former guest workers that the admission of their wives and children to France would grow increasingly difficult over time. For example, between the national censuses of 1975 and 1982, the balance of European and non-European foreigners shifted in the latter's favor for the first time. Second, illegal immigration from Tunisia and Morocco rose concurrent with a decrease in labor migration from southern Europe (most notably Spain). Third, native-born generations of Muslims have developed and grown at a higher rate than is true of the French population overall.[16]

Initially, communities of Muslim guest workers in France resided in government-subsidized hostels, with their members anticipating short-term stays to accumulate the requisite resources to enjoy prosperous lives in the future in their countries of origin. Their contact with French society was limited to daily labor in a given industrial occupation and did not involve the public practice of Islam. Once immigrant families reunified in France, they increasingly placed a greater emphasis on the cultural and religious values common to their places of birth. This shift in religio-cultural focus included elements of Islam that featured a more publicly visible expression of their Islamic beliefs, one that stood in stark contrast to French societal norms. As Jocelyne Cesari explains, first generation North Africans "do not want to disappear into French society; they want to be recognized and considered as Muslim."[17]

With the development of subsequent generations of Muslims known as *beurs*, the communities in which they lived became more deeply rooted fixtures in France. Tariq Ramadan identifies two related issues that grew out of this demographic transformation. First, returning to the countries from which the guest workers of the 1950s and 1960s emigrated was no longer a realistic option. Notwithstanding *Maghrebians*' cultural and religious affinity for the past, their present realities and future prospects clearly lay in France. Second, those Muslims who have spent their formative years in France possess two identities—one North African and one French—that are by no means complementary.[18] As Ramadan notes, the second and third generations "were French and they were Muslim. This, in itself, did not solve any problems but, on the contrary, created a new, more complex and intricate difficulty . . . the question was not only 'how to be Muslim in France' but 'how to be Muslim and French'."[19]

Characteristics of Muslim Communities

The preceding discussion of the genesis and subsequent development and entrenchment of Islamic communities in France provides a necessary foundation for a deeper examination of those entities in the contemporary context. That examination, in turn, requires descriptions of the demographic, economic, socio-religious and political characteristics of French Muslims in the 1990s and 2000s. For purposes of clarity, the categorical particulars of these indicators are as follows. The demographic category focuses on the ethnic extraction, geographic dispersion and specific locations of Islamic communities in France. The economic category places an emphasis on types of jobs held by and rates of unemployment among French Muslims. The socio-religious category deals primarily with fertility rates, construction of mosques, and availability of *halal* meats. The political category features measurements of the extent to which Islamic communities have achieved representation at the local, regional and national levels.

The Muslim segment of the French population is composed principally of individuals and families from the *Maghreb*. It also includes communities from sub-Suharan Africa, Middle Eastern states such as Turkey and Lebanon, and French converts. A 2000 estimate by the French High Council on Integration report classified the number of Muslims in France as follows: Algerians (1.5 million), Moroccans (one million), Tunisians (500,000), Turks (350,000), other Middle Easterners [Arabs, Iranians and Kurds] (400,000), and Sub-Saharan Africans (250,000).[20] While Muslims account for no more than eight percent of the French population nationally at present, their numbers are increasing at a 3.7 percent rate annually and they are not evenly dispersed geographically.[21] Franco-Islamic communities are located almost exclusively in low-rent housing projects in the suburbs (*banlieues*) that ring major urban centers, most notably Paris, Marseille, Lyon and Lille. The Muslim presence is more pronounced—and thus more publicly visible—in local *banlieues* than is the case regionally or nationally. As a result, places such as Mantes-la-Jolie and Sartrouville (Paris), Bricarde-Castellane-Plan d'Aou (Marseille) and Vaulx-en-Velin (Lyon) are associated with Muslims who live in abject poverty and are perceived as threatening by the societal mainstream.

Fueled mainly by the development of the second and third generations since 1973, growth in these *banlieues* has left some French metropolitan areas with populations that are as high as one-third North African Muslim in ethno-religious orientation. Similarly, the French Interior Ministry estimates that Muslims account for proportions as high as 11 percent in particular regions.[22] As Christopher Caldwell notes, in "some places, France already looks like a Muslim country."[23] In Marseille, which is closer than any other major French city to the North African coastline, a quarter of the members of the population—roughly 200,000—are Muslims. In the *La Bricarde* housing project north of the city center, for instance, some 200 satellite dishes spring from rooftops, pointing south across the Mediterranean. More than 85 percent of *La Bricarde*'s residents have roots in the *Maghreb*, including approximately 2,000 *beurs* living in the project.[24]

With the aging of the Muslim pioneers of the 1950s and 1960s—former guest workers and their wives—the younger generations have gained more prominence within Islamic communities across France. The growth of these generations has altered the demographics of the country's Muslim population. For example, one-third of its Muslims are natives, 60 percent have lived there for at least 10 years and nearly half are French citizens.[25] These shifts have fostered a gradual trend toward the evolution of a hybrid Franco-Muslim identity. However, the speed of that process is contingent upon the economic opportunities available to Muslims. Unfortunately, present prospects are not particularly encouraging in that respect.

Put simply, Muslims face considerably worse economic circumstances than the majority of others living in France, both natives and immigrants of European ethnic extraction. Although unemployment was a serious national problem throughout the 1990s and continues as such today, its impact is markedly greater in Muslim communities. In January 1999, for example, the unemployment rate in France was 10.2 percent nationally. However, among North African Muslims, it stood at 33 percent.[26] Unemployment is even more pronounced in the *banlieues*. According to Didier Bonnet, who directs a social-service organization in Marseille, unemployment in October 2000 was 20 percent in the city overall and 50 percent in *La Bricarde*.[27]

As opposed to workers of European ethnicity, three quarters of whom work in service-oriented professions, *Maghrebians* are almost exclusively limited to blue-collar industries, which have undergone considerable downsizing over the past two decades.[28] In 1999, on average, for example, unemployment rates among individuals of European and non-European ethnic extraction in France, were as follows: Spanish (8.5 percent), Portuguese (eight), Algerian (32.5) and Moroccan (38). Similarly, among employed members of these ethnic groups, 58.2 percent of Moroccans and 48.7 percent of Algerians worked in blue-collar industries as opposed to 38.3 percent of Spaniards and 37.7 percent of Italians.[29]

Given their employment travails, Muslims in France face a perpetual struggle for subsistence, one they most often attribute to the state, whether in the form of the national government or the local officials with whom they more frequently interact. As Rémy Leveau argues, aside from President Jacques Chirac, the "mayor is the most immediate authority in [French Muslims'] lives and the one most often blamed for inadequate or hostile policies from which they suffer. It is true that most of the time problems of housing and employment create the conditions for exclusion and that the response to them comes in the form of a neo-communalism."[30] Leveau's assertion that the internal composition of Muslim communities in France reflects their exclusion from mainstream society is valid. However, the contextual articulation of such exclusion, whether economic, socio-religious or political, is complex and requires the consideration of a combination of related analytical factors. Financial shortcomings related to unemployment, for instance, often have a greater impact upon Muslim communities, because their fertility rates are higher than is the case among other minority groups. In 1990, the following percentages of couples residing in France had three or more children: Italian (16.6), Spanish (15.2), Portuguese (16), Algerian

(27.4), Tunisian (33.5) and Moroccan (40.1).[31] The national average fertility rate in France was 1.3 births per woman in 1990 and is now 1.89.[32]

While high fertility rates are symptomatic of the cultural traditions common to Islamic communities generally and the *Maghrebian* culture specifically, other indicators suggest the isolation of Muslims in France is decreasing. As increasing numbers of second and third generation Muslims have come into contact with French men and women socially, the number of mixed marriages has increased. Between 1970 and 1990, for example, the number of mixed marriages between North African women and French men rose from 433 to 3,892.[33] Similarly, between 1981 and 1992, the number of mixed marriages between individuals of French and *Maghrebian* ethnic extractions rose in the following proportions: Franco-Algerian (2,568-5,726), Franco-Moroccan (1,101-5,015) and Franco-Tunisian (747-1,309).[34]

Divisions between Muslim communities and the French state are more pronounced in public education. While the government has the option under the previously cited 1905 law separating church and state affairs to provide public funds to religious schools administered by organizations not directly associated with the state, it does not do so equitably with respect to all faiths. Under the auspices of this provision, the state regularly dispenses subsidies to private schools sponsored by Catholic, Jewish and Protestant groups. Collectively, these institutions educate approximately one-fifth of the school-age children in France.[35] As Jurgen Neilsen notes, by virtue of the tacit agreement reached between the French government and representatives of the county's principal faiths at the start of the twentieth century, "religious communities are entitled to run their own schools with public funding covering much of the costs."[36] However, the French national government has remained generally dismissive of Muslim requests for public funds to assist in the construction and administration of Islamic schools.[37]

The government has been similarly inflexible vis-à-vis the provision of public funds for the construction of mosques and the maintenance of exclusively Muslim sections in cemeteries in French cities and towns (as stipulated under the tenets of Islam). At present, there are a scant nine mosques in France that can accommodate 1,000 or more worshippers. Four are located in the Paris metropolitan area, two in Lille and one each in Lyon, Marseille and Reims. As a result, most Muslims in France are relegated to the 1,300 Islamic prayer rooms that often double as apartments for the *Meghrebians* residing in a given locale.[38] In Marseille, for instance, there is just one *mosque cathedral* to serve nearly 250,000 Muslims.[39] Additionally, the placement of the prayer rooms in squalid housing projects contributes to the marginalization of the communities they serve. As Wihtol de Wenden explains, it "is the poverty . . . of the prayer rooms [that] strikes the negative image of mosques in the neighborhood in French public opinion, rather than the challenge to French identity brought by minarets in the French landscape."[40]

While Muslims in France are divided among several distinctive ethnic groups, their communities—whether Algerian, Moroccan, Tunisian or Turkish in orientation—are perceived by most Frenchmen as a monolith, one characterized by Islamic fundamentalism rather than moderation or modernity. In reality, French Muslims are, on the whole, by no means radical in their practice of Islam. While the majority of

Muslims tend to eat ritually slaughtered *halal* meat or at least what they believe is such,[41] most do not pray every day or attend weekly Friday services at a mosque or prayer room. A pair of 1994 *Sondage* polls, for example, suggested that just 31 percent of Muslims in France pray daily and only 16 percent go to weekly services. In the former case, the 31 percent figure was 10 percent lower than in a *Sondage* poll that asked the identical question in 1989.[42]

Given the growing proportion of Muslims in the population (in terms of religious allegiance, they are outnumbered only by Catholics) interaction between French government officials and Islamic communal representatives is essential to ensure that each side acknowledges—and ideally attempts to discuss and resolve—differences of opinion on particular issues. However, despite common misperceptions to the contrary, there is no single body that accurately represents the collective interests of the Muslims of France. Consider the arguments of Olivier Roy and John Esposito on this topic. Roy stresses that in "spite of the efforts of missionaries and a few Islamic intellectuals, there is no religious solidarity in the Muslim community in France capable of transcending ethnic, linguistic and national divisions."[43] Similarly, Esposito notes that the "challenge today is to appreciate the diversity of Islamic centers and movements, to ascertain the causes or reasons behind confrontations and conflicts, and ... to respond to specific events and situations with informed, reasoned responses rather than predetermined presumptions and reactions."[44]

There are two paths leading to political representation for Muslims living in France. The first is through election to political office at local, regional or national level. The second is by way of organizations—defined according to ethnicity, religion or both—with the capacity to present the concerns of Muslim communities to government officials and extract concessions ranging from the provision of funds for the construction of mosques to the rights of schoolgirls to wear *foulards* while attending public school classes. Thus far, what limited success Muslims have achieved on each of these issues has been confined almost exclusively to local level. For example, while no Muslim has ever been elected to the French Parliament, 130 were elected as municipal councilors in 2001.[45]

Efforts to forge a collective Islamic identity among French Muslims and develop representative bodies to express their communal concerns have unfolded in three general contexts over the past 20 years. First, in the early 1980s, Muslim elites founded the initial national Islamic organizations, most notably the *Federation National des Musulmans de France* (FNMF) and the *Union des Organizations Islamiques de France* (UOIF).[46] A similar initiative in the early 2000s resulted in the establishment of the slightly more broad-based *Conseil de l'Islam en France* (CIF).[47] Second, in 1989, then French Interior Minister Pierre Joxe created the *Conseil de Reflexion sur l'Islam en France* (CORIF) to act as an interlocutory arm of the state.[48] Similarly, in April 2000, then French Interior Minister Jean-Pierre Chevènement instituted a joint government-Muslim council designed to improve domestic Franco-Muslim relations, the mandate of which was extended by Chevènement's successor, Daniel Vaillant, in May 2001.[49] Third, lay preachers—often connected with international Islamic organizations—have undertaken what Roy describes as "a 'grass roots' reconversion of the Islamic community, severing it from French society . . . as a means of ensuring Islam's position as a minority."[50]

Organizations in the first two contexts—those associated with Islamic elites and the French government—have thus far proven ineffective, largely because unemployed Muslims in their teens and twenties do not identify comfortably with representatives in either forum. Instead, they have grown more likely to seek and find solace—and a common purpose—in the teachings of foreign Imams who extol the virtues of orthodox Islam and berate the culture and values of a French society from which they feel excluded. As Wihtol de Wenden contends, "[n]ew wave Imams are using the loss of identiary values and the feeling of exclusion to develop a 'catch all' strategy all around. Across their network of so-called cultural associations, some of them are socializing the excluded to integrism, intolerance and radical Islam as a denial of citizenship."[51]

Clashes of Identity

The exclusion of Muslims from an equitable and productive position in the French societal mainstream is based fundamentally on differences in the identities of the individuals of whom Islamic communities and the majority of the population, respectively, are composed. This section discusses those differences and the extent to which they are reconcilable in three related areas. First, it examines the basic elements of French national identity, focusing primarily on the secular principles of the state. Second, it describes the tenets of Islam generally and the precepts of that faith most germane to the development of Muslim communal identities in France, placing an emphasis on *Maghrebian* ethnicities. Third, it evaluates the potential for the construction of a hybrid Franco-Islamic identity through an analysis of the evolving role of second and third generation Muslims (known as *beurs*) within French society.

European secularism is rooted in the rational principles of the seventeenth and eighteenth century Enlightenment. Seminal writers of this period, including Englishman John Locke, and Frenchmen Julien Offray de la Matrie and the Abbé Cordillac, encouraged individuals to interpret events themselves rather than give credence to the whims of religious leaders.[52] More pointedly, according to Norman Davies, the Enlightenment served as a means to illuminate and perhaps erase "all of the unthinking, irrational, dogmatic attitudes with which European Christianity had become encrusted."[53] As Davies notes, Locke's *Essay Concerning Human Understanding* "advanced the proposition that the mind is blank at birth" and, therefore, human knowledge "is the fruit of experience, either through the senses, which process data from the external world, or through the faculty of reflection, which processes data through the mind's internal workings."[54]

French secularism draws broadly on these ideas, particularly with respect to the primacy of individual over religious communitarian thought processes, but it focuses principally on the role of the state in society. The French national government acknowledges the importance of religion in people's lives but insists that residents—citizens and non-citizens alike—profess allegiance to the state first and religious institutions second. As Maxim Silverman asserts, "[s]ecularism is the sign *par excellence* of the rational, progressive, equal, universalist tradition of the French republic, counterposed to the particularist tradition of the 'Anglo-Saxon' model."[55] It follows that, as Liah Greenfeld contends, French "society (body politic, Republic, State, Sovereign or People) is law unto itself. All authority, all values emanate from it. It is, by definition, infallible."[56] Yet, given that the French government encourages individuals to think and act independently only if those thoughts and actions coincide with the interests of the state, it is essentially a self-, rather than collective-serving entity.

The French secular approach dictates that religion always remains confined to the private sphere, which is why the 1989 *foulard* affair and similar imbroglios in subsequent years have sparked vigorous debates over church-state relations, both nationally and internationally.[57] The 1905 French law separating church and state affairs stipulates that the government is not permitted to directly subsidize religious schools.[58] In accordance with this line of reasoning, students—irrespective of faith (Islam, Catholicism, Judaism, or any other denomination)—may not overtly practice any aspects of their religions while attending a publicly funded school. Generally, Catholics and Jews have come to accept this and thus play by the state's rules, relegating their religious identities to French cultural ones.[59] Comparable responses, however, have yet to occur on as broad a level among France's Muslims.

Prior to engaging in a discussion of the particulars of the practice of Islam in the French context, it is useful first to describe some of the most broadly accepted tenets of that faith.[60] Islam is by nature a religion that permeates all aspects of its adherents' lives, in both the public and private spheres. Fundamentally, it is based on five pillars, which Muslims must adhere to in order for consideration as strict observers of the faith. First, Muslims must profess their allegiance to Allah as the one true God and acknowledge Mohammed's role as his prophet. Second, they must pray five times daily while facing the holy city of Mecca, which is located in the Saudi Arabian desert. Third, they must abstain from the consumption of all food and beverages between sunrise and sunset during the holy month of Ramadan each year. Fourth, they must donate alms to the poor if they possess the resources to do so. Fifth, if financially able, they must make one pilgrimage (*hadj*)—to Islam's most holy shrine, the Kaba at Mecca, during their lifetimes. Additionally, Islam's holy book—the Koran—calls for females to wear veils when outside of their homes (as men are not permitted to gaze at the visages of women aside from their own wives and other family members) and forbids the consumption of pork and alcohol.[61]

While the rules one must follow for strict adherence to Islam are somewhat if not wholly out of place within Western societies, Muslims do not all practice their faith in the same manner. Even in the context of the Greater Middle East, there are divisions among Muslims regarding the interpretation of the Koran and the role of Islam in society and governance. Religion plays a predominant role in the political systems of some states and a less significant one in others. Islam itself is divided into Sunni and Shia strains, which are central to daily life in Saudi Arabia and Iran, respectively. Yet, one of the world's most populous Muslim-majority states—Turkey—has a secular government. As Esposito explains, Islam has "incorporated a variety of beliefs and activities that grew out of religious and historical experience and the needs of specific Muslim communities. . . . The inherent unity of faith, implicit in statements like 'one God, one book, one [final] prophet,' should not deter one from appreciating the rich diversity that has characterized the religious (legal, theological and devotional) life of the Islamic community."[62] In France, the practice of Islam varies distinctively by generation, with Muslims who immigrated in the 1950s and 1960s more likely to adhere strictly to the five pillars than is the case among their descendents. The results of a 1983 poll of *Maghrebians* residing in France were illustrative of this trend. First, the majority of first generation men openly declared themselves Muslims, whereas more than one-quarter of their children declined to identify themselves with Islam. Second, just over half of first generation parents continued to perform prayers five times a day as opposed to three percent of their children. Third, 45 percent of the parents read the Koran compared to 13 percent of the children.[63] Similar, a 1997 study indicated that just 23 percent of Muslims in France tended to partake in public prayer at least five times a day.[64]

The growth of the younger generations of Muslims in France has presented a welcome opportunity for the cultivation of a hybrid Franco-Islamic identity. However, the development of such an identity is contingent upon the creation of an equitable place for Muslims in mainstream French society, one that does not entail the unequivocal subjugation of religious practice to loyalty to the state. There is a perception in Islamic communities in France, for instance, that the majority of Frenchmen view North African Muslims as undesirable at best and threatening at worst, irrespective of the ways in which they express their religious beliefs. As Mustapha Tougui, a Muslim living in Paris, notes, the "world now doesn't accept racism because it doesn't look good. . . . So they make the same record, they just turn it over on the other side, and when they want to say the same thing about Arabs, they use Islam. If they say Arab, it's definitely racist, but if they say Islam, it's something intellectual, something different, they can pretend it's some kind of analysis."[65]

There are two distinctive paths present and future generations of young Muslims in France may follow with respect to identity formation. The first path, fostered by the bitterness that accompanies exclusion, is introverted in nature. Put simply, shunned by the French state and majority citizens therein, *Maghrebian* youths will turn inward in search of political, economic and social support. The end result, Wihtol de Wenden concludes, is that as "for the youngest, Islam grows all the more as exclusion increases: in some suburbs, the beard-wearing ('*barbus*') are the only [ones] present to propose [to] them structures of belief, of life, even a family or job and sometimes a valuable identity: 'It is better to say we are Muslims than unemployed.' "[66] Similarly, Leveau stresses that among Muslims in France, "[n]eo-communalism comes about because neighborhood organization around Islam is the only recognition available to excluded youths. Religion is the totem capable of attracting the interest of global society."[67]

The second path is progressive and considerably more encouraging. Given that they can openly practice the five pillars while residing in France, it is possible if not necessarily probable for Muslims to develop identities that include a mixture of Islamic and North African and French cultural characteristics. According to Cesari, second and third generation North Africans have had some success in cultivating precisely such an identity. As she puts it, they "distinguish between practicing religion and believing religion to describe their relationship with Islam. It is a part of the cultural legacy within the private sphere, with no direct influence on their social and political behavior. Especially for those who are upwardly mobile, Islam is an ethic, a source of moral values giving significance to their life but without implication for their practice."[68]

Examination of French Integration Process

In July 1998, the French national soccer team clinched the World Cup title with a 3-0 victory over Brazil in Paris. The star of the game was midfielder Zinedine Zidane, a French citizen born to Algerian parents in Marseille's *La Bricarde*. Given the team's diverse ethnic makeup—it featured players of French, North and Sub-Saharan African, and Afro-Caribbean ethnicity—in general and Zidane's starring role specifically, President Jacques Chirac and then Prime Minister Lionel Jospin described it as a shining example of the development of an equitable, multicultural French society. Chirac awarded Zidane and his teammates the *Legion d'honneur* and one French writer penned a work entitled *Zidane: The Novel of a Victory*. As Caldwell notes, there was a sudden sense within the French populace that Zidane "was living proof that France was great because France was welcoming. . . . People marked a changing attitude toward immigrants in general and Arabs in particular, and named it the Zidane effect."[69]

Yet, while France's World Cup victory helped to rally individuals of myriad ethnic backgrounds and social classes behind the flag in the short term, it by no means fully redressed the long-term economic, social and political exclusion of Muslims. Although Zidane's rise to prominence after spending his formative years in one of France's poorest *banlieues* demonstrates that all those with North African backgrounds are not condemned to lead desperate lives, he is clearly the exception rather than the rule. On the whole, the Muslims of France lack a middle class comparable in relative size to that existing within the societal majority. That shortcoming is a clear indicator of governmental inability if not unwillingness to fully integrate Muslims. In order to identify the reasons why, a chronological examination of French integration policies is necessary. The ensuing discussion pursues that objective by describing and evaluating French governmental efforts to integrate Muslims from the 1970s to the 2000s, placing an emphasis on the past 20 years.

The initial wave of North African migrants to France associated with the guest worker programs of the 1950s and 1960s did not trigger a concurrent need to integrate those individuals into mainstream society. Both the French government and the migrants felt at the time that their reciprocal interactions would not extend beyond the postwar recovery. Once the domestic labor supply increased, the demand for foreign workers would subside, causing the immigrants to return home. For their part, *Maghrebian* laborers generally did not try to anchor themselves in French society, preferring instead to return to the hostels after work and send most of what they earned back to North Africa in anticipation of prosperous futures in the communities from which they originated.

The issue of minority integration increased in significance when the government's decision to end foreign labor migration programs in 1974 triggered an unanticipated wave of family reunifications and the resultant entrenchment of Muslim communities in *banlieues* across France. Historically, the French have integrated foreigners by assimilating individuals rather than incorporating communities with distinctive minority identities based on factors such as class, culture, ethnicity and religion. The logic behind that approach is understandable given the importance of republicanism in the development of the modern French nation. As Karen Bird explains, "French republicans define democracy in terms of universal aspirations, and view the enlarged, centralized 'nation-state' as the ideal vehicle of progress. . . . The fundamental identity of all individuals must be as citizens."[70] However, the French model of integration based on assimilation was problematic for Muslim guest workers and their families, who wanted to retain their own identities, which were anchored in Islam. In short, the philosophical differences between French secularism and Islam have rendered the integration of Muslims a complex and—thus far—not fully surmountable task. As James Corbett contends, "France has never been a multicultural society. Foreigners are expected to fit into the French mold, French thought processes [and] the French value system."[71]

On balance, France has treated foreigners in a reasonably liberal manner in terms of the acquisition of citizenship over the past two centuries. Under the *jus soli* of the eighteenth century *ancien regime*, anyone born on French soil—irrespective of national origin—became a French citizen. Similarly, under the *jus sanguinis* of the revolutionaries, anyone with one French parent or anyone who married and then lived with a French citizen for at least six months could claim French citizenship.[72] However, while citizenship entitles an individual to equal treatment under the law in principle, such is not always the case in practice, particularly if citizens are determined to retain their own cultural and religious identities rather than adopt the political and cultural precepts of the state. As Silverman notes, "[a]ssimilation contains a double-bind at its very core; for the community which the outsider is required to join is, at all times, just as ready to reject this figure on the grounds of ethnic, national or cultural difference."[73]

Despite the generally liberal wording of the *jus soli* and *jus sanguinis*, the nineteenth and twentieth centuries are replete with examples of government initiatives designed to qualify both the means to acquire and rights derived from citizenship. Examples include the conditioning of citizenship rights on civil behavior under the constitution of 1793,[74] denial of suffrage to women until 1946, the loss of civil rights after condemnation in a criminal proceeding and a five-year waiting period to vote following naturalization (in force until 1973).[75] These types of qualifications have had a disproportionately negative effect on Muslims. While approximately 100,000 foreigners have acquired French citizenship annually since 1975, the percentages of citizens vis-à-vis non-citizens among first generation North African immigrants is considerably lower than for Europeans. In 1999, for example, the proportions of immigrants with French citizenship by nationality were as follows: Italian (55), Spanish (54), Tunisian (40), Algerian (24) and Moroccan (23).[76]

The appearance and subsequent growth of younger generations in Islamic communities across France from the mid-1970s to the 1990s increased the proportion of Muslims with citizenship to approximately 50 percent at the start of the twenty-first century. It also intensified the need to develop a more inclusive model to equitably integrate Muslims—particularly those born in France—into mainstream society. Cesari argues that such a model must bridge the gap separating multiculturalism from assimilation and the unequivocal acceptance of Muslim identity through full communal integration, stressing that "Islam has changed the balance between the three major 'pillars' of French political life: unity, respect for political pluralism and liberty. If pluralism is linked with democracy, it no longer refers to the integration of dominated groups or to the representation of the diversity of citizens, but to the balance between multiculturalism and communities."[77]

While successive French governments have made superficial attempts to mitigate the marginalization of Muslim communities over the past two decades, a comprehensive national framework to achieve substantial progress toward that end has yet to emerge. Following the wave of family reunifications in the late 1970s, for example, government officials shifted their rhetoric, replacing the historical emphasis on assimilation to a more accommodating "insertion" of minority communities into the majority.[78] Similarly, President François Mitterand's Socialist Party (PS) focused on improvements in human rights accorded to immigrant groups in the 1980s and early 1990s.[79] In addition, Chirac and Prime Minister Jean-Pierre Raffarin have both encouraged more open dialogue between the government officials and Muslim communal representatives since the 2002 presidential and parliamentary elections. On a particularly positive note, Raffarin has backed his rhetoric with concrete political action by naming two North African Muslims to national cabinet posts.[80]

Over the last decade, two trends were evident with respect to government engagement with Muslim communities. The first, manifested in the 1993 Pasqua Laws—named after then Interior Minister Charles Pasqua and imposed by the ruling Conservative government—was unequivocally negative. Prior to the 1993, all persons born on French soil to legal residents gained automatic citizenship at the age of 18. Under the Pasqua Laws, on the other hand, all foreigners born in France were required to apply for citizenship upon turning 18 or forfeit that right. The second, implemented after the Socialists defeated the Conservatives in June 1997 parliamentary elections, was considerably more tolerant. Legislation introduced by Chevenèment and passed by the National Assembly by a slim 276-254 margin in December 1997 included two provisions that eased citizenship burdens for foreigners. First, automatic citizenship is now granted to children born of foreign parents in France provided the latter had lived there legally between the ages of 11 and 18. Second, those parents can apply for citizenship on behalf of their children once they turn 13.[81]

Notwithstanding its conditional nature and the margin by which it was approved, the Socialist measure was encouraging, particularly given that the integration of minority groups—irrespective of descriptive characteristics, whether culturally, linguistically, racially or religiously based—has proven a daunting challenge in myriad national contexts. For instance, although the United States is known as a "melting pot" of assorted races and ethnicities, the integration of African-Americans since the Civil War has divided its society repeatedly, and skeptics still contend that that process is not yet complete. Similar hurdles await Hispanics, whose communities are the fastest growing among American minority groups. In referring to the work of sociologist Andre Siegfrid, Gerard Noiriel notes that in the United States, it "took three generations to transform an immigrant into a genuine American. The first generation generally remained foreign. The second was apparently assimilated in the sense that its representatives 'learned English, rapidly became used to no longer speaking other languages and held their parents in contempt.' Yet to the extent that they remained influenced by their origins, their assimilation was incomplete. Only with the third generation was the process fully accomplished."[82]

Following Noiriel's and Siegfried's logic, the time is now ripe to achieve progress on the integration of French Muslim communities, many of whose youngest and most impressionable members are from the third generation. Second generation Muslims began to acquire their French political wings in the late 1980s. Yet, by the early 2000s, young Muslims remained largely jobless and disillusioned, particularly in the urban *banlieues*. This has led to increased societal polarization. Such cleavages are particularly evident at the local level, where conflict between Muslims and members of the societal majority is the most pronounced. As Cesari explains, the "forms of mobilization (associations rather than political parties) and the types of demands (housing, improved conditions of life in the suburbs, citizenship for people who are not French nationals) reveal a new conception of citizenship. It emphasizes the different cultural and ethnic groups within civil society. . . . Political life in France is changing, because local and specific boundaries are more visible."[83]

Implications of Integrative Shortcomings

The implications of the exclusion of Muslims from the French societal mainstream are most pronounced in four interconnected issue areas, those relating to economics, social stratification, security and politics. An effective examination of such implications, in turn, requires a three-part discussion, which is conducted as follows here. First, a description of the ways that the economic travails of Muslims communities foster divisions in French society, particularly among the state's most recent two generations of members. Second, an articulation of the manifestations of social stratification with the greatest potential to threaten France's internal security and thus affect its domestic political system. Third, a discussion of the related implications pertaining to international politics and security.

The wretched living conditions many young Muslims face in the *banlieues* of cities such as Paris, Marseille and Lyon are primarily the result of a lack of income, which is attributable to the staggering unemployment levels prevalent in Islamic communities throughout France. Granted, joblessness has proven a largely insoluble problem across the European continent generally and in France in particular over the past dozen years. But when coupled with widespread accounts of employment discrimination against Muslims, unemployment has led to a growing sense of alienation among second and third generation *beurs*.[84] As a result, youths are often less willing to believe integration is possible, let alone probable. Franco-Algerian writer Sadek Sellam, for example, argues that young Muslims "see what France has done to their parents, they see the bad housing, and they see that France is not interested in helping them make a better life, and they discover radicalism. Their parents said: 'We are Muslims, why not?' But these kids are saying: 'We are Muslims. Now what?' "[85]

Negative perceptions cut in both directions. As is true of many Westerners, Frenchmen often mistakenly associate all Muslims with Islamic fundamentalism and the terrorist attacks some adherents of that religious belief system endorse and perpetrate. The facts that Algeria was formerly a part of France and Tunisia and Morocco were under the jurisdiction of the French colonial empire further exacerbate Franco-North African tensions. As Wihtol de Wenden explains, the "specificity of Islam in France lies in the fact that it is mainly viewed as a religion of colonized, of poor people, of obscuratanism, unable to adapt itself to French values and in contradiction with French political rules."[86] Furthermore, although she notes that the "image has now changed with collective identity expressions of the excluded youth, using Islam as an instrument of communitarist expression or as an alternate way of life . . . the public representations tend to amalgamate all these new Muslims to integrism and political terrorism."[87] The resultant social stratification has had sweeping consequences with respect to France's internal security, the dynamics of its political system and the government's development and implementation of domestic and foreign policy.

The issue of security has two related elements—one domestic and one foreign—that intermingle in the *banlieues*. The bitterness many young *beurs* feel toward the French government leads to confrontations with the police in a particular locality. The most socially destabilizing manifestation of rising urban violence in the past decade came in the form of a series of subway bombings in 1995 carried out by a group of disillusioned *Maghrebians*, some of whom grew up in the Lyon *banlieu* of Vaulx-en-Velin and were recruited by the radical Algerian Armed Islamic Group (GIA). The bombing spree, which left 10 dead and more than 100 injured—most in an attack on the Paris metro—was carried out in part by a terrorist cell headed by Khaled Kelkal, an unemployed 24-year-old Algerian who settled in Vaulx-en-Velin after a short stint in a French prison. Ultimately, Kelkal was fatally shot by French paratroopers in

September 1995, a controversial episode that itself sparked riots among North Africans in *banlieues* across the country.[88] These actions and reactions were products of the deep hybrid of ethnic, class and religious divisions pervading French society in the 1990s. As Franco-Algerian artist Kamel Khelif asserts, "there's a lot of hate on both sides in the suburbs. This is what [*beurs*] suffer . . . hate, racism, rejection. A human being cannot see himself in the mirror and like himself, because he has been rejected so much, so they become aggressive and start a war."[89]

Terrorism is a serious national problem in France for two reasons. First, once rejected by French society, individuals like Kelkal often prove fertile recruits for groups such as the GIA. For example, Alec Hargreaves notes that "Kelkal . . . turned his back on a society from which he had come to feel irremediably excluded. Kelkal's dissatisfaction made him a willing ally of Islamic militants in Algeria."[90] Second, the French government retains close ties to Algeria, which have been manifested in political support for the military-backed regimes of President Abdelaziz Bouteflika and his predecessor, Liamine Zeroual. Since the Algerian government's decision to cancel the 1992 national election, which the opposition Islamic Salvation Front (SLA) was poised to win, members of the GIA—the SLA's de facto military wing—have subjected France to numerous, albeit intermittent, attacks.[91]

More generally, according to the French Interior Ministry, incidents of urban violence increased by more than 400 percent from 1993-97, and resulted in 15 deaths and 1,347 injuries to North African youths in their teens and twenties, and 1,228 injuries to policemen in 1997. Similarly, 70 percent of crime in France in 1998 occurred in the *banlieues*.[92] Comparable trends were evident in 1999, 2000, 2001 and 2002.[93] As a result of these developments, the French national police have singled out more than 1,000 Muslim neighborhoods for special monitoring, which entails the permanent assignment of above average numbers of officers in those areas. In terms of categorization, 700 Muslim neighborhoods are classified as "violent" and 400 as "very violent," with the latter distinction meaning both that organized crime and the possession of firearms are prevalent and that residents have developed a systematic strategy to keep the police out.[94] In addition, the raft of opening initiatives put forth by the Raffarin government in July 2002 included proposals to add 11,000 prison places to the 47,000 already in use, put children as young as 13 into protective custody and hire 18,000 more police and *gendarmes*.[95]

Security threats, whether posed to the minority, majority or both, naturally affect the dynamics of the French political system with respect to both domestic and foreign affairs. In the domestic context, immigration flows initially engendered a threat in the form of instability generated by popular support for Jean-Marie Le Pen's far-right National Front (FN). On 21 April 2002, Le Pen stunned governments and citizens within and beyond the borders of the EU by finishing second and thus qualifying for the final round of the French presidential election. Le Pen, who garnered 16.9 percent of the vote as opposed to 19.9 for Chirac and 16.2 for Jospin, is head of the FN, the most well-known and influential far-right political party to emerge in Western Europe since the conclusion of World War II.[96] And, although Le Pen lost to Chirac by 64 percentage points in the second round and the FN failed to win a single seat in the subsequent June 2002 National Assembly elections, his mere presence on the final presidential ballot was indicative of a disturbingly successful rise in support for extremist parties across Western Europe since the end of the Cold War.[97]

Le Pen, a fiery orator and deft politician, founded the FN in 1972 on a racist platform that played on concerns over the growth of Islamic communities in France. The FN's cornerstone 50-point action plan—drafted by party ideologue Bruno Mégret and promulgated by Le Pen—included propositions to withdraw citizenship from all naturalized immigrants and segregate French schools.[98] Le Pen's party first made notable political headway by earning 10 percent of the vote in regional elections in 1986. The FN increased its share to 14 percent in regional balloting in 1992 and Le Pen himself polled 15 percent in the 1995 presidential election. From there, the FN garnered 15 percent of the vote in the 1997 parliamentary election and equaled that mark at the regional level in 1998.[99] A dispute between Le Pen and Mégret led to the division of the FN into two parties in December 1998, resulting in a drop in support to seven percent in the June 1999 European Parliamentary elections and the subsequent failure of either wing to put forward candidates in the 2001 municipal elections.[100] Nonetheless, each faction maintains a reasonably solid base of constituents who are unlikely to stray too far to the left without the emergence of a new scapegoat for the periodic travails of the French economy.[101]

The impact of Muslim communities on French government policy has equally significant external dimensions, especially vis-à-vis the Quai d'Orsay's relationship with its troubled former territorial department of Algeria. The mistaken association of all Muslims with Islamic fundamentalism, and the acts of terrorism the more radical adherents of that philosophy fund, plan and carry out, buttresses the perception of a monolithic community in opposition to French societal norms. However, in reality, Algerian Muslims within France themselves are split between supporters and adversaries of Bouteflika's secular, albeit military-oriented, government.[102] Ultimately, France's foreign and domestic policy dilemmas with respect to Algeria are rooted in an intransigent cycle of violence in that state. More than 100,000 Algerians—most of them civilians—have perished in a series of largely indiscriminate attacks perpetrated by the GIA and its offshoots that commenced immediately after the 1992 electoral abrogation.[103] If the unrest spreads beyond Algeria's borders, it could trigger a new wave of pan-North African migration to a France already struggling to integrate its present Muslim communities. Given its worries over this issue, the French government continues to support Bouteflika and his military masters, which renders cities such as Paris, Lyon and Marseille all the more enticing as targets for the GIA. Essentially, French policymakers are caught in a double bind. Support for the Algerian government or lack thereof each have the potential to foster French internal political and social instability, whether through acts of terrorism in the former case or increased immigration flows—primarily of the illegal variety—in the latter. Thus far, Paris has given primacy to the first rather than the second threat.

French statesmen must also consider the common religious bonds *Maghrebians* share with the citizens of many Middle Eastern and Persian Gulf states when fashioning policies affecting these volatile regions. For example, a perception among Muslims in France that an unfavorable government policy toward a given state is based strictly on anti-Islamic sentiments has the potential to trigger domestic unrest. Consider, for instance, the sentiments of French Muslims during the Persian Gulf War. A January 1991 SOFRES poll indicated that among North Africans residing in France, 68 percent were hostile to Western intervention in the Gulf, including 27 percent in that group between the ages of 15 and 24 who claimed they would fight on behalf of Iraq if given the opportunity.[104] Since the end of the war, the French government has repeatedly declined to support American military initiatives to force Iraqi President Saddam Hussein to comply with United Nations (UN) sanctions that mandated the monitoring of Iraq's chemical and biological weapons programs. Most recently, Chirac refused to back the U.S.-led Operation Iraqi Freedom, which was carried out in March and April 2003 and resulted in Saddam's removal from power.[105]

That stance is driven in part by concerns over the reaction within France's own Islamic communities. Similarly, the Arab-Israeli peace process is a matter of profound concern to the Muslims of the *banlieues* and thus also to the French government. *Maghrebian* support for the Palestinians, for example, was manifested in a rash of nearly 100 attacks on synagogues in several French cities allegedly carried out by Muslims over the first three weeks of October 2000. The attacks, which coincided with the outbreak of a new *intifada* in Israel, were illustrative of widespread Franco-Muslim support for the Palestinians in their ongoing struggle against the Jewish state.[106]

In addition to the internal security threats posed by rising minority-majority tensions in member states across the EU, even more troubling international linkages between Western European Muslims and transnational terrorist networks have emerged in the weeks and months that have elapsed since the tragic events of 11 September 2001. The case of Zacarias Moussaoui is one example of such linkages. Although the hijackers responsible for the attacks on the World Trade Center in New York City and the Pentagon on the outskirts of Washington, D.C. all had Middle Eastern citizenship, Moussaoui, a French citizen of Moroccan heritage, has also been linked to Al Qaeda and charged with complicity in planning and carrying out those crimes.[107]

Since the attacks against the United States, more than 200 Al Qaeda suspects have been arrested in six Western European states, most of whom were picked up in Britain, Italy, Germany and Spain. In July 2002, for example, German police arrested seven individuals they believed were attempting to replicate 9/11 hijacker Mohammed Atta's former cell in Hamburg. Seven other suspected Al Qaeda operatives were detained by Italian authorities in Milan during the same month. The Milan suspects were caught with forged documents of "good enough quality to ensure them entry into the United States." [108] Three months earlier, four Algerians went on trial in Frankfurt for conspiring to bomb the Strasbourg Cathedral. The four are alleged to have connections with Islamic groups in Belgium, France, Italy, Spain and the United Kingdom.[109]

Many of these arrests were the direct result of the establishment of a 50-person

Europol task force set up to coordinate intelligence on Al Qaeda. Why set up such a task force? According to an August 2002 report in the *Economist*, anti-terrorism experts on both sides of the Atlantic cite five European features that render Islamic terrorist organizations more likely to establish bases within the EU than in the United States: "geography, ethnic demography, communications and coordination, finance and availability of targets."[110] Of these features, two—ethnic demography and availability of targets—are particularly relevant in this book. First, the ethnically diverse Muslim communities situated in the EU serve as ideal places for terrorist groups to establish cells whose members can easily escape detection. The most significant reason why is the marginalization of such communities has alienated and embittered their inhabitants—citizens and non-citizens alike—to such an extent that they are unwilling to report suspicious activities to the police. Second, it follows that once transnational terrorist groups penetrate these excluded Islamic communities, they may find larger and larger numbers of disaffected young Muslims willing to plan and carry out attacks on civilian targets within an EU that has just as many large population centers as the United States.

Measurement of Integrative Progress

The integration of Muslim communities into French society is a long-term project, with progress in the short term best measured on a gradual basis, whether at the local, regional or national level. While French governments in office over the past two decades have generally focused on integrative initiatives applicable at the national level, most implications arising from the exclusion of Muslims are played out locally. Thus, it is logical to address the issue at the local level first, before attempting to implement a universal integrative framework applicable at either the regional or national level. This section does precisely that by proposing a model for integration with the potential for applicability locally, regionally and nationally over the long term, but emphasizing the need to begin at the micro rather than the macro level. The model is based upon a set of demographic, economic, social and political indicators, which are applicable to contemporary France as well as to the German and British contexts under consideration in the ensuing chapters.[111]

In order to develop an effective model for the integration of a minority group within the population of any state, it is first necessary to lay out a set of indicators that serve to describe that group's societal standing. These indicators are applicable at a variety of political levels, ranging from city or municipality to state or region and country. Demographically, the model focuses on the geographic distribution of a minority group and its growth within a population. Economically, it draws primarily on levels of income and unemployment. In terms of social interaction, it examines minority fertility levels and rates of intermarriage with members of the majority. Politically, it considers levels of representation, citizenship rates and government accommodation of minority cultural and religious requests.

The above clusters of indicators are employed to determine how the characteristics of a given minority group compare with those of the societal majority, and the resultant implications vis-à-vis the integration process. While related, each of these clusters features distinctive elements, which merit and thus receive specific attention in the context of the following discussion.

Demography

When measuring the extent of a minority group's integration within a given society, demography is a logical place to begin for two reasons. First, interaction among members of the minority and majority is necessary to improve the social standing of the former. Geographic dispersion is an indicator of the potential for such interaction, whether low if members of a minority group are concentrated in an esoteric enclave and have little contact with the majority or high if they are more evenly distributed throughout the territorial confines of a particular country. Second, as the growth rate of a minority group and thus its proportion in the population relative to the societal majority increase, integration becomes essential to mitigate if not preclude social instability. For example, for as long as a minority group's growth rate exceeds the societal average, even if that group remains clustered in one neighborhood, its expansion will eventually necessitate contact with the majority. The lower the degree of previous interaction between members of each group, in turn, the higher the likelihood for contentious relations when they do eventually meet.

Economics

Fundamentally, in order to enjoy a reasonably high standard of living, an individual must earn money, which requires employment in one profession or another. The measurement of income levels and unemployment rates thus help determine the extent to which minorities have an opportunity to prosper in a given society. In short, the gaps between minority and majority norms in terms of these benchmarks indicate the shortcomings in the integrative process in the context within which they are measured. This is true at any level of analysis, whether local, regional or national. Furthermore, examination of job types—blue and white collar generally—and levels of educational attainment serve as a means to discern the deeper causes of the economic deficiencies of minority groups.

Social Interaction

Generally speaking, the higher the level of interaction among members of the minority and majority, the more comparable at least some of the characteristics of each become over time. Two indicators in particular are instructive here—one direct and the other indirect. First, the measurement of rates of minority-majority intermarriage indicate the prevalence—or lack thereof—of interaction among members of each group and, in turn, the extent to which such behavior is deemed socially acceptable. This is particularly true with respect to marriages of partners with disparate religious beliefs. Second, fertility rates—which are naturally affected by marriages that mix ethnic, racial or religious backgrounds—are useful benchmarks to determine changes that reflect a gradual confluence of minority and majority norms.

Politics

This category of indicators is placed last primarily because it draws broadly on each of the previous three sets of benchmarks. The higher the proportion of the population composed by a minority group, for example, the more likely members of that group are to have an impact on the political system, particularly at the local level. That impact, in turn, is most easily measured in two related ways. First, in direct representative terms gauged by the number of minority candidates appearing on electoral lists and attaining positions on local and regional councils and in national and supranational parliaments. Second, indirectly through the willingness of government bodies to accede to minority demands on a variety of issues, whether culturally or religiously based. Examples include accommodation related to religious expression in public schools and the provision of government funding to minority organizations.

This model—as denoted in abstract terms through the description of the above indicators—serves as a useful analytical framework to measure the extent to which Muslims have been equitably integrated in French society specifically. An emphasis is placed on the local level here given the prevalence of Muslim communities in particular municipalities, with reference to the requisite empirical information drawn primarily from the previous sections of the chapter, most notably those addressing the exclusion of Muslim minorities and resultant implications.

In terms of demographics, the concentration of North African communities in the *banlieues* of Paris, Marseille, Lyon, Lille and Toulouse are indicative of the marginalization of Muslims. The limited interactions between the minorities and majorities of these urban areas are most often of a confrontational nature resulting from innate fear, mistrust and bitterness on both sides. Economically, unemployment rates among Muslims in the *banlieues* are typically twice and in some cases three, four or five times the national average. Such inequality fuels feelings of disillusionment if not desperation in Islamic communities, particularly among second and third generation *beurs* who believe the French government has not given them an opportunity to succeed. As Gilles Kepel explains, the central minority-majority conflict in France is between " 'insiders' and 'outsiders': those who have a paid job and access to social protection, and those who are excluded from the system because of their age, their educational attainment, their origin, the sound of their name or the color of their skin."[112] Similarly, Ramzi Tadras, a worker at the foreign reception center in Marseille, argues that "[i]f you want the second and third generations to respect French laws, you must show them that they are respected. This is the way to integrate. There is no other."[113]

Notwithstanding these figures, there are some indicators of progress with respect to the integration of Muslims in France in the 1990s and 2000s, most notably in terms of social interaction and political representation. An increase in the rate of intermarriage between North Africans and Frenchmen is an encouraging sign. Higher levels of interaction among youths of *Maghrebian* and French ethnicity the end result of which is marriage help demonstrate the potential to overcome minority-majority differences, whether rooted in class, race, religion or a combination of these and other factors. While reconciliation takes time, it is by no means unattainable, particularly if cultivated in the *banlieues* first and then expanded to the broader regional and national levels.

Similarly, the political strength of Franco-Muslim communities is on the rise. As is the case with social interaction, this phenomenon is also most evident at the local level. In the March 2001 municipal elections, for instance, the presence of *beurs* on electoral lists no longer created the stir that it had in the past and discussion of issues such as the construction of mosques was deemed politically expedient in the campaigns of candidates on both the left and the right.[114] As Vincent Geisser notes, "[w]e are no longer in 'beurmania'. The political system has righted this problem, and we talk about it less."[115] Given the concentration of *beurs* in the *banlieues*, Muslims have become an increasingly potent political force in places like Oise, where, according to North African PS member Eric Montes, "[o]ur candidates are almost all blacks or beurs. The Socialist Party has solicited our support as much as any group."[116] Raffarin's aforementioned North African cabinet appointment reflects this growing Muslim electoral influence.

While the progress North Africans have made in the local political arena over the past dozen years serves as a valid reason for optimism, it is also best viewed as a point of departure. In order to achieve the full integration of Muslims into French society in the future, considerable gains are necessary in each of the four major issue areas—those related to demographics, economics, social interaction and politics—featured within in the integrative model proposed here. The model is useful primarily as a means to measure that progress, with movement toward or away from a confluence of minority and majority characteristics viewed as success and failure, respectively. Granted, long-term integration necessarily entails interactive policy formulation, coordination and implementation at the local, regional and national levels. However, in light of the prevalence of Islamic communities in particular municipalities and the resultant higher degree of interaction among Muslims and governmental authorities in those contexts as opposed to the limited dispersion of Muslims regionally and nationally in France, a local level approach is more desirable in the short term. Once the full integration of Muslim minorities—or at least positive progress in that direction—is realized in given municipalities, wider-ranging regional, national and supranational level projects are likely to prove more feasible in light of insights drawn from the micro level.

Conclusions

This chapter had six fundamental objectives. First, to explain the development of Islamic communities in France. Second, to examine the characteristics of those communities to determine the extent to which they have been excluded from mainstream society. Third, to compare and contrast the identities of Muslims and Frenchmen in order to discern what elements of those identities foster the greatest societal divisions. Fourth, to describe the French integration process, placing emphases on its strengths and weaknesses as pertains to Islamic communities. Fifth, to discuss the implications of the failure to fully integrate Muslims into French society. And sixth, to suggest a model to more effectively facilitate the integration process in the future.

The establishment of Islamic communities in France unfolded through a three-stage process. First, Muslims migrated from North Africa to France through guest worker programs designed to utilize foreign unskilled labor to build the French economy in the 1950s and 1960s. Second, although France halted foreign labor migration in the aftermath of the 1973-74 oil crisis, the guest workers stayed and their communities acquired a more culturally North African and religiously Muslim character as a result of the large-scale reunification of family members. Third, Muslim communities grew in the *banlieues* surrounding France's major cities through the emergence of second and third generation *beurs* who possess both *Maghrebian* and French characteristics.

Unfortunately, Muslims are largely excluded from the benefits that accompany acceptance by if not full inclusion within the societal mainstream. Their communities are clustered predominantly in the urban *banlieues*, where jobs are scarce and prosperity all but nonexistent. The relegation of Muslims to these environs is partly attributable to a clash of identities that is based as much on misperception as reality. The inaccurate societal perception of Islam as a radical religion whose adherents are fundamentalists wholly at odds with modern Western civilization has fostered deep divisions between the majority and Muslim minorities in France. While legitimate political and religious differences exist on both sides, there is the potential to further develop a middle ground, within which Muslims already can practice the five essential pillars of Islam without undermining the authority of the secular French state. Similarly, accommodation on issues such as public subsidies for Islamic organizations and facilities would serve as an effective olive branch for the government to offer to facilitate an improvement in interfaith relations across France.

Although the full integration of Muslims is necessarily a long-term project, it is by no means unattainable. Initially, past French governments focused on the traditional method of individual assimilation in attempting to incorporate guest workers and their families into the mainstream. However, this model has proven largely ineffective, particularly with respect to the younger generations, whose members were born in France, possess citizenship and still feel alienated because of their desperate economic travails and social and political marginalization. Regrettably, many *beurs* have reacted to their plights by striking out against the majority as evidenced by increases in urban crime generally and periodic eruptions of violence manifested in riots in the *banlieues* of cities such as Lyon and Marseille in particular.

While it is possible to apportion blame on both sides of the social equation, it is more constructive to discuss the potential for cooperation. Present and future generations of North Africans are and will remain permanent members of French society. Continued minority-majority interaction is thus inevitable. Whether such interaction is constructive or destructive, on the other hand, is contingent upon the extent to which Muslims are integrated. Measurement of the demographic, economic, social interactive and political indicators in the model proposed here is a useful means to push the integration process forward—municipally first and later at the broader regional and national levels. Local progress, manifested in greater confluence between the characteristics of and norms acceptable to the minority and majority is possible but will occur in a gradual manner and thus require patience. Put simply, integration is a long-term process rather than a short-term solution and all interested parties must view it as such.

Interaction, whether pursued at the individual, local, regional or national levels, often results in differences of opinion. In order to mitigate if not preclude instability within French society, both Muslims and Christians must work to overcome such differences en route to the construction of more conciliatory relationships. However, in order to co-exist peacefully if not cooperate fully, one side must accommodate the other. The extent to which each side is amenable to that course of action will determine the nature of the relationship between the two at a given point. In order to facilitate greater bilateral minority-majority congeniality in France, it is essential that the two sides bridge the middle ground in a manner that allows for the discussion if not comprehensive resolution of the concerns each expresses in the future.

The effective integration of Muslims into French society is an indispensable long-term objective largely because of the ongoing evolution of the state's demographics. As is true of states throughout Western Europe, France's majority population is aging at a rate significantly greater that it is reproducing. Statistical estimates suggest that 35 percent of the French population will have reached age 60 or older by 2050, representing an 85 percent increase over 2000. Similarly, the number of individuals 60 and older will surpass those 20 and younger by 2011.[117] The resultant decline in the "working-age" supply pool (individuals between the ages of 15 and 64) of Europe generally and France specifically poses a significant threat to economic growth in these contexts in the twenty-first century. The best way to stem the decline, in turn, is through the use of foreign labor, which entails an increase in immigration. One report suggests that in order to satisfy the impending need for labor, France will need to attract 100,000 immigrants annually from 2001-05 and 11 million overall between 2010 and 2020.[118] Another study projects that for Europe to satisfy that demand, it needs to draw 1.8 million net newcomers annually through 2050.[119]

As was true in the aftermath of the economic boom of the 1950s and 1960s, France is likely to require laborers from its former colonial possessions in North and perhaps Western Africa in order to fuel economic growth from 2001-50. Given the demographic makeup of those regions, such migration flows will almost certainly include vast numbers of Muslims. Their classification as temporary workers is not likely to prove as politically feasible as was the case following World War II in light of the growing electoral strength of Islamic communities in France, particularly at the municipal level. Demands for accommodation of cultural and religious needs of migrants will almost certainly increase and require the prompt attention of French politicians at the local, regional and national levels.

Ignorance of the implications of these demographic trends—while possible albeit imprudent in the short term—is simply not a practically feasible course of action over the long term. Integration is both a present and potential future problem in France, one that, if not redressed, possesses increasing potential to threaten French social and political stability, internal security and perhaps economic prosperity as well. The remedy is relatively simple to state but will require a firm, long-term commitment to achieve. It entails the following four related steps:

First, acknowledge the significance of the problem rather than its mere existence. The French government has taken steps in this direction over the past decade, but more wide-ranging, coordinated action is necessary at the local level. For instance, although Chevenèment's creation of a national consultative body to improve relations between government policymakers and Muslim communal representatives and Raffarin's Muslim cabinet appointments were constructive measures, their practical implications have been limited by the continued sense of alienation felt by the young Muslims of the *banlieues*. More minority-majority engagement would likely prove most useful at the municipal level, where French initiatives to date have been manifested through a bolstered police presence rather than the frank discussion of governmental-Muslim differences.

Second, focus on the reduction of barriers between younger generations of Muslims and their counterparts in the societal majority in cities such as Marseilles, Paris, Lyon and Lille. The elimination of negative stereotypes will not occur in days, months or even years. But it is by no means impossible. Rather, a concerted effort to change attitudes through increased interaction at the local level has the potential to foster gradual progress. By setting and achieving short-term goals such as the improvement of living conditions in the *banlieues*—approached one at a time rather than collectively—local officials can demonstrate to *beurs* and their children that improvement is possible at broader and broader levels over the long term.

Third, gauge progress toward integration at the municipal level through the model proposed here. The indicators in the model are most immediately useful if applied locally. This is true of benchmarks ranging from decreases in unemployment and the resultant increases in income among Muslims in a particular urban district to the dispersion of those individuals across a given metropolitan area and subsequent increases in interaction with members of other ethnic and religious groups. The collection of data on these and the assortment of other benchmarks articulated previously is least elusive locally and thus easier to utilize expeditiously to more fully integrate minorities at the micro than the macro level.

Fourth, once positive results are achieved locally, apply the model regionally and nationally. If Muslims and majority Frenchmen are able to overcome their differences in one city or district, that context may serve as a model for the positive alteration of wider societal perceptions. Ultimately, through these means, the development of a more equitable and thus more socially and politically stable France is possible if not probable in the future. Without the discussion, development and eventual implementation of such a plan, on the other hand, the consequences of the exclusion of Muslims will only grow more pronounced over time.

Notes

1. Silverman, *Deconstructing the Nation*, 1; DeBula Baines, "L'Affaire des Foulards"; Kepel, *Allah in the West*, 180-90.
2. "Islam: France's Second Religion."
3. LeBor, *A Heart Turned East*, 163-64.
4. "A Question of Colour, a Matter of Faith," *Economist* (16 November 2002); Gourévitch, *La France africaine*, 189-90; "Islam: France's Second Religion"; Caldwell, "Crescent and Tricolor," 22.
5. Quoted in LeBor, *A Heart Turned East*, 166.
6. Julien Boëldieu and Catherine Borrel, *La proportion d'immigrés est stable depuis 25 ans* (Paris: L'Institute National de la Statistique et des études Economique [INSEE], 2000).
7. Walter F. Wilcox, ed., *International Migrations*, vol. 2 (New York: Gordon and Breach Science Publishers, 1931), 222. Wilcox cites French, Belgian and Italian government figures specifying the migration of 277,500 Italians and 51,700 Belgians to France from 1876-1910.
8. Ibid., 226-27. Wilcox cites French government statistics specifying the migration of 420,000 Italians, 124,000 Poles and 32,000 Czechs to France from 1920-25.
9. Silverman, *Deconstructing the Nation*, 47.
10. François Caron, *An Economic History of Modern France* (New York: Columbia University Press, 1979), 183. France's Gross Domestic Product grew at an average annual rate of five percent from 1951-69.
11. Steffen Angenendt and Peter Pfaffenroth, "France," in *Asylum and Migration Policies in the European Union*, ed. Steffen Angenendt (Berlin: Research Institute for the German Society for Foreign Affairs, 1999), 151.
12. Silverman, *Deconstructing the Nation*, 52-53. The right of immigrants to enter France to rejoin their families was suspended on 19 July 1974. It was restored on 21 May 1975, then redefined under more stringent guidelines on 29 April 1976.
13. Philippe Bernard, *La part des immigrès dans la population françaises n'a pas augmenté depuis vingt ans* (Paris: INSEE, 1998).
14. Patrick Festy, "Les populations immigrès en France," *Population* 13-6 (1993): 8.
15. Catherine Wihtol de Wenden, "Immigrants as Political Actors in France," *West European Politics* 17-1 (1994), 92.
16. Ibid., 97-98.

17. Jocelyne Cesari, "Islam in France: Social Challenge or Challenge of Secularism?," in *Muslim European Youth: Reproducing Ethnicity, Religion, Culture*, ed. Steven Vertovec and Alisdair Rogers (Aldershot, UK: Ashgate, 1998), 28-29.

18. Tariq Ramadan, *Muslims in France* (Leicester, UK: Islamic Foundation, 1999), 37.

19. Ibid.

20. "A Question of Colour, a Matter of Faith". A reliance on estimates is necessary here because the French census does not include any questions on religion.

21. Gourévitch, *La France africaine*, 191-92.

22. Michel Gurfinkiel, "Islam in France: Is the French Way of Life in Danger?," *Middle East Forum* (March 1997), 3. Specifically, these estimates set the percentages of Muslims in particular regions as of March 1997 as follows: Provence-Côte d'Azur (11), Ile-de France (10), Rhône-Alpes (6.8) and Nord-Pas-de-Calais (5).

23. Caldwell, "Crescent and Tricolor," 22.

24. Ibid.

25. Rémy Leveau, "The Political Culture of the 'Beurs,' " in *Islam in Europe: The Politics of Religion and Community*, ed. Steven Vertovec and Ceri Peach (London: Macmillan, 1997), 148.

26. Suzanne Thave, *L'emploi des immigrés en 1999* (Paris: INSEE, 2000).

27. Caldwell, "Crescent and Tricolor," 30.

28. Angenendt and Pfaffenroth, "France," 151.

29. Thave, *L'emploi des immigrés en 1999*.

30. Leveau, "Political Culture of the Beurs," 152-53.

31. Patrick Festy, "Les populations immigrès en France," *Population* 13-6 (1993), 9.

32. "La population de la France en 2000," *Population et Societés* 31-3 (2001), 3.

33. Philippe Bernard, *L'immigration* (Paris: Le Monde Poche, 1993). Reference made in Ramadan, *Muslims in France*, 49.

34. A.N. Malbet, *Migrations et Conditions Sanitaire* (Paris: L'Harmattan, 1995). Reference made in Ramadan, *Muslims in France*, 48.

35. Jorgen S. Nielsen, *Muslims in Western Europe* (New York: Pinter Publishers, 1992), 21.

36. Ibid.

37. Ibid.

38. Ramadan, *Muslims in France*, 8.

39. LeBor, *A Heart Turned East*, 163.

40. Catherine Wihtol de Wenden, "Muslims in France," in *Muslims in the Margin: Political Responses to the Presence of Muslims in Western Europe*, ed. W.A.R. Shadid and P.S. Van Konigsveld (Kampen, Netherlands: KOK Pharos Publishing House, 1996), 59.

41. Chris Kutschera, "Murky Business Behind the 'Halal' Label in France," *Middle East* 50-4 (1996). While *halal* meat accounts for 10-15 percent of the meat market in France, many Muslim leaders and French experts agree that no more than 5-10 percent of the meat sold as *halal* has been slaughtered in accordance with Islamic precepts.

42. *Sondage IFOP* poll numbers cited in Ramadan, *Muslims in France*, 47.

43. Olivier Roy, "Islam in France: Religion, Ethnic Community or Social Ghetto?," in *Muslims in Europe*, ed. Bernard Lewis and Dominique Schnapper (New York: Pinter Publishers, 1994), 55.

44. Esposito, *Islamic Threat*, 1995.
45. Wihtol de Wenden, "Immigrants as Political Actors," 102.
46. Jocelyne Cesari, "Remarks on Political Participation of Muslims in Europe," *Muslims in Europe Post-9/11 Conference*, Oxford University (April 2003).
47. Omer Taspinar, "Europe's Muslim Street," *Foreign Policy* 135-2 (2003), 76-77.
48. Ibid., 58.
49. Caldwell, "Crescent and Tricolor," 34; "Bientôt une instance représentative du culte musulman en France," *Le Monde* (Paris), 4 July 2001.
50. Roy, "Islam in France," 61.
51. Wihtol de Wenden, "Muslims in France," 56.
52. Davies, *Europe*, 597-98.
53. Ibid., 596.
54. Ibid., 597-98.
55. Silverman, *Deconstructing the Nation*, 111.
56. Liah Greenfeld, *Nationalism: Five Roads to Modernity* (Cambridge: Harvard University Press, 1992), 173.
57. Esposito, *Islamic Threat*, 1-2.
58. Wihtol de Wenden, "Muslims in France," 57.
59. James Corbett, *Through French Windows: An Introduction to France in the Nineties* (Ann Arbor: University of Michigan Press, 1994), 184. Corbett notes that "French Catholics accept readily enough the social mission of the church, its pronouncements on arms sales, racism, human rights, nuclear deterrence and unemployment, but they deny it any authority in cultural and private matters."
60. To avoid repetition, this definition of the basic tenets of Islam appears only in the French case study, although it also applies to the identity sections of the forthcoming German and British case studies.
61. John L. Esposito, *Islam: The Straight Path* (New York: Oxford University Press, 1998), 88-114.
62. Ibid., 114.
63. Nielsen, *Muslims in Western Europe*, 19-20.
64. INED estimate cited in Gurfinkiel, "Islam in France," 6.
65. Quoted in LeBor, *A Heart Turned East*, 165.
66. Wihtol de Wenden, "Muslims in France," 56.
67. Leveau, "Culture of the 'Beurs'," 154.
68. Cesari, "Islam in France," 29.
69. Caldwell, "Crescent and Tricolor," 20-21.
70. Karen Bird, "Group Recognition in the Civic Republic: Citizenship, Equality and Pluralism in France," in *Mistaken Identities: The Second Wave of Controversy over "Political Correctness"* ed. Cyril Levitt, Scott Davies and Neil McLaughlin (New York: Peter Lang, 1999), 223-24.
71. Corbett, *Through French Windows*, 202-03.
72. Ibid., 196.
73. Silverman, *Deconstructing the Nation*-State, 33.

74. Catherine Wihtol de Wenden, *Citoyennete, Nationalite et Immigration* (Paris: Arcantere, 1987). Reference made in Catherine Wihtol de Wenden, "Citizenship and Nationality in France," in *From Aliens to Citizens: Redefining the Status of Immigrants in Europe*, ed. Rainer Baubock (Vienna: European Centre Vienna, 1994), 87-88.

75. Wihtol de Wenden, *Citoyennete*, 74, 87; Festy, "Les populations," 8.

76. Boëldieu and Borrel, "La proportion d'immigrés est stable."

77. Cesari, "Islam in France," 36.

78. Wihtol de Wenden, "Immigrants as Political Actors," 96.

79. Ibid., 97-98.

80. Taspinar, "Europe's Muslim Street," 77.

81. Gary P. Freeman and Nedim Ogelman, "Homeland Citizenship Policies and the Status of Third Country Nationals in the European Union," *Journal of Ethnic and Migration Studies* 24-3 (1998): 27.

82. Gerard Noiriel, *The French Melting Pot: Immigration, Citizenship and National Identity*, trans. Geoffroy de Laforcade (Minneapolis: University of Minnesota Press, 1996), 266; Andre Siegfried, "La France et les problemes de l'immigration et de l'emigration," *Les Cahiers du Musee Social* 2-3 (1946).

83. Cesari, "Islam in France," 35.

84. Philippe Bataille, *Le Racisme au Travail* (Paris: Le Découverte, 1987). Bataille was the first to document the widespread discrimination and workplace racism experienced by persons of non-European origin residing in France.

85. Quoted in Bruce Wallace and Barry Came, " 'The Islamic Peril': A Right-wing Crackdown Targets France's Muslim Immigrants," *Maclean's* (November 1994).

86. Wihtol de Wenden, "Muslims in France," 64.

87. Ibid.

88. "Pour decourager les autres," *Economist*, 7 October 1995; Alex G. Hargreaves, "The Beurgeoisie: Mediation or Mirage," *Journal of European Studies* 28-2 (1998): 94-95.

89. Quoted in LeBor, *A Heart Turned East*, 177-78.

90. Hargreaves, "Beurgeosie," 94.

91. John Newhouse, *Europe Adrift: The Conflicting Demands of Unity, Nationalism, Economic Security, Political Stability and Military Readiness Now Facing a Europe Seeking to Redefine Itself* (New York: Pantheon Books, 1997), 269.

92. "Why he has his Admirers," *Economist* (4 May 2002).

93. Gurfinkiel, "Islam in France," 4-5.

94. Ibid.

95. "Soft on Politicians, Hard on the Rest," *Economist* (11 July 2002).

96. "After the Catacylsm," *Economist* (25 April 2002); "France's Shame," *Economist* (25 April 2002); "Qui a voté Le Pen," *Le Monde* (23 April 2002).

97. "Jacques Chirac Wins by Default," *Economist* (11 May 2002).

98. Silverman, *Deconstructing the Nation*, 58-59.

99. "A Fear in Provence: The Far-Right Xenophobes of the National Front May Hold the Balance," *Economist* (14 March 1998); "Smooth Bigotry," *Economist* (21 March 1998).

100. "Les deux partis d'extrême droite abordent municipales et cantonales en position de faiblesse," *Le Monde* (6 March 2001).

101. "A Split of the Far Right," *Economist* (12 December 1998).

102. Andrew Borowiec, "New President Warms up to France," *Washington Times* (3 August 1999).

103. Ibid.

104. Wihtol de Wenden, "Muslims in France, 60.

105. "Very Well, Alone," *Economist* (15 March 2003).

106. Michel Gurfinkiel, "Black October: The Unreported Attacks Against the Jews of France," *Weekly Standard* (30 October 2000).

107. "France to Assist Terror Suspect," *BBC News*, www.bbcnews.co.uk (12 December 2001).

108. "They're on Both Sides of the Pond," *Economist* (10 August 2002).

109. "The Elusive Prey," *Economist* (20 April 2002).

110. "They're on Both Sides of the Pond."

111. The model is outlined in detail here. It is also applicable to the German and British case studies appearing subsequently and will be noted as such when necessary.

112. Kepel, *Allah in the West*, 208.

113. Quoted in LeBor, *A Heart Turned East*, 185.

114. Jean-Baptiste de Montvalon and Sylvia Zappi, "Les parties politiques considèrent les candidates issus de l'immigration comme un atout electoral," *Le Monde* (7 March 2001); Xavier Ternisien, "La construction de mosques n'est plus un sujet tabou des municipals," *Le Monde* (9 March 2001).

115. Quoted in Montvalon and Zappi.

116. Ibid.

117. Elisabeth Bursaux and Pascale Krémer, "L'Insee prédit un 'vieillissement inéluctable' de la population dans les prochaines décennies," *Le Monde* (27 March 2001).

118. Ibid.

119. Nicholas Eberstadt, "The Population Implosion," *Foreign Policy* 123-2 (2001): 42-50.

Chapter 4

Islam in Germany

Introduction

In January 1999, the government of the southeastern German *Länd* of Bavaria deported a 14-year-old boy of Turkish descent to Istanbul on the pretext of a series of minor criminal infractions. The youth—identified generically in media accounts as Mehmet—was born in Munich to Turkish immigrant parents and had lived there throughout his life. However, he did not possess German citizenship, a circumstance that enabled Bavarian authorities to enact deportation proceedings.[1]

Mehmet's deportation was carried out concurrent with the development of a heated national debate over a proposal by the ruling Social Democratic Party (SPD) government to reform a 1913 law mandating that only those of purely German ethnicity receive citizenship.[2] Crafted by Chancellor Gerhard Schröder's administration, the initiative was designed to enable more ethnic and religious minorities—predominantly Turkish and Kurdish Muslims—to obtain German citizenship while retaining the nationality of and accompanying access to economic opportunities in their countries of origin. It generated widespread protests, undertaken both by disillusioned Germans residing in the economically depressed *Länder* of the former East Germany and by supporters of the opposition Christian Democratic Union-Christian Social Union (CDU-CSU), a high proportion of whom reside in Catholic-majority *Länder* such as Bavaria and Baden-Württemburg.[3] The SPD measure was initially tabled and ultimately passed in a less publicly controversial and thus politically more acceptable form. The new law, which was enacted on 1 January 2000, granted immediate citizenship to all children born to foreigners with at least one parent possessing legal German residency since age 14 or younger but required those individuals to choose one form of nationality—foreign or domestic—by their 23rd birthdays.[4]

These related developments are demonstrative of the generally contentious nature of the relationship between Muslim communities and the societal majority in contemporary Germany. Intolerance, such as that illustrated by the deportation of Mehmet and political conflict over the dual citizenship issue, has the potential to generate widespread social instability, particularly given that Muslims with ancestral roots in Turkey are the Federal Republic's fastest growing minority group. There are currently between 2.8 and 3.24 million Muslims living in Germany, including at least 2.7 million Turks and Kurds. This total represents approximately four percent of the German national population, a figure that while by no means unmanageable at present, demands informed, evenhanded governmental engagement—principally in local and regional contexts rather than at the national level—in order to ensure stability in an increasingly ethnically and religiously diverse society.[5] As Nadeem Elyas, head of the Central Council of Muslims in Germany notes, "[I]integration is difficult but not impossible, because the laws are already there and because Germany already is a multi-cultural and multi-religious society. It is an immigrant's country despite the denial of that fact by German politicians. Different religions and worldviews have been present for a long time, so it is not the foundations we have to lay. But co-existence has to be transformed into one state of togetherness with each other."[6]

With these related observations as a point of departure, this chapter discusses the issue of Islam in Germany through the presentation of the following seven sections:

Development of Muslim Presence

This section describes the genesis, and subsequent entrenchment and growth of Muslim communities in Germany over the latter half of the twentieth century in three parts. The first part addresses the initial development of flows of Muslim migrants to Germany from Turkey through related pull and push factors in the 1960s and early 1970s.   The second part discusses the changes in composition and character undertaken by these communities as a result of family reunifications in the 1970s and influxes of Iranians in the 1980s and Iraqis and Bosnians in the 1990s. The third part examines the entrenchment of Islamic communities in urban centers such as Berlin, Duisberg and Frankfurt-am-Main concurrent with the development of German-born second and third generations of Muslims in those contexts.

Characteristics of Muslim Communities

This section offers quantitative and qualitative descriptions of Muslims residing in Germany in the 1990s and 2000s. Its four related parts focus on demographic, economic, socio-religious and political indicators, respectively.

Clashes of Identity

This section discusses, in three parts, the philosophical and practical issues that separate Muslims from the majority citizenry of Germany. The first part examines briefly the historical and contemporary elements of the German national identity in both political and social terms. The second part defines the principal components of Islamic identity in the German context. The third part addresses the evolving identities of Muslims in the Federal Republic, emphasizing the extent to which members of the younger generations are likely to forge the synthesis necessary to create a progressive Germano-European variant of Islam in the future.

Examination of German Integration Process

This section focuses on German governmental efforts to integrate Muslim communities into society in two parts. The first part describes the basic facets of the models utilized by German government officials in attempting to fully integrate Muslims. It stresses the applications of those models to the second and third generations given the emphasis the book places on the past 20 rather than 50 years. The second part evaluates incisively the strengths and weaknesses of German approaches to the minority integration process.

Implications of Integrative Shortcomings

This section discusses the implications of the government's attempts to fully integrate Muslim communities into German society over the past two decades, particularly with respect to the second and third generations. It does so in four related parts, which address in turn the implications as they pertain to economics, social stratification, security and politics.

Measurement of Integrative Progress

This section applies the general model proposed in the French case study to the Federal Republic in order to determine where the integration process stands at present in the context of German society.

Conclusions

This section reviews the chapter's key points incisively, then discusses the extent to and speed at which the integration of Muslim communities in Germany is likely to proceed in the twenty-first century and the potential consequences of any shortcomings in that process.

Development of Muslim Presence

The initial large-scale flow of Muslim migrants to Germany was triggered by the Federal Republic's First Employment Agreement with Turkey in 1961.[7] The agreement, which facilitated the migration of guest workers, followed similar pacts with Italy in 1955 and Spain and Greece in 1960, and preceded deals with Portugal in 1964, Tunisia and Morocco in 1965 and Yugoslavia in 1968.[8] These agreements came in response to the increasing demand for cheap unskilled labor to drive the West German industrial engine as the nascent Federal Republic emerged from the post-World War II reconstruction process. Collectively, they paralleled similar programs in Western Europe generally and France in particular, all of which were triggered in part by the creation of the European Coal and Steel Community in May 1951 and the establishment of the European Economic Community (EEC) in June 1957.

An implicit sense of reciprocity was central to each of the above pacts. Germany lacked the requisite unskilled labor force to fuel appreciable economic growth. This was especially evident as the Germans joined their Western European partners in the construction of an integrated regional economy in the 1950s and 1960s. The immigrants, for their part, traveled abroad because of a dearth of employment at home. In short, cheap foreign labor drawn from the developing world drove the German industrial engine when rapid growth was indispensable and marks from governmental coffers enabled immigrants to raise funds in anticipation of more prosperous futures in their countries of origin. As Gerd Nonneman explains, "[t]hese immigrant communities . . . were still defined by the host community by their economic function [as guest workers], their color or their nationality, and only to a much lesser extent by their culture or religion. This reflected the migrants' own perception of their place in their [German] surroundings, and their relative lack of concern with opportunities for socio-religious expression within the context of the host society."[9]

The Turks recruited to help satisfy the labor demand in the West German context were predominantly young males drawn by wages significantly higher than those prevailing in the cities, towns or villages from which they originated. The government's intention was to utilize these workers to fill a transitory domestic employment gap. As Christian Joppke argues, the "assumption of return migration is the very rationale of a guest worker regime, which sees foreign labor as a conjuncturally disposable commodity without social reproduction and education costs."[10] Therefore, when recession enveloped Western Europe the aftermath of the October 1973 oil embargo, the German government responded by halting the recruitment of any further guest workers in an attempt to stem the inflow of migrants and encourage the eventual departure of those foreign laborers who remained.

However, Turkish guest workers residing in the Federal Republic at that juncture did not leave. As was true of North Africans in France, rather than return home, Turkish laborers capitalized on relatively liberal German policies to allow for the reunification of children and wives with their husbands, which served both to augment the size and alter the composition of Turkish communities in Germany. In addition, periodic influxes of ethnic Kurds seeking to escape government repression in Turkey further swelled the populations of these enclaves. As a result, Turkish communities in the Federal Republic rapidly assumed more traditional characteristics, which entailed a greater emphasis on cultural and religious values—those associated with Sunni Islam (the predominant denomination among Kurds and Turks) in particular.

The rise of Turks to numerical prominence among foreigners in Germany paralleled that of North African immigrants in France. Migratory flows from Turkey began as a trickle—just 6,500 in 1961—relative to Western European nationals such as Italians and Spaniards, then increased substantially from the mid-1960s to the early 1970s. When the government ended its guest worker recruitment program in 1973, for example, there were more than 700,000 Turks living in the Federal Republic. Growth accelerated through the reunification of families, with total numbers increasing to 910,500 in 1974, 1.07million in 1975, 1.1 million in 1977, 1.2 million in 1979 and 1.5 million in 1981, at which point Turks became Germany's largest minority group.[11]

Turkish communities expanded by 30 percent in that context between 1979-81 alone. However, government measures designed to reduce family reunifications and encourage guest workers to return to their places of origin forced a stagnation of Turkish growth rates in the mid- to late-1980s. In the wake of two measures in particular—most notably the Decree on the Socially Responsible Regulation on Family Reunification (1981) and the Law of Voluntary Repatriation for Foreigners (1983)— the number of Turks living in Germany increased by less than 100,000 from 1981-89.[12]

The 1990s, on the other hand, saw a resurgence of growth in Turkish communities, engendered principally by the development of the younger generations. Between 1992 and the end of the decade, the Turkish population rose from 1.8 to 2.1 million, with the latter total accounting for 28 percent of foreigners residing in Germany.[13] In addition to Turkish communal growth, influxes of migrants from Iran in the 1980s and the Greater Middle East and South and Central Asia in the 1990s boosted the number of Muslims in the Federal Republic past the 2.5 million mark.[14] Between 1989 and 1999, for instance, the number of Afghans and Bosnians living in Germany increased from statistical insignificance to 167,690 and from 22,500 to 71,955, respectively, in large part because of escalating civil wars and political instability in their countries of origin. Similarly, nearly 47,000 Iraqis migrated to Germany in that period.[15]

So long as Turks accepted roles as guest workers and thus temporary migrants, Germans proved generally tolerant. However, by the late 1970s and early 1980s, this was clearly no longer the case.[16] When members of Turkish and other ethnic minority communities attempted to assert cultural identities rooted in Islam and alien to the sense of conformity prevalent within mainstream German society, the level of public tolerance decreased rapidly. Bereft of citizenship and the accompanying economic and social benefits, Muslims were left to struggle within esoteric communities characterized equally by abject poverty, and ethnic and religious homogeneity. This marginalization was at least partially attributable to the disparate ethnic and religious identities of Germans as opposed to those of Muslim minorities generally and Turks specifically. Put simply, German society thrives on political consensus and ethnic homogeneity. As Nonneman and Yasemin Karakasoglu note, "Germany does not see itself as a country of settler immigration. This is . . . linked with the German concept of nationality. 'Germanness' is essentially seen as depending on ethnicity, not place of birth."[17] Unfortunately, this construct undermines the consensus it was designed to facilitate in that it has the potential to consign minority groups to the societal periphery.

Characteristics of Muslim Communities

Muslim communities in Germany are composed of groups from a wide range of ethnic backgrounds. Three-quarters of Muslims living in the Federal Republic are of Turkish national origin, including more than 400,000 Kurds.[18] However, Germany is also home to Muslims with ancestry—whether immediate or one or two generations removed—in countries as geographically wide ranging as Bosnia-Herzegovina, Iran, Morocco and Afghanistan. One widely accepted study listed the following breakdown of German residents possessing roots in Muslim-majority states (Turkey is excluded because that figure was cited previously): 167,690 Bosnians, 116,446 Iranians, 81,450 Moroccans, 71,955 Afghans, 55,600 Central Asians from Azerbaijan, Kazakstan, Kyrgystan, Tajikistan, Turkmenistan and Uzbekistan, 54,211 Lebanese, 51,211 Iraqis, 38,257 Pakistanis, 24,260 Tunisians, 17,186 Algerians, 12,107 Albanians and 8,350 Somalis.[19] Among these groups, only the size of the Bosnian community is on the decline, having fallen by nearly 50 percent since 1997.[20]

As is true of the French and British contexts, Muslim communities in Germany are prevalent in low-rent housing zones on the peripheries of major to mid-size cities such as Berlin, Munich, Frankfurt-am-Main, Duisberg and Cologne. More than three-quarters of Turks residing in the Federal Republic, for instance, are concentrated in urban areas, including 136,400 in the Berlin district of Kreuzberg. Regionally, 35 percent of Turks live in North Rhine-Westphalia, which houses most of the industrial plants that attracted guest workers during the 1960s. This *Länd* includes the cities of Cologne and Duisberg, each of which houses Turkish enclaves of at least 30,000 residents.[21] Most Muslims of other ethnic groups living in Germany—Bosnians in particular—are similarly situated in urban rather than rural areas.

Among the most significant demographic differences between these esoteric communities and the societal majority are those associated with age, culture, and the related issues of linguistic proficiency and educational attainment. One 1990 study, for example, found that just five percent of ethnic Turks in Germany were aged 65 and older compared with 17 percent of the population overall.[22] Similarly, birth rates in Turkish communities are substantially higher than is the case nationally,[23] which helps to explain why nearly 70 percent of individuals in the former context are under 30 years of age.[24] These figures suggest the likelihood if not certainty of further increases in the proportion of Turks both among minorities in Germany and in the national population in the future.

Yet, while largely stratified by generation in terms of age, most Turkish communities in German cities have retained distinctive elements of the culture of the original guest workers' national—and often regional and local—places of origin. As one journalist explains, nearly three-quarters of Turkish residents in Germany "live in ethnic enclaves with extensive Turkish networks of shops, restaurants, mosques and professional services. They can even watch Turkish TV on more than a dozen channels available via cable or satellite."[25] While particularly convenient for older Turks content to retain their native culture and abstain from interaction in German society, this support system often limits the capacity of members of the younger generations for educational and related economic achievement in the Federal Republic. Consider the case of Duisberg's Marxloh district—known locally as "Little Istanbul"—where, as 15-year-old Turk Hanim Han puts it, "[y]ou just don't need any German to get along."[26]

A general lack of proficiency of the German language permeates Turkish communities in cities across Germany. According to Ali Ucar, most "third-generation Turks in Germany do not have a sufficient knowledge of German even though most of them have been born and raised here."[27] A 2001 study conducted in Berlin's Kreuzberg district is demonstrative of this trend. Among a sample group of 273 pre-school children from Turkish families living in Kreuzberg, Ucar found that 63 percent spoke little or no German and thus failed to "meet the linguistic requirements for primary school."[28] Such linguistic deficiencies have contributed to striking gaps between Turks and ethnic Germans regarding educational and vocational qualifications. One 1999 report found that Turks had 4.5 years less of schooling than Germans on average and that twice as many members of the latter group had high school degrees than was true of the former.[29] A 1998 study documented two similar trends. First, only 14 percent of Turkish secondary students qualified for university admission, as opposed to more than 30 percent of their German counterparts. Second, nearly 40 percent of Turks ages 20-29 had no vocational qualifications compared to just eight percent of Germans of the same age group. As Friedrich Maroner, principal of Marxloh Comprehensive School, where 65 percent of the 800 students are of Turkish descent, notes, they "come to school with incredible linguistic deficits. It's impossible for us to ever work off those deficits with the staff resources that we have."[30]

The inability to communicate effectively in German, and related deficiencies of educational attainment and vocational training among most Muslims in the Federal Republic have had markedly negative effects on their economic status. As guest workers, for example, Turks were limited all but exclusively to unskilled jobs in the industrial sector of the economy, where the need for extensive interaction with German-speakers was minimal if it existed at all. However, the decline in demand for unskilled laborers in the wake of the 1973 oil crisis, followed by the gradual modernization of the German economy with concurrent shifts in emphases to the technology and service sectors in the 1980s and 1990s, had profound effects on Turkish job seekers. Influxes of migrants from Eastern and Central Europe and the Balkans, triggered by the collapse of the Soviet empire in 1989-90 and the civil wars of 1992-95 in Bosnia and 1998-99 in Kosovo, only exacerbated matters by increasing the supply of idle blue collar labor. As a result of these factors—in part if not fully—the jobless rate among Turks in Germany is—on average—roughly twice and in many cases triple the present national rate of 10.7 percent.[31]

Among those Muslims who are employed, income levels are substantially lower than the national average and generally on a par with those prevalent in many of the *Länder* of the formerly Communist East, such as Mecklenburg-West Pomerania, Thuringia and Saxony.[32] The results of one 1997 study focusing on the economic conditions prevalent among past guest workers and their extended families is particularly instructive with respect to this issue. According to the study, which was based on comparisons of foreign workers and German citizens, 91 percent of the former were employed in blue-collar professions—including 62.3 percent in manufacturing—as opposed to just 43.8 percent of the latter. Similarly, foreigners with jobs earned an average of 700 marks less per month than Germans.[33]

In terms of economic progress among Turks in particular, most has come in the form of private enterprises launched in metropolitan areas over the last decade. A 1999 KPMG Peat Marwick study, for example, projected that the number of Turkish entrepreneurs in Germany would reach 106,000 by the end of 2001 as a result of a 50 percent annual growth rate since 1996.[34] Collectively, these entrepreneurs own more than 35,000 companies, the vast majority of which cater predominantly to the distinctive needs of Turkish communities. These achievements have come despite the marginalization of Muslims in the context of a German society with many built-in hurdles to advancement, including the antiquated ordinances that require shops in many cities to close by 8 p.m. and thus obstruct one path open to industrious immigrants in other Western countries: running late-night restaurants and 24-hour convenience stores.[35]

Economic shortcomings among Muslims are also related in part to the socio-religious characteristics of their communities.   The growth of Turkish-owned enterprises is itself a product of the significance of religion and culture in the lives of Muslims in contemporary Germany, particularly with respect to members of the first generation. As Zehra Onder asserts, the "identity of a Muslim family is widely determined by Islam. The passage into a foreign culture occurs via a social change. Many of the still dominant traditions in Turkish behavior take their origin from religion. Some families can overcome the norms and values of traditions, especially if from large Turkish cities. But, for the majority, the Islamic norm-value system keeps its validity."[36]

Prior to the family reunifications of the 1970s and 1980s, Islam did not play a significant role in the lives of guest workers residing in government-provided housing complexes in the Federal Republic's central and northern industrial centers. The reunification sparked an increase in the desire among Muslims to place an emphasis on their cultural and religious traditions. As a result, Islamic communities increasingly pressed for the construction of mosques and the establishment of accompanying social associations across Germany in the 1980s and 1990s. According to Germany's Central Islam Institute Archive, for example, the number of mosque associations has grown from single figures to more than 2,200 over the past two decades.[37]

Initially, virtually all of the mosques administered by these associations were situated in contexts ranging from abandoned factories to temporarily converted Turkish apartment buildings. This was related both to a lack of funds for the construction of traditional mosques with prominent domes and minarets, and opposition by the societal majority to accept the existence of these structures in German cities. Take Berlin, where construction of the German capital's first cathedral mosque did not commence until 2000. As Katherine Pratt Ewing explains, "[b]uilders of the mosque faced considerable obstacles. Arguments against the mosque included objections that such a building would disrupt the Berlin skyline, being a constant and permanent reminder of the presence of foreigners in the heart of Germany. People were also concerned that Muslim practices associated with the mosque—such as the Muslim call to prayer—would disturb the peace."[38] On a positive note, recent trends point to a gradually increasing prevalence of recognizably Islamic mosques in Germany, most often in Turkish communities but also in those inhabited by Muslims from a variety of other ethnic groups. The number of mosques that can hold at least 1,000 worshippers has increased from 32 to 66 since 1997, with an additional 30 under construction.[39]

The hurdles the Turks of Berlin had to overcome before moving forward with construction of their first cathedral mosque was attributable in part to a German misperception of Islam as a monolith whose adherents share fundamentalist Islamic beliefs. Yet, in reality, Muslim communities in Germany are diverse in ethnic extraction as well as in the particulars of religious denomination and practice. Ethnically, such communities are predominantly Turkish in national origin. But nearly one quarter of these enclaves are composed of Kurds, who left Turkey because of government repression and generally shun interaction with Turks. Similarly, while the majority of Muslims living in the Federal Republic practice Sunni Islam, sizable Iranian and Iraqi communities in that state are composed predominantly of members of the Shia strain of the faith. Further divisions are evident vis-à-vis orthodox versus modernist interpretations of Islam among Turks and other ethnic minorities.[40]

The lack of socio-religious homogeneity has complicated the efforts of Islamic communities to achieve political representation to a degree proportionate to the Muslims' share of the German population, glaringly so when broken down nationally. In order to examine the roles of Muslims in the political life of the Federal Republic accurately but incisively, brief analyses of two types of representation are necessary. First, the endeavors of individual politicians catering to the needs of Muslim communities, whether through seeking—and at times achieving election to—office in the national parliament or on a local council. Second, the pursuit of Islamic communal objectives by political parties and organizations, some sponsored internally and others externally.

Muslim communities in Germany are severely limited in terms of formal political representation—at the *Länd* and national levels. To date, two Muslims (both Turks) have been elected to office in the German Parliament—Green Party MP Cem Ozdemir in the lower house (*Bundestag*) and Berlin Green state senator Ismail Kosan in the upper house (*Bundesrat*).[41] Ozdemir, the 36-year-old son of guest workers who settled near Stuttgart in the 1960s, has been particularly outspoken on minority issues since first gaining a *Bundestag* seat in 1993. His lobbying was instrumental to the eventual passage of the 2000 law reducing hurdles to citizenship for foreigners born in Germany. The measure rendered 40 percent of Turks—principally those of the second and third generations—eligible for immediate citizenship and thus qualified to run for political office.[42] Ozdemir, who was re-elected in 1998 and stepped down to focus on his research and writing endeavors vis-à-vis the Muslims of Germany in 2002, notes that these "babies born today won't experience what I went through. They will grow up as citizens, and it will change the future of the country. . . . There are going to be Ozdemirs at every level, local, state and federal. That's for sure, because the law will change the attitudes of the society and because there could soon be two million new voters, enough to swing an election. One day it will be very normal for a non-German like myself to be a member of the government."[43]

Ozdemir's points are well taken. Statistical estimates, for example, suggest that approximately 500,000 Turks voted in the 2002 national election, most of whom supported the SPD-Green coalition, helping to re-elect Schröder by a slim margin over CDU-CSU challenger Edmund Stoiber of Bavaria. As Omer Taspinar notes, these "Muslim Germans punished the anti-immigrant Christian Democrats who oppose Turkey's membership in the EU. And they expressed their gratitude for efforts by the SPD-Green coalition to change the archaic laws of German citizenship." In addition, if Turks continue to take advantage of the new citizenship law at the present rate of 160,000 per year, studies indicate that one million will be on the voting rolls by 2006 and perhaps three million by the end of the decade.[44]

Yet, notwithstanding such electoral advances, there remains a relative dearth of effective cross-ethnic political advocacy groups among the Muslims in the Federal Republic. A 1999 study of minority behavior in Western Europe, for example, found that ethnicity—not religion—is the primary motivating factor in the establishment of political organizations by foreigners residing in Germany. According to the study, 82.5 percent of minority claims filed with the German government from 1990-95 came on behalf of groups identifying themselves by ethnicity or nationality rather than religious denomination. Specifically, of those claims, 33, 15 and .4 percent were made by individuals referring to themselves as Kurds, Turks and Muslims, respectively.[45] Additionally, among all minority claims made during the above period, 41.5 percent were related to contemporary issues in their countries of origin as opposed to just 6.3 percent associated with the integration and civil rights of foreigners in Germany.[46]

The diversity of organizations claiming to serve the interests of Muslims in Germany—most of which define themselves in terms of ethnicity and culture rather than by religion—reflect the figures highlighted in the study. Notwithstanding the establishment of the cross-ethnic Central Council of Muslims at the national level in 1994, there are currently more than 2,000 organizations with Islamic linkages—however subtle—operating at the regional level. These organizations are composed of 50,000-100,000 active members, who provide services—most notably the free distribution of copies of the *Koran*, repatriation of remains to Turkey and the arrangement of annual pilgrimages to Mecca—to more than 500,000 Muslims. However, their financial backers comprise a wide range of ethnic and national sources, including the fundamentalist *Aurupa Milli Görüs Teskilatlan*, secular *Diyanet Isleri Türk Islam Birligi* and militant *Kurdistan Workers Party* (Turkey), *Muslim World League* (Saudi Arabia) and *Muslim Brotherhood* (Egypt). Predictably, these groups pursue self-serving agendas that often have little to do with the daily lives of Muslims in Germany. *Diyanet*, for instance, is administered by the Turkish government and often used as a means for Ankara to gather information on political dissidents who have settled in the Federal Republic. The Kurdistan Workers Party, on the other hand, advocates the creation of a breakaway Kurdish republic in Turkey and is often in violent street protests that threaten civil order in Germany.[47] In sum, as Karakasoglu and Nonneman argue, there "is thus far no all-encompassing umbrella organization for all Turkish Islamic groupings."[48]

Clashes of Identity

The exclusion of Muslims from an equitable and productive position in mainstream German society is attributable—in part if not fully—to differences in the identities cultivated within minority Islamic communities and the majority population of the Federal Republic. While the development of German national identity was historically –and remains—a complex process, an incisive description with an emphasis on the past century is sufficient here. In short, the formation and subsequent refinement of the composition and meaning of German nationhood resulted from a series of internal and external shocks to the peoples—past and present—residing in the confines of what is now the Federal Republic. These shocks were sparked by inter-state warfare, domestic economic, political or social transformation, or, in many cases, a combination of these factors.

Four such periodic shocks had a profound collective impact on modern German identity. First, the Napoleonic Wars of the late eighteenth and early nineteenth centuries and subsequent unification of Germany in 1871. Second, the World War I and World War II eras, with the rise, decline and defeat of Adolph Hitler's Third Reich as the focal point. Third, the division of the Cold War years generally and the rebirth of the German nation in the West in particular. Fourth, the reunification of Germany in October 1990 and continuing efforts to redefine the Federal Republic's image to reflect its present and future promise rather than its troubled past.

Among Western Europe's predominant three powers, Germany was the last to emerge as a formal territorial nation-state. Prior to unification through its triumph over France in the war of 1870-71, Germany was composed of a loosely connected patchwork of regional and municipal entities sharing similar bloodlines but lacking a common government. The Federal Republic retains some of the underlying elements of this system, which are most notably manifested in the semi-autonomous nature of its *Länd* governments and dissimilar cultural and political tendencies prevalent within the constituencies they serve. However, the foundation of the modern German nation laid by Chancellor Otto von Bismarck over the final third of the nineteenth century has remained generally intact despite the development of periodic cracks and fissures in the proverbial mortar in the ensuing decades.

Bismarck's victory over France was the crowning achievement in the context of a long-term social and political process that grew out of Prussia's initial defeat to the forces of French Emperor Napoleon Bonaparte in 1806. According to Liah Greenfeld, the "idea of the nation was known in Germany throughout the eighteenth century; it was almost commonplace. But until the fall of Prussia and the dismemberment of the Empire, it did not ring a bell. ... It was the defeat of Prussia in the course of the French revolutionary wars that finally ushered German nationalism into the world."[49] While military victories and diplomatic acumen provided Bismarck's nascent state with geopolitical legitimacy, a confluence of the ideals of the eighteenth and nineteenth century Enlightenment and subsequent age of European Romanticism contributed to the development of a common German social consciousness based upon shared race, culture and allegiance to government authority. As Greenfeld asserts, "German rationalism was akin to French rationalism. It was the belief in human reason as the reason of those elect and superior humans who were able to arrive at the right philosophy, the cultivated reason, the reason of the educated, reason as a distinguishing characteristic among—rather than of—humans, and therefore an admission ticket to superior status."[50]

Ultimately, the emergence of a united Germany in the heart of Europe and the growth of nationalist tendencies among the racially homogeneous population therein served as related preconditions for one of the most destructive periods in global history. Together, World Wars I and II and the inter-war years provided the contexts for a series of drastic highs and lows that altered some elements of German identity and perpetuated others. The Allies' victory in World War I in 1918 and their subsequent imposition of the Treaty of Versailles upon defeated Germany in 1919, led to a transitory shift in governance from authoritarianism to democracy. Yet, most Germans retained an innate susceptibility to the allure of nationalist fervor rooted in racial homogeneity, which Hitler used proficiently to construct a National Socialist state that proceeded to initiate a global conflict that ended in its own destruction and left future generations with a ghastly historical burden to bear.

While the end of World War II fostered rebirths of Western Europe generally and Germany—most notably its Western segment—in particular, it left at least one element of German national consciousness largely intact. Notwithstanding the democratization of governance domestically and inclusion in Western military, economic and political institutional structures—the North Atlantic Treaty Organization and EEC— internationally, the cornerstone of the Federal Republic's constitution (the Basic Law) left room for the subjugation of minority groups. Specifically, the Basic Law made distinctions between two categories of rights—general and reserved—which are defined as follows. First, "[g]eneral rights apply to all individuals in the Federal Republic, and include freedom of expression, liberty of person and freedom of conscience."[51] Second, "[r]eserved rights are restricted to German citizens, and include the right of peaceable assembly, freedom of movement, freedom of association and freedom of occupation."[52] Put simply, the linkage to citizenship entailed in the second set of rights denoted above denied those freedoms to non-Germans (whether born in the Federal Republic or not) based strictly on race.

The final shock to the system—reunification—both resurrected visions of Germany's dark history but also provided an opportunity to finally put at least some of those memories to rest. Schröder's triumph over four-term CDU Chancellor Helmut Kohl in the October 1998 election signaled the start of a necessary transition to a generation of leaders born after rather than before World War II. Indeed, it was in part the result of a growing sentiment among Germans to redefine the nation's identity in a manner reflective of present realities as opposed to past nightmares. Given the legacy of the Holocaust, one means to this end—which Schröder was quickly pursued—was the improvement of the standing of minority groups in German society. The enactment of the previously discussed measure reducing barriers to citizenship for foreigners in Germany at the start of 2000 was a laudable first step in that process of amelioration. Similarly, it is reasonable to assume that further measures to more fully integrate minorities, if implemented effectively, are likely to contribute to a higher level of domestic heterogeneity in the future. However, the broad popular acceptance of a more multicultural German society is necessarily a long-term project.

The most daunting challenges to the achievement of the above integrative end are those associated with the inclusion of Muslim communities, in large part because of widespread German and Western misperceptions of Islam as a radical monolithic faith. As Abdul Hadi Hoffmann, a former CDU official who converted to Islam in 1989, notes, "German Muslims face the same challenge that confronts Muslims everywhere: that all Muslims are made to be responsible by the media for everything any single Muslim does at any place in the world in the name of Islam. . . . To cut through these layers of public prejudice and misinformation is the first prerequisite to a wider acceptance of Islam in Germany."[53] In order to correct these misperceptions, a discussion of the diversity of Islam as practiced by followers of disparate ethnic groups and denominations in Germany is particularly instructive.[54]

The evolution of the identities of Muslim communities in the Federal Republic since the end of World War II has unfolded in three transitional stages, which have taken into account related factors such as place of origin, family structure, generation and social environmental surroundings. First, the limited practice of Islam by male guest workers in the 1960s. Second, the increasing prominence of religion in the lives of Muslims following the surge in family reunifications in the 1970s and early 1980s. And third, the gradual development of a hybrid Turko-German Islam among the younger generations from the mid-1980s to the early 2000s.

Pioneer migrants from Turkey to Germany were generally content to practice Islam within the confines of the government-provided barracks in which they resided. The construction of mosques was limited to isolated cases through the provision of funds from Middle Eastern governments, and daily prayers and Friday services were thus typically conducted in a relatively informal fashion, with guest workers assuming the role of *imam* before, after or between shifts on a given factory production line. Karakasoglu, for instance, explains that "[b]ased on the somewhat naive popular faith of the Turkish homeland that contained strong elements of Sufism, this kind of religious observance was not grounded in orthodox Islamic theology, especially since few of the migrant workers were themselves strictly religious."[55] The role of Islam in these workers' lives changed markedly as a result of the proliferation of guest worker family reunifications concurrent with the oil crisis-induced recession of the mid-1970s. As Karakasoglu notes, when "Turkish everyday life shifted from hostels to houses or flats [and] family reunion recast the social fabric of the Turkish minority, religion took on a new centrality. . . . In the hostels, Turks had lived apart from their families and segregated from German society. In their new residential neighborhoods, they set out to create their own distinctive way of life apart from a culturally different German society."[56]

The esoteric character of emergent Muslim communities, in turn, conflicted with the innate affinity for conformity permeating the societal majority in the Federal Republic. While this clash of identities was of minimal consequence to first generation migrants—who were content to focus exclusively on the retention of their own cultural and religious practices and thus fully disassociate them from the German mainstream—such exclusion is neither acceptable nor beneficial for second and third generation Muslims born and educated in Germany. As Unal Yuksel, a 31-year-old Turk who was born in Berlin and founded Germany's first Turkish-owned record production company, points out, the "first generation cannot speak good German but the second generation is more confident. . . . The first generation wants to make money and go back to Turkey. My problem is to stay here, make money and live here. What can I do in Turkey?"[57]

These generation gaps are even more pronounced vis-à-vis Muslims in their teens and 20s, who find themselves at odds with their parents over life within and without the Islamic enclaves of major metropolitan areas. As Onder contends, the "culture conflict is seen in everything. On one side are the parents with their efforts to establish their views about moral thinking and behavioral norms; on the other side are the children trying to convince their parents about the advantages of the German norm-and-value system in the new environment."[58] Ultimately, many young Muslims find themselves in the middle ground—neither traditionally Turkish nor contemporarily German but at least somewhat alienated from both cultures. Such alienation is encapsulated in the lyrics of a song describing the plight of young Turks composed by the band *Islamic Force*, which is under contract with Yuksel's company: "Hey ho house, we're neither liars, nor naturalized Germans nor foreigners. We're just guest worker kids."[59] Reflecting on the band's message, Yuksel concludes poignantly that the "music we make here is the music for the second generation and the problems of the second generation. . . . I think you have to choose to live either in Berlin, or in Turkey, but don't be in between, because then you go crazy."[60]

Examination of German Integration Process

The initial appearance, subsequent growth and eventual entrenchment of Muslim communities in the Federal Republic over the latter half of the twentieth century left the German national and regional political establishments with a dilemma. Successive governments, whether SPD or CDU-CSU in political orientation, had to determine how to respond to the presence of then unfamiliar minority groups domestically. They have employed three distinct strategies to that end over the past four decades. First, the recruitment of temporary foreign guest workers to boost industrial expansion in the 1950s and 1960s, and segregation of those minorities from mainstream society during their stays in Germany. Second, government efforts to reduce the flow of new migrants to the Federal Republic and encourage the departure of those already residing there between the early 1970s and the reunification of Germany in 1990. Third, gradual acceptance of the need to fully integrate minority groups through a series of inclusive initiatives in the post-Cold War 1990s and 2000s.

Since the end of World War II, governments of the left and right alike have proclaimed unabatedly that the Federal Republic is not "a country of immigration," a demographically inaccurate rhetorical stance belying the fact that foreigners account for 80 percent of Germany's population growth over the last 50 years.[61] The government's approach to the recruitment and subsequent use and treatment of foreign workers in the 1950s and 1960s was illustrative of this philosophy. From the outset of the guest worker programs, Germany officials viewed immigrants as a temporary solution to the shortages of labor caused by the loss of domestic manpower that occurred during the war. Theoretically, as soon as the native German labor pool was once again sufficient to satisfy the demand for blue-collar jobs, the guest workers would return to their countries of origin. Thus, there was no reason to develop a model for the integration of foreign minority groups. As Christian Joppke notes, "[e]xtolling the no-immigration maxim was part of the Federal Republic's response to its guest worker immigration: as a historical episode that was not to be repeated."[62]

However, when declining labor demand in the 1970s sparked a wave of family reunifications rather than an exodus of foreigners, the Federal Republic was forced to acknowledge and respond to ongoing increases in the number of immigrants and the resultant potential for permanent alterations in the demographics of German society. Over the ensuing two decades, national and *Länder* government officials did so through a pair of related legal and political strategies. First, they attempted to stem the flow of new migrants to Germany by ending foreign labor recruitment, gradually imposing restrictions on reunification of guest worker families and implementing programs to entice minorities to return home. Second, they sought to entrench clear distinctions between foreigners and Germans in the legal system in order to slow if not fully preclude the development of a multi-ethnic domestic society.

Notwithstanding the effects of the oil crisis, the rationale for the end of the guest worker programs in 1973 was not exclusively economic. As Joppke stresses, government action was "commanded by domestic security considerations alone—the problem of urban ghettoization and lacking social integration, which had been completely neglected during the first two decades of guest worker recruitment, and the problem of growing domestic unemployment at the end of the postwar boom, which fed the resentment of Germans against the foreigners."[63] That resentment had grown particularly strident over the latter half of the 1970s. One survey, for instance, found that the proportion of Germans favoring the return migration of foreigners increased from 39 percent in November 1978 to 66 percent in December 1981."[64] By that point, Turks outnumbered all other minorities in the Federal Republic and thus served as convenient scapegoats to blame for the economic downturn preceding the shift in federal administrations from Schmidt to the CDU-CSU coalition of Chancellor Helmut Kohl in 1982.

Unfortunately, rather than address the issue of integrating minorities over the long term, the German government—then under the mandate of an SPD-Free Democratic Party coalition led by Schmidt—tried to restrict family reunification through measures such as the Decree on the Socially Responsible Regulation of Family Reunification in December 1981. That measure, which was considerably more tolerant of foreigners than those enacted by the CDU-CSU *Länder* governments of Baden-Württemburg, Bavaria, Berlin and Schleswig-Holstein, had two key planks—those addressing the migratory rights of children and spouses of guest workers, respectively.[65] Regarding children, the cut-off age for legal reunification was lowered from 18 to 16, and offspring were no longer permitted to rejoin either single parents or parents in Germany exclusively for the purpose of attending a university. As for spouses, a distinction was drawn between the first and second generations, with no restrictions imposed on the former but the latter generally excluded unless the spouse seeking to immigrate was at least 18, the resident spouse had lived in the Federal Republic for eight years or longer and the marriage had already existed for a year or more.[66]

The development of a federal policy vis-à-vis family reunification neither eliminated the need to eventually incorporate foreigners into German society nor ensured uniform treatment of minorities across the Federal Republic. In light of the considerable autonomy accorded to *Länd* governments in the Basic Law, *Länder* governments often treat immigrants with differing levels of tolerance. This bifurcation was manifested in a series of legal and political conflicts—particularly after the change in administrations in Bonn in 1982—among officials at the federal and *Länd* levels and the minority communities they governed. Examples included an increase of the aforementioned federal family reunification stipulation on marriage from one to three years in Baden-Württemburg and Bavaria, Bremen's refusal to lower from 18 to 16 the maximum age for foreign children to rejoin their parents in Germany and Hesse's lowering of the second-generation marriage requirement from eight to five years.[67]

Ultimately, such contradictions resulted in a series of attempts to develop a universal policy on minorities, which culminated in the enactment of a new Foreigner Law in April 1990. The measure featured a mixture of old and new ideas vis-à-vis the treatment of foreigners under German law. Positively, it acknowledged that, by 1990, nearly 70 percent of foreigners residing in the Federal Republic were natives, including 1.5 million born there since 1970. It also refrained from the explicit encouragement of return migration. On the negative side, at least from the perspective of Islamic communities, the law retained one overarching element of past dogma: it "replicated the fundamental distinction between Germans and foreigners."[68] However, that distinction in itself served as the basis for the campaign to reduce hurdles to citizenship for foreigners that unfolded over the balance of the decade.

The political debate over the integration of minorities in Germany in the 1990s focused on two questions. First, should the national government concentrate primarily on protecting the rights of foreigners living in the Federal Republic or on easing restrictions on the acquisition of citizenship by members of those minority groups? Second, upon resolution of the initial question, what type of model would prove most useful in building a more inclusive society? The first question was resolved—albeit not until after the change of government from Kohl to Schröder and even then only after a full year of SPD-Green rule and over strident objections from the opposition CDU-CSU—in favor of the reduction of citizenship barriers to foreigners. The 2000 citizenship law included three revolutionary provisions with respect to residents previously defined as foreigners. First, children born in Germany to foreign parents acquired immediate eligibility for citizenship—both in the future and retroactively for those individuals 10 years of age or younger—if at least one parent has lived legally in the Federal Republic for at least eight years. Second, children obtaining citizenship under this provision were also given the right to hold dual passports until the age of 23, at which point they must choose German or foreign nationality. Third, the residency requirement was reduced from 15 to eight years for adult foreigners seeking German citizenship.[69]

Concurrent with progress toward higher levels of citizenship for foreigners—both preceding and in the time since the enactment of the 2000 law—the resolution of the second question continues to revolve around the development of an effective integration model.[70] Governmental discussions on the issue have been limited to two general options. First, the assimilation of minorities—either as individuals or communities—into mainstream German society. Second, the acknowledgement and gradual acceptance of the co-existence of majority and minority cultures in the Federal Republic. The latter option has proved the most amenable to date, particularly so with respect to the federal and *Länder* governments and ethnic German population but also to a large extent among minority groups. As Joppke explains, in "both nationally exclusive and post-nationally inclusive perspectives, immigrants are not expected to assimilate. The rejection of assimilation is the one continuity in the unprincipled, wavering German approach to immigrant integration."[71] The contemporary German definition of multiculturalism reflects this philosophy in what Joppke describes as a two-pronged "attack on the principle of the nation-state." Initially, multiculturalism "figures as the description of a society in which immigration has taken place." Ultimately, the "description of the society diversified by immigration is transformed into the normative claim that the nation could no longer be the legitimizing principle of the state."[72]

Granted, the German brand of multiculturalism is a noble and often effective means to acknowledge the relevance of a variety of ethnic and religious perspectives, whether expressed by the majority or a given minority community. Nonetheless, even once these distinctive groups are recognized, the existence of a multicultural national mentality in and of itself does not ensure that the individuals and communities that compose the societal majority and minority will develop the cooperative multilateral relationships—public and private—that are required to form an inclusive whole. Thus, the case of Muslims in Germany is demonstrative both of the daunting challenges associated with the integration of minority groups and the societal implications that grow out of the successes and failures encountered along the path to that end.

Implications of Integrative Shortcomings

As is true of any modern democratic state, the exclusion of minority groups from the economic benefits that accompany acceptance by the majority has the potential to foster social and political instability in Germany. This is particularly evident in the urban districts of major metropolitan areas, where the vast majority of Muslims—whether of Turkish, Kurdish, Bosnian, Iranian or Arab ethnic extraction—reside. In short, the low income levels and above average unemployment rates prevalent in these districts tend to exacerbate relations among minority Muslims and members of the societal mainstream.

However, unemployment rates and income levels higher and lower than the national average, respectively, are just two of myriad factors that contribute to the social exclusion of Muslims. The existence of ethnic and religious enclaves, most notably those of Turkish and Kurdish orientation, is also attributable to the unwillingness of most of their original inhabitants—first generation guest workers and their wives—to attempt to forge a productive place for themselves in German society. Growth in the number of Turkish-owned companies, which are typically based in these enclaves and cater to Muslims, reduces the need for daily interaction with Germans among the young to the detriment of the minority and majority alike. It would likely prove more constructive to strike a balance, one that enables Turks to retain their cultural and religious identiies but also to develop and maintain constructive roles within rather than remain segregated from society at large. As Bilal Yuksel, a 51-year-old Turk who owns a stationery and toy shop in Kreuzberg, asserts, "I give my culture to my sons, the street and the school gives the German mentality. This is something not German, not Turkish, but something new. When you want to live in another country, first you must learn the language, secondly you must integrate yourself into the culture. When you do both of these, you won't have many problems."[73] Similarly, Central Council of Muslims Chairman Elyas stresses that "[w]e define ourselves as Muslims in Germany or German Muslims. We reject dependency [on the Islamic world] and demand that Muslims in Germany should show loyalty for Germany, they should make Germany the focus of their life and activities."[74]

One institutional context in which regular give-and-take interactions among federal and *Länd* governments and minorities are essential, is that related to education. Turkish demands directed toward government officials in this context have focused on issues including the provision of separate-sex gym classes and acceptance of the wearing of veils by females in public schools, which are administered by the *Länder* as opposed to federal government. Summarizing the Islamic communal stance on these issues, M. Abdullah notes that "Muslims should be able to have qualified religious education for their youths on the same basis as the Christian community, as a normal subject. Islamic religious education must have the same space in public schools as Christian religious education."[75] The often-uncooperative manner in which regional officials respond to such requests reflects the exclusionary nature of the 1990 Foreigner Law. In a 1995 case in North Rhine-Westphalia, for example, rather than accede to demands for the establishment of a religiously oriented education program in its school system, the *Länd* government unilaterally imposed one based on the development of a cultural Islamic identity with underlying German features.[76] Put simply, the government sought to accommodate Turkish concerns without undermining the societal conformity indispensable to Germany's national identity. In order to allow for the practice of Islam to any extent whatsoever in the public sphere, North Rhine-Westphalia had to do so on its own terms.[77]

A similar case, which unfolded from 1980-2000 in Berlin, demonstrated shortcomings on both the government and minority sides in reaching mutually acceptable compromises with respect to religion in the public education system. In 1980, the Islamic Federation of Berlin (IFB), an umbrella group acting on behalf of a group of the city's Muslims, applied for permission to conduct religious instruction in the city's schools.[78] After an initial rejection of the request and subsequent dismissals by Berlin's administrative court in 1987, 1993 and 1997, the city acceded to the IFB's wishes in January 2000. Yet, once the IFB received government recognition as a religious organization and was thus authorized to offer instruction in Islam to Muslim school children, other Islamic groups—*Diyanet* and fundamentalist *Milli Gorus* most prominent among them—protested. These groups suggested that the IFB was not representative of the wishes of Muslims in Berlin (and, in doing so) illustrated the internal divisions that often serve as roadblocks to the integration process.[79]

In addition to such internal hurdles to minority integration, the rising proportion of foreigners in Germany's population has led to the development of a popular backlash against the acceptance of immigrants in general, whether from Turkey or former communist states to the east and southeast such as Poland, Ukraine and Bosnia. One of the most violent manifestation of this trend to date came in May 1993 with the neo-Nazi firebombing of a home in Solingen that left five Turkish women dead and triggered a half-week of riots by disillusioned second and third generation Turks in that northern German town.

While the Solingen incident also sparked a wave of solidarity marches by German citizens in support of minority communities in cities across the Federal Republic, anti-foreigner perceptions continue to pervade the societal mainstream. More than five years after the bombings, for instance, a Forsa survey conducted for *Die Wöche* indicated that 52 percent of the population felt there were too many foreigners in the country.[80] Such sentiments have had many violent manifestations in the 1990s. There were 2,500 racially motivated attacks reported in Germany in 1996, 10,000 crimes described as right-wing extremism in 1999 and another 10,000 in 2000.[81] Over the course of the decade, right-wing attacks have resulted in 100 deaths, including 16 Muslims. Among those cases were an April 1997 firebombing that claimed the lives of three Turks in Krefeld and the February 1999 killing of an Algerian refugee in Guben.[82]

Anti-Muslim violence is in part the product of a German unemployment rate that hit double digits for the first time since World War II less than one year after reunification in 1990 and presently stands at 10.7 percent nationally and more than twice that in some eastern *Länder*.[83] As is the case with terrorism, perception plays an important role regarding blame for high unemployment rates. Typically, citizens blame migrants for occupying jobs that the former would otherwise fill. However, in the German case in particular, immigrants in general and Muslims in particular often accept jobs that individuals in the societal majority would never consider occupying.

Given the importance of perceptions, rising unemployment in the Federal Republic has provided an opening to far-right parties to mobilize political support by using foreigners as scapegoats. Turks, Kurds, Arabs and Iranians are more susceptible than other minority groups because of widespread German misperceptions of all Muslims as advocates of Islamic fundamentalism and thus a threat to domestic security. As Karakasoglu and Nonneman point out, there "has been a growing fear of xenophobic attacks, which have increased with the host society's economic problems, the 'different' migrant population being an easily identifiable scapegoat. Ironically, this tends to drive those groups which are targeted further into that very 'difference'— Islam."[84] Anti-foreign opinions are particularly strident in the Eastern *Länder*, where the radical German People's Union (DVU) polled 13 percent in April 1998 Saxony-Anhalt regional elections through the use of campaign slogans such as "foreign bandits" and "German jobs for Germans." It was the highest total for the far right in a German election since Hitler was in power.[85] While support for the far-right in Germany is considerably lower than that engendered by the National Front of Jean-Marie LePen and Bruno Mégret in France and Jorg Haider's Freedom Party in Austria, negative attitudes toward foreigners extend beyond the constituencies of parties such as the DVU.[86]

Notwithstanding the rising potential for improvement in the societal standing of Muslims in the Federal Republic in light of the reform of the citizenship law, German popular impressions of minority groups remains decidedly unfavorable, particularly when compared with averages in the European Union (EU) overall. Consider the results of a 2000 study undertaken by the EU to gauge public attitudes toward ethnic and religious minorities in its member states.[87] The following three sets of comparative statistics drawn from the study are particularly instructive. First, just six percent of Germans think the government should accept workers from Muslim countries without any restrictions compared to 16 percent of Brits, 14 percent of Frenchmen and an EU average of 17 percent. Second, 61 percent of Germans feel the presence of minority groups increases unemployment rates as opposed to 54 percent of Frenchmen, 48 percent of Brits and an EU average of 51 percent. Third, 62 percent of Germans believe immigrants are more often involved in criminality than the national average; the comparative totals among Brits and Frenchmen are 31 and 71 percent, respectively.[88]

Public divisions—both among Muslims and the societal majority—over government encouragement of the coexistence as opposed to local if not national incorporation of distinct cultures are in part a result of the practical impact of minority integration upon the development and implementation of domestic policy in Germany. In short, the coexistence of within but relegation to the fringes of society of Muslim communities whose members retain esoteric religious and cultural values but are economically disadvantaged is a source of local and national instability rather than integrative progress. This is particularly true of members of the second and third generations, who are more likely to choose to withdraw from rather than seek prosperity within the societal mainstream. As Ali Yamasaki, a Turkish journalist who has lived in Berlin since 1970, explains, the "new generation is more self-confident and refuses to allow itself to be oppressed or discriminated against. They have reacted to the discrimination by forming their own networks. Young Turkish men used to date German women and even marry them. But now that trend is reversing, where Turks will only date and fraternize among each other. Now there are special Turkish discos, and some of the contact between the nationalities has been severed."[89]

Measurement of Integrative Progress

The integration of Muslim communities into German society is a long-term project, with progress in the short term best measured on a gradual basis in a given context, whether at the local, regional or national level. While German governments in office over the past two decades have generally focused on integrative approaches applicable at the national level, the majority of the implications arising from the exclusion of Muslims are played out locally. As a result, it is logical to apply the general model proposed in the French case study to contemporary Germany in order to determine where Muslim communities stand in comparison to the majority in given municipalities in that context.

Demographically, Muslim communities are situated in homogeneous clusters in urban areas rather than dispersed evenly across the Federal Republic. This settlement pattern has not changed appreciably since the first guest workers arrived from Turkey in the early 1960s. In addition, younger generations born to guest workers and their descendents have increased the proportion and public visibility of Muslims in Germany, a trend that is likely to continue in the future given birth rates—among Turks specifically—that are considerably higher than the national average. However, the isolation of Muslim communities has continued and is reflected in the enclave mentality that limits contact among ethnic groups such as Turks, Kurds, Iranians and Iraqis and the societal mainstream—primarily to the detriment of the members of the minority.

In terms of economics, the unemployment rate among Muslims is typically twice the national average and in extreme cases triple that rate. Such inequality fuels feelings of disillusionment if not desperation within Islamic communities, particularly among second and third generation Turks who believe the German government has not afforded them reasonable opportunities to prosper. While increases in ownership of private businesses by Muslims are indicative of economic progress, most employed members of that minority group remain confined to the unskilled labor sector of the German economy and thus continue to earn lower incomes than is true of the national majority. Such disparities are in part the product of an inability of most Muslims residing in the Federal Republic to speak fluent German that is in itself a result of their communal isolation. A greater commitment to linguistic and related educational advances on behalf of the younger generations is necessary to speed the incorporation of Muslims into the skilled labor sectors of the economy, which, if achieved, will help improve the integration process overall.

Minority-majority social interaction in national contexts where that type of behavior has long been deemed atypical is understandably difficult. The reversal of such trends demands commitment on behalf of government officials, community leaders, citizens and non-citizens alike on both sides of the social equation. In the case of the Federal Republic, considerable progress is necessary vis-à-vis the issue of minority-majority interaction, both between ethnic Germans and distinctive foreign ethnic and religious communities and among Muslims themselves. Increases in the number of inter-ethnic religious organizations such as the Central Council of Muslims in Germany is one way to both deepen and widen the interaction necessary to mitigate if not fully erase minority-minority and minority-majority differences over particular issues. Political dialogue among federal and *Länd* officials—elected, appointed or otherwise—and representatives from minority communities is another. As relates to the latter, for example, Ozdemir notes that ethnic German politicans "come to me and ask, 'I have a mosque in my constituency, I don't know whether I should go there or not. What do you think?' I feel like a kind of ambassador."[90]

The Schröder administration's reform of the citizenship law has the potential to expand the scope and utility of the types of interactions that Ozdemir describes over both the short and long terms. Prior to the reform enacted at the start of 2000, the principal barrier to Muslim electoral power in the Federal Republic was a lack of citizenship. Now, as increasing numbers of second, third and eventually fourth generation Muslims—the vast majority of whom meet the qualifications for citizenship under the provisions of the new measure—acquire voting rights, politicians are likely to gradually recognize a greater need to address Islamic communal concerns. This is all but certain to prove the case in those local districts at the *Länd* governmental level with substantial proportions of Muslim residents. Additionally, albeit over the long as opposed to the short term, the appearance of Muslim candidates—whether of Turkish or other foreign ethnic extraction—will become the rule rather than the exception on local, regional and national electoral lists.

However, while the increased likelihood of greater political representation for Muslims in the future engendered by the Schröder citizenship law serves as a valid reason for optimism, it is also best viewed as a point of departure. In order to achieve the eventual full integration of Muslims into German society, considerable gains are necessary in each of the four major issue areas—demographic, economic, social interactive and political—featured in the integrative model proposed here. The model is useful primarily as a means to measure that progress, with movement toward or away from a confluence of minority and majority characteristics viewed as success and failure, respectively. Granted, long-term integration necessarily entails interactive policy formulation, coordination and implementation at the local, regional and national levels. But in the light of the high concentration of Muslims in given German municipalities and the resultant likelihood of a higher degree of interaction among Islamic communal leaders and governmental authorities in those contexts, a local level approach is more desirable in the short term.

Conclusions

This chapter set six fundamental objectives. First, to explain the development of Islamic communities in Germany through the recruitment of Turkish guest workers during the 1960s and early 1970s and subsequent refugee flows in the 1980s and 1990s. Second, to examine the characteristics of those communities as a means to determine the extent to which they have been excluded from the benefits of an equitable place in mainstream German society. Third, to compare and contrast the identities of Muslims with those of Germans generally in order to discern what elements of each tend to foster the greatest societal divisions. Fourth, to describe the German integration process, placing emphasis on its strengths and weaknesses as they relate to Muslims. Fifth, to discuss the implications of the German government's failure to fully integrate Muslims. And sixth, to apply the model proposed in the French case study to the Federal Republic.

The establishment of Islamic communities in Germany unfolded through a three-stage process. First, Muslims migrated predominantly from Turkey through government-sponsored guest worker programs designed to utilize foreign unskilled labor to build the German economy in the 1960s. Second, although Germany attempted to stem immigration flows through a variety of legal initiatives in the 1970s and 1980s, the pioneer migrants—whether employed or not—remained in the Federal Republic, and their communities acquired a more culturally Turkish and religiously Muslim character as a result of the large-scale reunification of family members. This trend grew even more pronounced with influxes of Iranians in the 1980s and Bosnians and Central Asians in the 1990s. Third, Muslim communities grew on the peripheries of Germany's major cities through the emergence of second and third generations possessing both German and foreign cultural characteristics.

Unfortunately, Muslims are largely excluded from the benefits that would likely accompany acceptance by if not full incorporation within the societal mainstream. Their communities are clustered predominantly in urban districts on the peripheries of large cities, where jobs are scarce and prosperity rare if not nonexistent. The marginalization of Muslims in these environs is partly attributable to a clash of identities that is based as much on misperception as reality. The inaccurate societal perception of Islam as a radical religion whose adherents are fundamentalists wholly at odds with modern Western civilization fosters deep divisions between the majority and minority groups in Germany. While legitimate political and religious differences exist on both sides, there is still potential for the development of a middle ground, within which Muslims could practice the five pillars of Islam without undermining the authority of the Federal Republic's national and *Länd* institutions.

Although it is possible to apportion blame on both sides of the social equation, it is more constructive to discuss the potential for cooperation. Present and future generations of Muslims are and will remain permanent members of German society. Interaction with the majority is inevitable, most notably so at the local level, where the eventual amelioration of German-Muslim relations is essential. Interaction, whether pursued at the individual, local, regional or national levels, inevitably results in some differences of opinion. In order to mitigate if not preclude instability in the Federal Republic, both Muslims and Christians must work to overcome such differences en route to the construction of more conciliatory relationships. However, in order to co-exist peacefully if not cooperate fully, one side must accommodate the other. The extent to which each side is amenable to that course of action will determine the nature of the relationship between the two at a given point. In order to facilitate greater bilateral minority-majority congeniality in Germany, the two sides must bridge the middle ground in a manner that allows for the discussion if not comprehensive resolution of the concerns each expresses in the future.

The effective integration of Muslims into German society is an indispensable long-term objective primarily because of ongoing shifts in the Federal Republic's demographics. As is true of states throughout the EU, the majority population in Germany is aging at a rate significantly greater that it is reproducing. The resultant decline in the "working-age" population (individuals between the ages of 15 and 64) of EU member states broadly and Germany specifically poses a significant threat to economic growth in those contexts this century.[91] In the case of the Federal Republic, one study projects that the proportion of individuals 60 or older will increase from 23 percent to 35.8 percent over the next 50 years.[92] The best way to stem that decline, in turn, is through the use of foreign labor, which demands higher levels of immigration. Statistical estimates, for example, indicate that for Europe generally and Germany in particular to satisfy the impending need for labor, they must attract 1.8 million and 100,000 net newcomers, respectively, each year from 2001-50.[93] Given the ethnic makeup of present Germany minority communities, many such migrants—albeit perhaps not the majority—are likely to come from states and regions (Turkey and the Balkans among others) with high percentages of Muslim inhabitants. Their relegation to the margins of society is not likely to prove as politically feasible as was the case previously in light of the growing electoral strength of Islamic communities in Germany, especially in urban districts with high concentrations of Muslims. Demands for accommodation of cultural and religious needs of migrants will almost certainly increase and thus require the prompt attention of German government officials and political parties at the local, regional and national levels.

Ignorance of the implications of these demographic trends—while possible albeit not prudent in the short term—is not feasible over the long term. Integration is both a present and likely future dilemma in the Federal Republic, one that, if not redressed, possesses increasing potential to threaten German social and political stability, internal security and perhaps economic prosperity as well. The remedy is simple to state but will require a firm commitment to achieve. It entails the following four related steps:

First, acknowledge the growing significance of the presence of Islam in Germany and do so in a positive rather than negative manner. The Schröder government took an important step in that direction by focusing on the issue of the treatment of minorities during the 1998 election campaign and subsequently crafting and securing passage of the 2000 citizenship reform. As a result, the proportion of Muslims possessing German citizenship is on the rise. Whether the increased political rights accompanying that status leads to higher levels of formal representation for Muslims— and, if so, how much time is required for such progress to occur—remains open to question. What is all but certain, on the other hand, is the fact that future improvements in the public standing of Muslims—or lack thereof—will be more pronounced at the local than the national level and have a greater impact upon the younger generations. This is likely to prove true in light of the higher proportions of Muslims in particular districts and growing majorities of individuals under 30 in ethnic and religious minority communities across Germany.

Second, work to ameliorate the exclusion of Islamic communities, placing an emphasis on the reduction of barriers between younger generations of Muslims and members of the societal majority. The elimination of negative stereotypes will not occur in days, months or even years. But it is by no means impossible. Rather, a concerted effort to change attitudes through increased interaction at the local level has the potential to foster gradual progress. By setting and achieving short-term goals such as the improvement of living conditions in urban areas—approached one at a time rather than collectively—local officials can demonstrate to Muslims and their children that improvement is possible at broader and broader levels over the long term. The high level of autonomy enjoyed by German *Länder* serves as a built-in opportunity for regional officials to accomplish these tasks without extensive national governmental oversight. However, it is up to individual *Länder* officials to take advantage of— rather than waste—that opportunity. Similarly, Muslim leaders must work to overcome their own intra-communal differences, whether defined in terms of religious denomination, ethnicity or national ancestry. Social turbulence within Islamic communities will only render Christian-Muslim engagement more difficult.

Third, gauge progress toward integration at the municipal level through the model proposed here. The indicators in the model are most immediately useful if applied locally. This is true of benchmarks ranging from decreases in unemployment and the resultant increases in income among Muslims in a particular urban district to the dispersion of those individuals across a given metropolitan area and subsequent increases in interaction with members of other ethnic and religious groups. The collection of data on these and the assortment of other benchmarks articulated previously is least elusive locally and thus easier to employ expeditiously to more fully integrate minorities at the micro than the macro level.

Fourth, once positive results are achieved locally, apply the model regionally and nationally. If Muslims and majority Germans are able to overcome their differences in one city or district, that context may serve as a model for the positive alteration of wider societal perceptions. Ultimately, through these means, the development of a more equitable and thus more socially and politically stable Federal Republic is possible if not probable in the future. Without the discussion and eventual implementation of such a plan, on the other hand, the consequences of the exclusion of Muslims will only grow more pronounced over time. In either case, the German outcome will reverberate regionally to a greater extent than is true of the integration or exclusion of Muslims in other EU member states such as France and the United

Kingdom. Because of Germany's size, geographic placement and history, it is perhaps
the most indispensable piece in the integrated continental puzzle that European leaders
have been putting together since the end of World War II. Put simply, the cultivation
of ethnic and religious harmony within the Federal Republic—or lack thereof—has the
potential either to enhance or threaten the potential for the successful completion of the
European integration project. Naturally, the former path is the most desirable.

Notes

1.   "Turkish Germans"; Geitner, "14-year-old boy finds himself at center of German storm."
2.   "Turkish Germans." Only 160,000 of the 2.1 million Turks residing in Germany had
      German citizenship when the proposal was made following the September 1998 national
      election.
3.   "Germany: Lift the Roadblocks to Citizenship," *Business Week* (1 March 1999).
4.   German Information Center, *Citizenship Reform and Germany's Foreign Residents*
      (Berlin: German Information Center, 2000).
5.   *Muslims in Germany*; *Foreign Population from a Choice of Islamic Countries in
      Germany*.
6.   Quoted in Juliane Hammer, "Making Islam Part of Germany," *Islam Online*, www.islam-
      online.net (2000).
7.   Yasemin Karakasoglu and Gerd Nonneman, "Muslims in Germany with Special Reference
      to the Turkish-Islamic Community," in *Muslim Communities in the New Europe*, ed. Gerd
      Nonneman, Tim Niblock and Bogdan Szajkowski (Ithaca, NY: Ithaca Press, 1996), 241.
8.   Christian Joppke, *Immigration and the Nation-State: The United States, Germany and
      Great Britain* (New York: Oxford University Press, 1999), 65.
9.   Gerd Nonneman, "Muslim Communities in the New Europe: Themes and Puzzles," in
      Muslim Communities, ed. Nonneman, Niblock and Szajkowski, 5.
10.   Joppke, *Immigration and Nation-State*, 65.
11.   German National Office of Statistics, *Population of Turks in Germany between 1961-1992*
      (Berlin: German National Office of Statistics, 1996). Reference made in Andreas
      Goldberg, "The Status and Specific Problems of Elderly Foreigners in the Federal
      Republic of Germany," *Journal of Comparative Family Studies* 27-1 (1996): 131.
12.   Goldberg, "Status and Problems of Elderly Foreigners," 131; Joppke, *Immigration and
      Nation-State*, 78-79.
13.   "Turkish Germans"; *Population of Turks in Germany Between 1961-1992*.
14.   Angenendt, "Germany," *see* Angenendt (1999), 168-70.
15.   *Foreign Population from a Choice of Islamic Countries in Germany*.
16.   Karakasoglu and Nonneman, "Muslims in Germany," 243. Karakasoglu and Nonneman
      note that all "surveys since the 1980s indicate that the majority of Muslims [in Germany]
      intend to stay long-term."
17.   Ibid., 244.
18.   "Whose Fatherland? A Proposal to Grant Citizenship to Members of Germany's Vast
      Immigrant Community Stirs Passionate Debate," *Time International* (25 January 1999).
19.   *Foreign Population from a Choice of Islamic Countries in Germany*.

20. Ibid. With the gradual return of stability to Bosnia-Herzegovina, 148,310 Bosnian refugees returned to their homes there from Germany between 1995 and 1999.

21. Ural Manco, "Turks in Europe: From a Garbled Image to the Complexity of Migrant Social Reality," *Center for Islam in Europe* (December 2000): 1-3.

22. German National Office of Statistics, *Distribution of Foreigners According to Age Groups and Selected Nationalities* (Berlin: German National Office of Statistics, 1992); Goldberg, "Status and Problems of Elderly Foreigners," 131-32.

23. Jochen Mayer and Regina T. Riphahn, *Fertility Assimilation of Immigrants: Evidence from Count Data Models* (Bonn, Germany: Institute for the Study of Labor, 1999), 9. In 1996, for example, the birth rates for Turkish and ethnic German women in the Federal Republic were 3.8 and 1.93 children, respectively.

24. David Lawday, "The Germans: Multiculturalism Thrives in Germany," *New Statesman*, (17 July 2000).

25. "Losers in the Language Gap: Failure to Learn German is Hurting Young Turkish Immigrants," *Time International* (30 April 2001).

26. Ibid.

27. Quoted in "Losers in the Language Gap."

28. Ibid.

29. Ira N. Gang and Klaus F. Zimmerman, *Is Child Like Parent? Educational Attainment and Ethnic Origin* (Bonn, Germany: Institute for the Study of Labor, 1999), 28.

30. Ibid.

31. "Economic Indicators," *Economist* (5 July 2003); "Losers in the Language Gap."; "Germany: Lift the Roadblocks to Citizenship."

32. "Germany's Ex-Communists Creeping Up," *Economist* (9 October 1999).

33. Christoph M. Schmidt, "Immigrant Performance in Germany: Labor Earnings of Ethnic German Migrants and Foreign Guest-Workers," *Quarterly Review of Economics and Finance* 37-1 (1997): 386-90.

34. "Germany: Lift the Roadblocks to Citizenship."

35. "Both Turkish and German," *Economist* (4 February 1999).

36. Zehra Onder, "Muslim-Turkish Children in Germany: Sociocultural Problems," *Migration World Magazine* 24-11 (1996): 21.

37. "New Data and Facts on the Islamic Associations in the Federal Republic of Germany," *Muslim Review* 10-2 (2000): 112-21.

38. Katherine Pratt Ewing, "Legislating Religious Freedom: Muslim Challenges to the Relationship between 'Church' and 'State' in Germany and France," *Daedalus* 129-3 (2000): 131.

39. "New Data and Facts on Islamic Associations."

40. LeBor, *A Heart Turned East*, 210-12; Sigrid Bafekr and Johan Leman, "Highly-qualified Iranian Immigrants in Germany: The Roles of Ethnicity and Culture," *Journal of Ethnic and Migration Studies* 29-1 (1999).

41. Ibid., 203-04.

42. William Drozdiak, "The New Year Brings a Wave of New Citizens in Germany: Law Eased to Fill Jobs with Foreign Workers," *Washington Post* (9 January 2000).

43. Quoted in Drozdiak, "New Year Brings Wave of New Citizens in Germany"; quoted in

"Whose Fatherland?"

44. Taspinar, "Europe's Muslim Street," 77.
45. Ruud Koopmans, "Germany and its Immigrants: An Ambivalent Relationship," *Journal of Ethnic and Migration Studies* 28-3 (1999): 637-38.
46. Ibid., 639.
47. For example, in February 1999, three Kurds were killed and another 16 wounded by guards at the Israeli Embassy in Berlin during a Kurdish protest over alleged complicity in the capture of Kurdistan Workers Party leader Abdullah Ocalan.
48. Karakasoglu and Nonneman, "Muslims in Germany," 257-61.
49. Greenfeld, *Nationalism*, 358.
50. Ibid., 312.
51. Elmar Hucko, ed., *The Democratic Tradition: Four German Constitutions* (Oxford: Berg Publishers, 1989), 194-95. Reference made in Douglas B. Klusmeyer, "Aliens, Immigrants and Citizens—the Politics of Inclusion in the Federal Republic of Germany," *Daedalus* 122-2 (1993): 82.
52. Hucko, *Democratic Tradition*, 196-97.
53. Abdul Hadi Hoffmann, "Muslims in Germany: The Struggle for Integration," in *Islam and the Question of Minorities*, ed. Tamara Sonn (Atlanta: Press, 1996), 52-53.
54. For a description of the general tenets of Islam, please consult the identity section of the chapter on Islam in France.
55. Yasemin Karakasoglu, "Turkish Cultural Orientations in Germany and the Role of Islam," in *Turkish Culture in German Society Today*, ed. David Horrocks and Eva Kolinsky (Providence, R.I.: Berghahn Books, 1996), 160.
56. Ibid., 160-61.
57. Quoted in LeBor, *A Heart Turned East*, 191.
58. Onder, "Muslim-Turkish Children in Germany," 23.
59. Quoted in LeBor, A Heart Turned East, 187.
60. Ibid., 191.
61. Joppke, *Immigration and Nation-State*, 62.
62. Ibid., 63.
63. Ibid., 77.
64. "Ausländerfeindlichkeit: Exodus erwünscht," *Der Spiegel* (May 1982). Reference made in Joppke, *Immigration and Nation-State*, 78.
65. Karl-Heinz Meier-Braun, *Integration oder Rückkehr* (Munich: Grünewald, 1988), 166-69. Reference made in Joppke, *Immigration and Nation-State*, 79.
66. Joppke, *Immigration and Nation-State*, 79.
67. Ibid., 81.
68. Ibid., 84.
69. German Information Center, *Citizenship Reform and Germany's Foreign Residents*.
70. German National Office of Statistics, *Naturalization of 186,700 Foreigners in 2000* (Berlin: German National Office of Statistics, 2001). The number of foreigners acquiring citizenship in 1999 and 2000 rose by 30 percent, an increase attributable in large part to the enactment of the new citizenship law. This group included 82,800 Turks.
71. Joppke, *Immigration and Nation-State*, 186-89.

72. Ibid., 193.

73. Quoted in LeBor, *A Heart Turned East*, 194.

74. Quoted in Hammer, "Making Islam Part of Germany."

75. Muhammad Abdullah, "Der Islam will in Deutschland harnisch werden," *Die Brucke* 58-1 (1992): 38.

76. Werner Schiffauer, "Islam as a Civil Religion: Political Culture and the Organization of Diversity in Germany," in *The Politics of Multiculturalism in the New Europe: Racism, Identity and Community*, ed. Tariq Modood and Pnina Werbner (New York: Zed Books Ltd., 1997), 155. The objectives of the program: "first, to provide the children with an Islamic identity ('the formation of identity through the use of tradition'); second, to enable the children to apply their knowledge of Islam to particular experiences in the Federal Republic; and third, to enable them to acquire the ability to enter into a dialogue with Christians in Germany."

77. Ibid., 153. Schiffauer notes that the German civil servants responsible for developing the program "claimed that they were best able to interpret religion, in the case of Islam, in accordance with the common good."

78. "Verwaltungsgericht Berlin," *Islamic Federation of Berlin* (19 January 1997). Reference made in Pratt Ewing, "Legislating Religious Freedom," 38.

79. Ewing, "Legislating Religious Freedom," 38-39.

80. Geitner, "14-year-old boy finds himself at center of German storm."

81. "Fascism Resurgent," *Economist* (9 October 1999); Peter Finn, "Germany's German Question: Demographics and Rising Xenophobia Bring Issue of Immigration to Forefront," *Washington Post* (25 November 2000).

82. *Turks in Germany* (College Park, Md.: Minorities at Risk Project, Center for International Development and Conflict Management, 1999); "A Decade of Death," *Searchlight* (November 2000).

83. "Economic Indicators."

84. Karakasoglu and Nonneman, "Muslims in Germany," 249.

85. "Dismal All Around," *Economist* (2 May 1998).

86. "Fascism Resurgent."

87. Eva Thalhammer, Viasta Zucha, Edith Enzenhofer, Brigitte Salfinger and Gunther Ogris, *Attitudes Towards Minority Groups in the European Union* (Vienna: SORA, 2001).

88. Ibid.

89. Quoted in LeBor, *A Heart Turned East*, 211-12.

90. Quoted in LeBor, *A Heart Turned East*, 209.

91. Eberstadt, "Population Implosion," 42-50.

92. German Information Service, *Population in Germany will Decline by more than 10 Million from Present 82 Million by 2050* (Berlin: German Information Service, 2000), 1-2.

93. Eberstadt, "Population Implosion," 42-50; *Population in Germany will Decline*, 1-2.

Chapter 5

Islam in the United Kingdom

Introduction

In January 1989, Muslim activists staged a demonstration in the city of Bradford in north-central England during which they burned a copy of British author Salman Rushdie's *The Satanic Verses*. The event, which received extensive local, national and international electronic and print media coverage, was organized by the Bradford Council of Mosques (BCM) in response to what it and other Muslim advocacy groups both within and outside of the United Kingdom interpreted as a derogatory portrayal of Islam in general and the prophet Muhammad specifically in the novel. It followed an unsuccessful request by the United Kingdom Action Committee on Islamic Affairs three months earlier for the British government to ban the release of Rushdie's work for public perusal. Subsequently, Iranian cleric Ayatollah Khomeini issued an Islamic decree (*fatwa*) demanding Rushdie's execution, a measure that also garnered the support of the BCM and served to heighten Muslim-Christian tensions across the United Kingdom.[1]

Twelve years later, ethnic and religious tensions boiled over once again in Britain. They came in the form of a series of riots pitting young South Asian Muslims and whites against each other and the police in several northern English cities between April and July 2001. The most violent rioting—the worst of its kind in Western Europe in two decades—erupted in Bradford on 7 July and continued for nearly three days, resulting in 164 injuries to police officers and 55 arrests. The episode, which was touched off by the stabbing of a Muslim youth by a member of the far-right British National Front, served as the culmination—at least to date—of a 2 ½-month long upsurge in violence in the region that commenced in Bradford in April and spread to lower-class Muslim neighborhoods in Oldham and Burnley in May and June.[2]

Though separated by time and particular points of contention, these developments reflect a generally contentious nature of the relationship between Muslim communities and the societal majority in the contemporary United Kingdom. In the context of the Rushdie imbroglio, the BCM responded stridently to a perceived lack of political will by the British government to acknowledge let alone redress its members' religious grievances. However, the BCM employed an imprudently inflammatory method—the burning of Rushdie's novel—to express its displeasure, which, in itself, unwittingly buttressed a misperception in the United Kingdom of Islam as a monolithic fundamentalist faith universally at odds with Western societal norms. Philip Lewis, for example, argues that "media images of angry demonstrations and inflammatory placards projected and fixed in the public imagination a fearsome and negative picture of Muslims and served to alienate rather than enlist support."[3] Similarly, Adam LeBor stresses that for "many non-Muslims, that picture symbolized every atavistic fear they had about Islam: that it was a faith irrevocably set on a collision course with the West, a religion of fury and rage, intolerance and censorship."[4]

The Rushdie affair and 2001 riots highlighted the potential for social instability arising from conflict—whether verbal or physical—between members of the societal mainstream and Muslims, who are Britain's fastest growing minority group. There are presently between 1.6 and 1.8 million Muslims residing in the United Kingdom, the vast majority of which are of Pakistani and Bangladeshi ethnic origin. This total represents, at most, just over three percent of the British national population, a figure that, while not unmanageable, is substantial enough to demand significant government attention—most notably in local and regional contexts rather than at the national level—in order to ensure stability in an increasingly ethnically and religiously diverse society.[5] As John Rex notes, there "is a significant Muslim voice in Britain today, which speaks for up to [two million] people and which perhaps has greater resonance and elicits a deeper response than the public voices of other religions and cultures."[6]

With these related observations as a point of departure, this chapter discusses the issue of Islam in the United Kingdom through the presentation of seven sections, which unfold in the following manner:

Development of Muslim Presence

This section describes the genesis, and subsequent entrenchment and growth of Muslim communities in the United Kingdom over the latter half of the twentieth century in three parts. The first part addresses the initial development of flows of Muslim migrants to the United Kingdom from South Asia through related pull and push factors in the 1950s and 1960s. The second part discusses the changes in composition and character of these communities in the 1970s, 1980s and 1990s as a result of three factors. First, an influx of Bangladeshi migrants after the establishment of Bangladesh in 1971. Second, the family reunification that followed flagging labor migration to Britain in the aftermath of the 1973-74 oil crisis. And third, inflows of Arabs in the 1980s and 1990s. The third part examines the entrenchment of Islamic communities in urban centers such as London, Bradford and Birmingham concurrent with the development of British-born second and third generations of Muslims in those contexts.

Characteristics of Muslim Communities

This section offers quantitative and qualitative descriptions of Muslims residing in the United Kingdom in the 1990s and 2000s. Its four related parts focus on demographic, economic, socio-religious and political indicators, respectively.

Clashes of Identity

This section discusses the philosophical and practical issues that separate Muslims from the majority citizenry of the United Kingdom in three parts. The first part examines the historical and contemporary elements of the British national identity in both political and social terms. The second part discusses the elements of Islamic identity most germane to the British context. The third part addresses the evolving identities of Muslim minorities in the United Kingdom, placing an emphasis on the extent to which members of the younger generations are likely to forge the synthesis necessary to create a progressive Anglo-European variant of Islam.

Examination of British Integration Process

This section focuses on the British government's efforts to equitably incorporate Muslim communities into society in two parts. The first part describes the models utilized by the British government in attempting to fully integrate Muslims. It stresses the applications of those models to the second, third—and eventually fourth—generations given the emphasis the book places on the past 20 rather than 50 years. The second part evaluates the strengths and weaknesses of those models.

Implications of Integrative Shortcomings

This section discusses the implications of the government's inability to fully integrate Muslim minorities into British society over the past two decades, particularly with respect to the most recent generations. It does so in four related parts, which address in turn the implications that pertain to economics, social stratification, politics and security.

Measurement of Integrative Progress

This section applies the model proposed in the French case study to the United Kingdom in order to determine the extent to which Muslim minorities are making positive progress in the direction of full societal integration.

Conclusions

This section reviews the chapter's key points incisively, then discusses the extent to and speed at which the integration of Muslim communities in the United Kingdom is likely to proceed and the potential consequences of any shortcomings in that process.

Development of Muslim Presence

The initial appearance of Muslims in Britain dates to the scattered recruitment of sailors known as *lascars* by the East India Company 300 years ago.[7]   More permanent communities of Muslims emerged in the forms of Yemenis in Wales, Indians, Cypriots, Iraqis and Egyptians in Liverpool, London and Woking, who arrived over the last quarter of the nineteenth century and first four decades of the twentieth century, respectively.   Yemenis residing in Cardiff, for example, constructed one of Britain's first mosques in 1870.   Two characteristics linked these ethnically and nationally disparate communities.   First, their appearance was a product of the British colonial legacy in the states from which their members originated.   Second, they were minuscule in terms of proportion in Britain's population, numbering less than 50,000 collectively at the start of World War II.[8]

That changed after the war.   The genesis of a substantial Islamic presence in the United Kingdom was rooted in the de-colonization of the British Empire concurrent with Western Europe's concentration on physical and industrial reconstruction following the Allied victory over National Socialist Germany. Muslim migrants began leaving for Britain soon after London's accession to Indian demands for independence and the resultant division of the Indian subcontinent into the states of India and Pakistan in August 1947.   In short, military conflict between India and Pakistan in the wake of the departure of British forces triggered the first wave of South Asian immigration in the late 1940s and early 1950s.[9]

Geopolitical turbulence at home and the demand for inexpensive blue-collar labor to fuel the post-war British economy drew increasing influxes of South Asian workers to the United Kingdom in the 1950s and 1960s.   Eager to escape the economic deprivation of the subcontinent and perpetual military skirmishes between India and Pakistan over control of the disputed region of Kashmir (it straddles the northwestern and southeastern borders of those states, respectively) Pakistanis and Indians were quick to respond to recruitment campaigns organized principally by British textile manufacturers.   These campaigns functioned in the following manner.   First, representatives of British companies utilized commercial linkages dating from the colonial era to recruit unskilled laborers in South Asian cities and villages.   Second, after the initial wave of migrant workers arrived in Britain, familial linkages helped to generate future flows of workers to northern English factories.[10]   As a result, the number of Muslims in the United Kingdom increased from 23,000 at the end of World War II to 82,000 in 1961 and 360,000 in 1971.[11]   The largest short-term influx of migrants during this period—50,170 Pakistanis—matriculated over an 18-month span in 1961-62, in direct response to the anticipated imposition of the 1962 Commonwealth Immigration Act, which placed restrictions on the formerly automatic right of Commonwealth residents to receive citizenship upon arrival in Britain.[12]

Next, in the late 1960s and early 1970s, a wave of 200,000 East Africans swept into the United Kingdom.   This group, composed largely of individuals fleeing government persecution of minority groups in Kenya and Somalia, included 50,000 Muslims with origins in the Gujarati and Punjab states of north-central India.[13] It altered the ethnic composition of the Muslim population in Britain but not to the extent true of a largely concurrent flow of nearly 100,000 Bangladeshis who arrived in the decade after the transformation of East Pakistan into an independent Bangladesh in 1971.[14] Intermittent immigration of Arabs from the Greater Middle East in the 1980s and 1990s also further diversified British Islamic communities through additions of Iranians, Turks, Yemenis, Egyptians, Moroccans and Iraqis.[15] Collectively, these influxes helped boost the total of Muslims in the United Kingdom to 533,000 in 1981, one million in 1991 and 1.6 million in 2001.[16]

The two largest Muslim communities in the United Kingdom are those of Pakistani and Bangladeshi origin. These groups share many basic developmental characteristics. In each case, communal genesis and subsequent growth has occurred in the context of a four-stage migratory pattern that Lewis aptly describes as follows: "[f]irst the pioneers, then what is known as 'chain migration' of generally unskilled male workers, followed by the migration of wives and children and finally the emergence of a British-born generation."[17] Most Pakistani and Bangladeshi pioneer and chain migrants fled to the United Kingdom in the wake of geopolitical transformations emanating from the Indian subcontinent and did so in part because of expectations of the availability of blue-collar jobs upon arrival. Similar to North Africans and Turks in the French and German contexts, they helped to fuel British economic growth in the industrial sector, albeit to a considerably lesser degree in the case of Bangladeshis given their arrival amidst the stagnation of the 1970s and 1980s.

Initially, Muslim migrants—most notably those of Pakistani and Indian origin who arrived in the 1950s and 1960s—had little contact with British governmental authorities, in a large part because private-sector firms were responsible for the recruitment and housing of guest workers in the United Kingdom. Young Muslim men resided in homogeneous enclaves of workers who shared common ethnic, linguistic and religious backgrounds and sent much of what they earned back home to their wives and children in India and Pakistan. The same was true of the first Bangladeshi migrants. These examples suggested that Muslims had deep connections with their places of origin—typically esoteric villages rather than large urban centers in South Asia—and thus planned to return eventually.[18]

However, the tightening of migration requirements through the Immigration Act of 1971 altered both the compositions of Islamic communities in Britain and the relationship between minority Muslims and the societal majority. The act, which demanded proof of "personal connections" in order for entry to the United Kingdom, resulted in the proliferation of family reunifications as remittances decreased and Indian, Pakistani and Bangladeshi women and children joined their husbands and fathers in British urban areas such as metropolitan London, Bradford and Birmingham.[19] The reunification of families fostered the development of a greater emphasis on Islam—albeit of variant strains—in Muslim communities. Ensuing increases in demands by Muslims for government recognition and accommodation of religious needs, such as the provision of *halal* meats in public schools and workplaces, in turn, sparked related rises in minority-majority cleavages.

With the appearance and growth of second and third generations, Islamic communities have acquired a greater sense of permanence in British society. This is particularly evident at the local level, where Muslims in their teens, 20s and 30s are less likely than their parents to accept marginalization, whether defined in terms of race, ethnicity or religion. The burning of *The Satanic Verses* was in part a product of that marginalization. As Gilles Kepel notes, the Rushdie Affair "allowed Islam in Britain to move from a communalism of management, which at best perpetuated a traditional Islamic order transplanted from the subcontinent, to local British politics, to a communalism of radical mobilization."[20] As Muslim communities' collective political viewpoints increasingly reflect the opinions and thus the demands of the younger generations, the need for government engagement with their representatives will grow to the point of indispensability.

Characteristics of Muslim Communities

One of the most notable characteristics of the present Muslim population in the United Kingdom is its diversity. Notwithstanding widespread British popular perceptions to the contrary, terms such as ethnic, religious and social heterogeneity are more useful than radical Islamic solidarity when describing Muslim communities in the United Kingdom. Consider the arguments of Lewis and Charles Husband on this issue. Lewis stresses that it is necessary to speak of "Muslim communities in the plural to underscore the empirical fact that Muslims belong to a variety of linguistic, regional and sectarian groups. The making of a British Islam is an ongoing, unfinished process of experimentation, diversity and debate."[21] Similarly, Husband explains that there "are many cross-cutting variables of nationality, ethnicity, past background, current residence and work, and denominational commitment within Islam that fracture the notion of a homogeneous Muslim community in Britain."[22]

Islamic communities in the United Kingdom are composed of groups from a wide range of ethnic backgrounds. The majority of Muslims residing in Britain are of Pakistani, Indian and Bangladeshi extraction. However, the United Kingdom is also home to Muslims with roots—whether immediate or one or two generations removed—in countries such as Saudi Arabia, Yemen, Iran, Turkey, Malaysia and Nigeria. For example, a variety of statistical estimates, including but not limited to the 2001 census, categorize Muslims inhabitants in the following ethnic and numerical terms: 675,000 Pakistanis, 295,000 Indians, 257,000 Bangladeshis, 350,000 Middle Easterners and North Africans and 180,000 others (most notably Nigerians and Malaysians).[23] These totals, however, do not account for illegal immigration, which is understandably difficult to measure accurately.

As is true of North Africans in France and Turks in Germany, Pakistani, Bangladeshi and Indian Muslims in the United Kingdom are concentrated in low-rent housing blocks on the peripheries rather than in the city centers of major metropolitan areas such as London, Bradford, Birmingham, Manchester and Glasgow. The communities in which Muslims live are distinguished by a variety of ethnic, religious and social class characteristics, with Pakistanis, Bangladeshis, Indians and Arabs each clustered in distinct neighborhoods of a particular city. Geographically, for instance, more than two-thirds of British minorities are situated in the Greater London, West Midlands (Birmingham), Greater Manchester and West Yorkshire (Bradford) regions compared with less than one-fifth of whites residing in those environs.[24]

Pakistani communities in the United Kingdom are located predominantly in north-central England, an industrial region traditionally known for the production of textiles. Nearly 50 percent of British Pakistanis reside in the Greater Manchester, West Midlands and West Yorkshire regions, more than one-third of whom live in Birmingham (110,000) and Bradford (96,000), accounting for four and five percent of the populations of those metropolitan areas, respectively.[25] In each of the latter two cases, Pakistanis are concentrated in a low proportion of municipal wards—eight of 42 in Birmingham and seven of 30 in Bradford—which are culturally and religiously distinct, with mosques and *halal* butcher shops prevalent in most neighborhoods.[26] Similarly, almost half of Britain's Bangladeshis reside in London (36,955 in Tower Hamlets alone) and more than three-quarters of its Indian Muslims live in either London or Leicester.[27]

Demographically, Muslim communities in the United Kingdom are younger and possess higher growth rates than is true of the British majority. Fertility rates among Pakistanis and Bangladeshis in particular are considerably higher than the national average. Specifically, the average numbers of children in Pakistani and Bangladeshi families are 4.7 and 4.2 compared with 2.3 nationally.[28] Similarly, the Pakistani and Bangladeshi communities have twice the number of individuals 16 years old and younger than is the case in British society overall, and just four percent of the members of those minority groups are over 65 as opposed to 11 percent at the national level.[29] Given these growth rates, the number of Pakistanis and Bangladeshis is likely to double by the midway point of this century, most notably through the growth of present and future British-born generations.[30]

Economically, Muslims residing in the United Kingdom are forced to subsist at drastically lower levels than is true of the societal majority, in large part because of substandard income levels and high unemployment rates in the Pakistani, Bangladeshi—and to a lesser extent—Indian communities. Figures drawn from a 1998 British National Office of Statistics estimate of the population by ethnic group and area of residence are indicative of these general trends, which are related to both religious and ethnic characteristics. As Mark Brown notes, "some of the widest [economic] differences occur within broad racial groupings, particularly the South Asian population, within which Indians appear relatively successful, whereas

Pakistanis, and to an even greater extent Bangladeshis, stand out as disadvantaged communities within the Asian and national population."[31]

Robust growth rates concurrent with a reduction in the availability of blue-collar jobs have exacerbated the economic shortcomings among Muslims in the United Kingdom over the past three decades. The restructuring of the British economy from one based on manufacturing to one with an emphasis on service oriented professions in the 1970s and 1980s, for example, had a disproportionate effect on Pakistanis and Bangladeshis working in the textile industry. The number of jobs in textiles in the United Kingdom fell from more than two million in 1945 to 517,000 in 1986, a drop that contributed to unemployment rates among Pakistanis and Bangladeshis as high as 28.1 percent in 1991, 38.6 percent in 1994 and nearly 40 percent in 2001.[32]

The difference in economic prosperity between South Asian Muslims and members of the societal majority is particularly striking. A 1999 study conducted by the British Board of Health found that among those males 16 and over with jobs, 90 percent of Bangladeshis and 70 percent of Pakistanis earned 10,000 pounds or less per year as opposed to a national average of 28 percent. Similarly, just one percent of Bangladeshis and four percent of Pakistanis earned 30,000 pounds or more, whereas the national average was 23 percent.[33] These income levels are partly attributable to substandard levels of educational attainment among South Asians in Britain. According to a 2000 study, just 30 percent of Pakistani and Bangladeshi students attending primary and secondary schools received grades of C or higher in at least five courses compared with 38 percent of blacks, 50 percent of whites and 62 percent of Indians.[34]

Yet, notwithstanding the discouraging nature of these studies generally, Lewis argues that there is reason for optimism vis-à-vis the potential for economic improvement among South Asian Muslims in the United Kingdom. Most significantly, he cites a 1994 study suggesting both that the "proportion of Pakistanis in professional occupations exceeds the white norm [and that] even though a disproportionate number are currently found in manual occupations, they are in no sense comprehensively at the bottom of the pile, for . . . they are over-represented in the skilled manual category."[35] Similarly, a 1994 survey of South Asians, indicated that 31 percent of Muslims were self-employed at the juncture, 53 percent of whom held management positions.[36] Echoing these points, Pnina Werbner notes that in contemporary Manchester, the 20,000 resident Pakistanis "constitute a relatively prosperous community, including many professionals (accountants, solicitors, doctors, engineers), manufacturers (mainly clothing and knitwear) and small businessmen (shopkeepers, market traders, restaurant and hotel owners, taxi owners/drivers, property rental landlords)."[37]

Additionally, Lewis cites the growth of the Pakistani business community in Bradford, which has developed into a hub of sorts for Muslim religious, political and commercial activities over the past several decades, as an encouraging sign. He notes that the number of businesses owned by South Asian Muslims— predominantly Pakistanis—in Bradford increased dramatically, from five in 1959 to 260 in 1970 to 793 in 1980 to 1,200 in 1984. Approximately 75 percent of those ventures are in retail services designed to cater to Pakistani, Bangladeshi and Indian religious and cultural needs, such as the provision of *halal* meats, traditional Islamic herbal medications and Punjabi, Hindi and Urdu audio and video tapes. Two-thirds of all these business were established in the seven city wards where the vast majority of Bradford's Muslims live.[38] Comparably, at the broader national level, the growth of Muslim enterprises helped boost the proportion of ethnic minorities among all small business owners from five to seven percent between 1996 and 2000.[39]

The growth of Muslim-owned businesses reflects the importance individuals who practice Islam place upon their religious and cultural heritage as manifested in their daily lives in the United Kingdom. Similarly, increases in the number of mosques—typically in metropolitan areas—are indicative of the entrenchment of Muslim communities in British society. While there were just 18 mosques in the United Kingdom in 1966 and 36 in 1977, the number had risen to more than 1,000 by 1997, and the current growth rate is approximately 100 per year. While nearly all British mosques constructed prior to 1998 were converted from previously existing structures (usually warehouses and churches), the majority of those built since then are categorized as mosque cathedrals. These cathedrals typically have the capacity for at least 1,000 worshippers and feature more traditional Islamic elements such as prominent central domes and minarets.[40]

Notwithstanding the societal tendency to associate the growing presence of businesses and religious institutions catering exclusively to Islamic communities with the notion of a monolithic entity, the manner in which Muslims of different ethnic and denominational backgrounds practice their faith are by no means identical. For example, although Pakistanis and Bangladeshis are predominantly followers of the Sunni strain of Islam and generally more inclined to practice their religion regularly, their dispositions toward inter-faith marriages differ significantly. According to one poll, while 64 percent of Pakistanis view marrying outside of Islam negatively, only 35 percent of Bangladeshis share that viewpoint.[41] Similarly, although nearly three-quarters of Pakistanis and Bangladeshis consider religion "very important" in their lives and nearly 90 percent abstain from the consumption of alcohol as stipulated in the *Koran*, those living in close proximity rarely worship at the same mosque.[42] Instead, Muslims of variegated ethnic and ancestral backgrounds often pray at mosques employing imams from the villages to which they trace their familial ancestry. As a result, the points a given imam makes in the course of presiding at Friday services are at times more reflective of political circumstances on the Indian subcontinent than those germane to the contemporary United Kingdom. As s Ceri Peach and Gunther Glebe explain, Pakistani and Bangladeshi "mosque tradition has an extremely parochial tradition. Imams are often recruited in the sending village of the British congregation and sometimes represent narrow local practices as universal Islam."[43]

Comparable splits among Bangladeshi and Somali Muslims are evident in London's East End. Competition for scarce jobs, particularly as relates to the younger generations, fosters inter-faith divisions that are most evident in these groups' lack of attendance at common mosques. As Camillia Fawzi El-Sohl notes, though the "older Somali generation may invoke the common bond of Islam as a basis for cooperation, this ideal is not always confirmed by reality on the ground."[44]   Additional cooperative hurdles for British Muslims are rooted in differences in interpretation of Islam—typically orthodoxy versus modernity.

This lack of socio-religious homogeneity has complicated the efforts of Muslim communities to achieve political representation to a degree proportionate to their share of the population, glaringly so at the national level. In order to examine the roles of Muslims in British political life accurately but incisively, brief analyses of two types of representation are necessary. First, the endeavors of individual politicians catering to the needs of Muslim communities, whether through seeking—and at times achieving election to—office in the national parliament or on a local council. Second, the pursuit of Islamic communal objectives by political parties and organizations, some sponsored internally and others externally.

Just two Muslims have ever earned seats in the parliament. Muhammad Sarwar, a native of Pakistan who settled in the United Kingdom in 1976, was elected on the Labour Party ticket in the Glasgow Govan district in May 1997 and re-elected in June 2001. Khalid Mahmood joined Sarwar by winning Birmingham's Perry Barr District Seat in the latter election.[45] However, those electoral achievements did not come without controversy. For example, the Labour Party suspended Sarwar from his seat a month after the 1997 election over allegations of bribery that surfaced immediately following the election.[46] Sarwar, who joined Labour in 1984 and had previously served as a city councilor for Pollokshields, denied committing any illegal acts and was ultimately acquitted by a Scottish court in March 1999.[47] In addition to costing Sarwar nearly two years in office, the episode served to further exacerbate the already tenuous broader relationship between Muslim communities and the political establishment in Britain.

The dearth of Muslim representation in Parliament is at its core the result of a system whereby the hierarchies of political parties—most notably the governing Labourites and opposition Conservatives—decide on lists of candidates to contest seats in given electoral districts. In the June 2001 election, for example, a record 53 Muslim candidates ran for parliamentary seats, including 23 under the banners of the three main parties. Yet, only three were selected to contest seats perceived as "winnable" by party leaders. Sarwar and Mahmood won their races; Conservative Muhammad Riaz, on the other hand, came up short in his bid to upset Labour MP Marsha Singh in the Bradford West district.[48] As Sarwar explains, "I believe to be influential, you have to be in politics and to be elected, you have to be selected as a candidate. So it is up to the parties and particularly the leaders to do it. Labour [Prime Minister Tony Blair] says many fine things. But there needs to be the political will to do it."[49]

Notwithstanding their electoral shortcomings nationally, Muslim communities have made steady progress in achieving representation at the local level, especially over the past 18 years. Predictably, much of that progress has come in the context of Bradford, where the most politically active Islamic community in Britain is located. Muhammad Ajeeb, who migrated to Bradford from Kashmir in 1957, broke a significant barrier to minorities when he was elected as the United Kingdom's first Muslim Lord Mayor in 1985. According to Ajeeb, without more political representation on municipal councils, Muslims' frustration will only build—to the detriment of the majority and minority alike. As he contends, "[e]very section of society should have representation. If you don't have any avenue to express your grievances or anxieties, other than lobbying, you feel disenchanted, left out, alienated, to the extent that you vent your frustrations on undesirable outlets such as riots."[50]

Ajeeb's election was a watershed, which helped clear the path for higher levels of representation for Islamic communities in subsequent years. By 2001, the number of Muslims elected to local councils across the United Kingdom had risen to 217.[51] Through the election of councillors, Muslim communities gain opportunities to place their demands on the public political table. While the vast majority of Muslims elected to local offices to date have done so by standing under the flags of the mainstream Labour, Conservative and Liberal Democratic parties, some have run under the banner of the Islamic Party of Britain (IPB), which was founded in 1989 and contested its first electoral race in 1991.[52]

The IPB includes Islamic adherents from a variety of foreign and native-born ethnic groups in the United Kingdom, who endeavor to "give Muslims a voice in matters relating to the future of British society." Since its establishment, the IFB has sought to educate the British population on Islam by promulgating a party platform including positions on agriculture, education, the environment, health, law and justice, social affairs, youth, defense, the economy, foreign affairs, home affairs, religious affairs, and transport and communication. To date, it has proven more effective in the dissemination of information on general policy positions than in conducting formal political campaigns at either the local or national level. The IPB emphasizes the importance of the cultivation of mutual respect in minority-majority relations. Its platform, for instance, acknowledges that "[r]eligious differences between various beliefs and sects will always remain," but by focusing on the "common ground between various religions, it should be possible to maintain good relations between people of different religions."[53]

In addition to formal political parties, Islamic communities in the United Kingdom have established national political advocacy groups such as the Muslim Parliament, the United Kingdom Action Committee for Islamic Affairs, the Islamic Foundation and the Union of Muslim Organizations of the UK and Eire. These organizations have both strengths and weaknesses. On the positive side, they reflect the growing interest of Muslims in obtaining a political voice in British affairs, both nationally and locally, as evidenced by the results of a study indicating that Muslims administered 47.9 percent of minority organizations interacting with the British government from 1990-96. As Statham argues, in "a sense, the Muslim identity has replaced the Asian categorization and become a basis for collective mobilization against discrimination in society."[54]

The greatest weakness of umbrella organizations attempting to pursue the collective interests of British Muslims, on the other hand, is their inability to fully unify the diverse array of ethnic and cultural communities serving as their membership pool.   There are, for example, more than 950 active Muslim organizations in the United Kingdom at present, most of which serve what Steven Vertovec describes as "specific regional/linguistic or even family/culture-based groups in one part of a city or neighborhood."[55]   Sponsors of such groups vary from individual to local to regional to international actors advocating agendas that range from the improvement of living standards in given housing projects to the conduct of holy war against the West.   Put simply, the heterogeneity of such groups renders their unification under a common political banner a daunting challenge.

Clashes of Identity

The exclusion of Muslims from an equitable and productive role in British society is attributable—in part if not fully—to differences in the identities cultivated within minority Islamic communities and the majority population of the United Kingdom at large.   Those differences are most aptly identified by way of a three-part discussion. First, an explanation of the fundamental elements of British national identity. Second, an examination of the tenets of Islam associated with the process of identity formation within Muslim communities in the United Kingdom.[56]   Third, an evaluation of the potential for the development of a hybrid Anglo-Muslim identity through the evolving role of second and third generation Pakistanis and Bangladeshis in the societal mainstream.

In order to place an emphasis on the elements of British national identity most germane to the issue of Islam in the contemporary United Kingdom, it is necessary to focus the following discussion principally on the past 100 years.   While England's contact with Islam dates to the Crusades of the Middle Ages, widespread daily interactions among Muslims and individuals of British ethnicity in the United Kingdom are just under a half century old.   Ultimately, the aspects of British identity relevant here relate to the United Kingdom's transition from a global imperial power to a European regional player attempting to come to terms with growing internal heterogeneity resulting in a large part from the breakup of its colonial empire.

Religion has played a profound role in British history. The genesis of English nationalism, for example, was sparked by the Protestant Reformation, which is manifested in the Anglican Church's present status as an official state institution in the United Kingdom. As Liah Greenfeld notes, the "role of religion in the development of English nationalism . . . was much greater than that of a facilitating condition, because it was owing to the Reformation, more than any other factor, that nationalism spread as wide as it did in the sixteenth century, and a whole new stratum was added to the idea of those who could find the idea of the nation appealing."[57] As was true for Western European states generally, the eighteenth and nineteenth century Enlightenment tempered the influence of religion in British governmental affairs. Although the Enlightenment did not result in a divorce of church and state in the United Kingdom comparable to the one that prevails in modern France, it helped to ingrain further a traditional sense of pragmatism in the British national psyche. The lack of a written constitution to condition interpretations of governance is one practical product of this philosophy. As Christian Joppke explains, "[p]ragmatism, aversion to fixed first principles, and balanced empirical reasoning have characterized British democracy for centuries. . . . Sovereignty is firmly and unequivocally invested in Parliament, which knows no constitutional limits to its law-making powers."[58]

The most significant changes in the identity of the United Kingdom in the twentieth century were triggered by the devolution of its overseas empire in the aftermath of World War II. The de-colonization and subsequent division of British South Asia into the independent states of India and Pakistan in August 1947 both reduced London's power abroad and set the stage for the emergence of nascent ethnic and religious communities domestically. Flows of migrants from former colonial possessions to and resultant growth and eventual entrenchment of minority groups within the United Kingdom fostered a long-term shift in the makeup of British society from homogeneity to heterogeneity in ethnic, racial and religious terms. These developments, in turn, left successive governments to redefine the nation's identity—in particular who is or is not deemed British both legally and in terms of majority perceptions. As Joppke notes, "[i]mmigration policy both suffered from and aggravated the problem of identity, demolishing the Whig-imperialist illusion in excluding certain subjects of empire, while having no alternative model of membership and community to build upon."[59]

Popular misperceptions of Islam as a monolithic, radical, anti-Christian faith have perpetually undermined relationships between the government and Muslim minority communities. Such viewpoints are partly attributable to what William Montgomery Watt describes as four elements of innate but largely inaccurate British interpretations of Islam. First, "Islam is a falsehood and a deliberate perversion of the truth" in that its fundamental precepts run counter to Christian beliefs. Second, "Islam is a religion that spreads by violence and the sword: an implication of this view was that while Christianity was a religion of peace, which won converts through persuasion, Islam was proselytized through violence and threat." Third, "Islam is a religion of self-indulgence: particularly this invoked notions of sexual excess, and unreliability in other matters." Fourth, "Mumammad is the anti-Christ—since Muhammad had set himself up to create a religion in opposition to Christianity, he must be an agent of the dead."[60] In order to correct such misperceptions, a discussion of the diversity of Islam as practiced by followers of disparate ethnic groups and denominations in the United Kingdom is instructive at this juncture.

In Britain, the practice of Islam differs among ethnic groups, denominations and generations of believers within each of the former two contexts. As is true at the global level, the vast majority of Muslims residing in the United Kingdom ascribe to Sunni as opposed to Shia Islam. However, aside from the five pillars, which are generally recognized as absolute among Muslims of various ethnic, racial and national backgrounds, interpretations of the minutiae of the Koran vary. As Ayad Abu Chakra, an Arab journalist living in London, explains, "[y]ou cannot simplify Islam, just as you cannot simplify Christianity. Islam is a world culture, a global religion. Someone in Bradford, involved in a mosque with a puritanical approach to Islam does not behave in the same way as a secular Muslim in Istanbul, or as an Arab nationalist who thinks that Arab nationalism is based on Islam in Syria and Egypt. They are totally different."[61]

In examining the assorted religious philosophies of Muslims in the United Kingdom, it is useful to distinguish between two general groups—modernists and Islamic activists. Most British Muslims are modernists. As Rex contends, the majority of Sunnis in the United Kingdom "are followers of the Hanafi law school. This means that they are among the most pragmatic of Muslims . . . particularly when it comes to dealing with secular political administrations."[62] Modernists, including former Regent's Park Mosque Director Zaki Badawi, advocate engagement with local and national politicians and government officials and institutions as an effective way to improve the standing of Muslims in society. According to Badawi, Muslims "cannot act like King Canute, demanding that science and technology must retreat at our command. It is there. No one lives without television, radio, the airplane. People can no longer escape the consequences of modernity."[63]

Those characterized as Islamic activists are affiliated with organizations such as the Muslim Parliament and the fundamentalist *Hizb-ut-Tahrir* and *Tablighi Jama'at* movements. Rather than seek to forge a place for Muslims in British society, they reject Western secular norms and advocate the entrenchment of Islamic communities under the auspices of an orthodox interpretation of the *Koran*. These groups were particularly active in the contexts of the Rushdie affair and subsequent protests over the United Kingdom's participation in the American-led 1990-91 and 2003 Persian Gulf Wars against Iraq. Though clearly in the minority among British Muslims, these activists have served to buttress negative perceptions of Islam within the societal majority. As Akbar Ahmed explains, they "have had their fifteen minutes of fame, with the sensation of them threatening this and threatening that. The damage they are doing to Islam, which is a very rational, balanced system, which encourages dialogue [and] a much more serious exchange of ideas, the damage is incalculable. People just assume that Muslims are mad fanatics."[64]

The task of fashioning an Anglo-Islamic identity that strikes a balance between the five pillars and life in modern British society has fallen principally to second and third generation South Asians born and raised in the United Kingdom. Most children and grandchildren of the guest workers that migrated to Britain in the

1950s and 1960s, lack their forebears' connections—whether cultural, linguistic or national—to former British colonies. Although later generations share the religion of their parents and grandparents, they are more capable of encapsulating the practice of Islam in the cultivation of a communal identity that is both British and South Asian. As Sher Azam, former head of the BCM, notes, "Islam is a tablet. In the Middle East, or the Far East, or Eastern Europe, we have coated Islam with our own particular culture. British Muslims are coating that tablet with a British Islam which is different from ours, very different."[65]

One aspect of that emerging Anglo-Islamic identity is the development of media outlets catering to second and third generation Muslims who speak only English and are considerably less interested in the affairs of their states of ancestry than is true of their elders. Two notable examples are the *Q News* and *Muslim News* journals, each of which circulates nationally and features reports on issues germane to the lives of Muslims in the United Kingdom.[66] As Lewis explains, the "fact that increasing numbers of British Muslims are monolingual should not be dismissed as a liability. Mastery of English enables British Muslims from a variety of ethnic, regional and linguistic backgrounds to communicate and begin to work together."[67] Most significantly, the development of a hybrid Anglo-Islamic identity and related increases in political engagement among British Muslims have the potential to enhance the minority integration process.

Examination of British Integration Process

The initial appearance, subsequent growth and eventual entrenchment of minority Muslim communities in the United Kingdom over the latter half of the twentieth century left the British political establishment with a dilemma. Successive governments, whether Labour or Conservative in political orientation, had to determine how to respond to the presence of then unfamiliar minority groups in Britain. As opposed to the French and German cases, the migration of guest workers to the United Kingdom was triggered by a combination of private recruitment and individual initiative rather than formal government sponsorship. London's primary internal policy objective related to the collapse of the British imperial empire was to minimize immigration from former colonies in order to ensure the preservation of domestic homogeneity. As Joppke notes, "Britain rejected immigration because of political boundaries wider than the nation: its immigrants were formal co-nationals without substantive ties of belonging, capitalizing on political boundaries that had too expansively and indistinctly been drawn on the boundaries of the empire."[68]

In general terms, most legislative measures pertaining to the issue of minorities in the United Kingdom between 1948 and 1981 were designed either to reduce immigration flows or limit the citizenship rights of those migrants who had already settled in major British cities. Examples of this brand of legislation included the British Nationality Act of 1948, the Commonwealth Immigrants Acts of 1962 and

1968, the Immigration Act of 1971 and the British Nationality Act of 1981.[69] The Commonwealth Immigrants Act of 1962 limited citizenship to individuals born in the United Kingdom proper, thus excluding migrants from former colonies in South Asia and Africa. Similarly, the Commonwealth Immigrants Act of 1968 denied entry to 200,000 East African Asians fleeing repression in post-independence Kenya. The 1981 British Nationality Act was even more discriminatory: it redefined the traditional *jus soli*, which granted automatic citizenship to anyone born in the United Kingdom, in a manner that increased the legal hurdles for migrants' children born in Britain who attempt to obtain citizenship.[70]

In short, the above measures all served—whether consciously designed as such or not—to postpone if not avoid altogether the daunting challenge of fully integrating minority groups generally and South Asian Muslims specifically into British society.   However, notwithstanding government attempts to reduce immigration and thus limit the presence of ethnic, racial and religious minorities, Muslim communities grew and developed distinct cultural identities in a large part through the reunification of families in the 1970s. As a result, it was left to the Conservative and Labour governments of the 1980s and 1990s first to acknowledge and then to attempt to redress the exclusion of minorities from the benefits accompanying acceptance by the societal mainstream. Building on the limited work undertaken by their predecessors—both historically distant and recent—via measures such as the Race Relations Act of 1976, contemporary British leaders have addressed the issue of integration through a general framework that contrasts starkly with that described in the French case study: The recognition of the coexistence of distinctive minority communities as opposed to the assimilation of individuals into an overarching national culture. As Joppke asserts, "Britain's readiness to acknowledge immigrants as ethnic minorities has deep historical roots. British nationhood has always comprised various ethnicities, with no intention of swallowing them."[71]

The United Kingdom laid the foundation for its present approach to the integration of minority groups through the then Home Secretary Roy Jenkins' formal dismissal of the utility of assimilation as a workable policy in 1966. At that juncture, Jenkins stressed that "I do not think that we need in this country a 'melting pot.' . . . I define integration, therefore, not as a process of flattening uniformity but of cultural diversity coupled with equal opportunity in an atmosphere of mutual tolerance."[72] Essentially, Jenkins' statement implied both that there was room for the existence of myriad distinct cultures in the context of British society and that—irrespective of origin—those minorities not ascribing to the traditional norms of the mainstream were entitled to equal protection under the law.

Jenkins' formula was the initial public step in a process that continues—but as yet remains incomplete—in present-day Britain. The general rhetoric encapsulated in his multicultural approach was formalized through the Race Relations Acts of 1968 and 1976, the latter of which established a Commission for Racial Equality

(CRE) designed to respond to the concerns of the United Kingdom's minority communities. The Race Relations Act of 1976 sought to ameliorate the economic—and by association—class standings of minority groups by prohibiting two types of discrimination. First, direct discrimination on the basis of "color, race, nationality or ethnic or national origins." Second, indirect discrimination, "in which a 'condition or requirement' is applied that does not allow persons of a particular race to comply with it equally, is not 'justifiable' on non-racial grounds, and works to the 'detriment of these persons.' "[73]

The United Kingdom's multicultural formula for integration reflects the pragmatic nature of British national identity. Rather than facilitate protection of minority rights through constitutional means similar to those prevalent in the United States and Germany, the United Kingdom—at least in theory—uses multiculturalism to achieve the political flexibility necessary to accommodate minority concerns, whether defined in terms of race, ethnicity, nationality or an admixture of those elements. Joppke, for instance, argues that "[m]any of the ethnic-minority protections that in Germany and the United States are grounded in constitutional human-rights guarantees have been achieved in Great Britain by unprincipled common law and flexible statute-making."[74]

This flexible construct served as the basis for the CRE's development of two strategies to achieve progress toward the full integration of minority groups in the 1980s and 1990s. First, it pressed for and ultimately obtained government approval of a question on ethnic origin in the 1991 national census in order to more accurately gauge the number and needs of minorities residing in the United Kingdom. Second, it pushed for and has gradually achieved recognition of minority cultural requirements in government administered institutions such as prisons, schools, public services and the military. One of the more notable accommodations made to minorities, for example, was the exemption of Indian Sikhs from donning safety helmets at construction sites as their religion prohibits the cutting of hair and mandates that they wear turbans.[75]

However, notwithstanding the CRE's successful efforts to improve the status of minorities generally, the United Kingdom's multicultural approach has proved less effective vis-à-vis the integration of Muslims in particular. Consider the Race Relations Act of 1976, a measure that does not deal with religion and thus neglects to afford Muslims official minority status and the accompanying protections granted to other groups such as the Sikhs, which are designated as distinct ethnicities. As Lewis notes, "there was little attempt [by the British government in the 1980s and early to mid-1990s] to incorporate religion in race and ethnicity perspectives, either as an important component in self-description or as a vehicle for the expression and mobilization of collective minority interests."[76]

Put simply, while multiculturalism is a noble and often effective means to recognize the relevance of a variety of groups—both majority and minority— possessing distinct and disparate characteristics in a given society, it must include fully all communities that exist within that context. Additionally, even once all those groups are recognized, multiculturalism in and of itself does not ensure that the majority and minority will develop the cooperative multilateral relationships that are required to form an inclusive whole. The case of Muslims in the United Kingdom is demonstrative both of the daunting challenges associated with the integration of minority groups and the implications of that process.

Implications of Integrative Shortcomings

As is true of any modern democratic state, the exclusion of minority groups from the economic benefits that accompany equitable integration has the potential to foster social and political instability in the United Kingdom. This is particularly evident in the urban districts of major metropolitan areas, where the vast majority of South Asians live. The prevalence of low income levels and high unemployment rates in these districts exacerbates relations among minority Muslims and members of the societal mainstream. Perceptions among Muslims of government mistreatment over cultural and religious practices trigger more drastic reactions than would likely prove true if economic conditions were not so dire in Islamic communities. The more extreme the reaction, the higher the probability that negative stereotypes of Muslims will become more deeply ingrained in society at large. As Rex asserts, "there still is considerable space for dialogue which is prevented by prejudices on both sides. On the British side, there is widespread dismissal of all Muslims as fundamentalists, and on the side of the Muslims, there has been an unwillingness to extend their thinking to deal realistically with the problems of Muslims living as a minority in a non-Muslim society."[77]

Take the Rushdie affair. The burning of Rushdie's *The Satanic Verses* and support for Khomeini's *fatwa* mandating the author's execution polarized British society. The BCM's actions were a product of the deep reverence South Asian Sunnis display toward Muhammad, and the marginalization of Muslim communities in British society. By portraying Muhammad as a womanizer— whether an accurate depiction or not—Rushdie evoked a visceral reaction among Pakistanis and Bangladeshis.[78] According to historian Wilfred Cantwell Smith, for example, "Muslims will allow attacks on Allah; there are atheists and atheistic publications, and rationalistic societies; but to disparage Muhammad will provoke from even the most 'liberal' sections of the community a fanaticism of blazing vehemence."[79] In turn, the public nature of the BCM-orchestrated book-burning and subsequent demonstrations supporting the *fatwa* reinforced Western societal perceptions of Islam as a threatening fundamentalist faith. As Husband explains, the "Rushdie affair, and specifically Ayatollah Khomeini's *fatwa* . . . provided a linkage of 'oriental political pathology' to 'Islamic fanaticism.' "[80]

The 1990-91 Persian Gulf crisis sparked a similar heightening of Christian-Muslim tensions in the United Kingdom, which was manifested in BCM-sponsored demonstrations opposing the British government's political and military participation in the American-organized coalition against Iraq. Initially, the BCM condemned Saudi Arabia for allowing Western Christian states to station their troops on its sacred soil, issuing an August 1990 proclamation insisting that the "nation of Islam (ummah) is one . . . [and] national borders cannot be more sacred than the security of Muslim blood and land. The build up of non-Muslim military forces in the vicinity of Islam's holiest shrines is not acceptable."[81] Ultimately, once military operations to expel Iraqi forces from Kuwait commenced in January 1991, the BCM organized a national Muslim conference, whose representatives issued three anti-Western resolutions. First, they demanded that the "USA-led aggression against Iraq" must stop and Western forces must be withdrawn from Saudi Arabia. Second, they condemned Saudi King Fahd and his family for allowing those forces onto Muslim holy lands. Third, they stressed that it was every Muslim's duty to "restore custody [of those lands] to rightful hands."[82]

While each of these international imbroglios exacerbated majority-minority and intra-minority societal divisions in the United Kingdom, disputes pitting Islamic communities and British officials over local-level issues are more instructive vis-à-vis the dynamics of the integration process. Interactions among municipal governments and Muslim advocacy groups have typically proven the first step in facilitating minority-majority cooperation that has the potential for expansion to the regional and national levels over time. Consider the case of Bradford in the 1980s. In response to requests from Muslim advocacy groups—most notably the BCM—for instance, the Bradford Local Education Authority (LEA) inaugurated a program for the provision of *halal* meat to 1,400 Pakistani and Bangladeshi children attending public schools in the city in 1983. Additionally, the LEA made a commitment to extend this service to all of Bradford's 15,000 Muslim pupils within two years.

Yet, ensuing protests from animal rights activists objecting to Islamic requirements for livestock to remain conscious during slaughter prompted a March 1984 debate on the issue within the Bradford Council. Although the council voted to retain *halal* meat in the schools, its ruling did not fully defuse the underlying tensions between Muslims and Christians in the community.[83] Instead, a new dispute arose over the publication in a right-wing journal of an article in which Ray Honeyford, headmaster of Bradford's Drummond Road Middle School, downplayed the need to accommodate Muslim religious needs in the public education system. Granted, LEA officials ultimately forced Honeyford to resign in December 1985. But the affair was nonetheless illustrative of societal reluctance to adapt British institutions to the needs of ethnic and religious minorities.[84]

Interaction between the BCM and local officials in Bradford in the 1980s was significant primarily because it started a process of majority-minority engagement that has exhibited increasing levels of success—albeit on a gradual basis—in the years since. Consider, for example, a study undertaken by the European Union (EU) in 2000 to gauge public attitudes toward ethnic and religious minorities in its member states. The study indicates higher levels of tolerance in the British context than is true in the cases of France and Germany.[85] The following three sets of comparative statistics drawn from the study are particularly instructive. First, 16 percent of Britons think the government should accept workers from Muslim countries without any restrictions compared to 14 percent of Frenchmen and six percent of Germans. Second, 48 percent of Britons feel the presence of minority groups increases unemployment rates as opposed to 54 percent of Frenchmen and 61 percent of Germans. Third, 31 percent of Britons believe immigrants are more often involved in criminality than the national average; the comparative totals among Germans and Frenchmen are 62 and 71 percent, respectively.[86]

Despite these relatively positive figures, much work remains vis-à-vis the equitable incorporation of Muslims within British society. This is in part the result of the shortcomings of the government's policy of multiculturalism. Public divisions—both among minority Muslims and the societal majority—over government encouragement of the coexistence as opposed to local if not national incorporation of cultures are in part a product of the practical implications of multiculturalism in terms of internal stability and the related development and implementation of domestic and foreign policy in the United Kingdom. In short, the coexistence of within but relegation to the fringes of society of Muslim communities whose members retain esoteric religious and cultural values but are economically disadvantaged is a source of local and national instability rather than integrative progress.

Such instability is manifested in desperation—most notably among the second and third generations—with the potential to erupt in civil unrest in minority communities in places such as Bradford, Oldham and Burnley, the sites of inter-ethnic rioting in the spring and summer of 2001. These riots, which included violent altercations between South Asian and white youths and members of these groups and the police were illustrative both of the distrust Muslim youths feel toward the British government generally and the police force in particular, and their own ongoing struggle to define themselves. As Muslim writer Arun Kundnani argues, the "fires that burned across Lancashire and Yorkshire through the summer of 2001 signaled the rage of young Pakistanis and Bangladeshis of the second and third generations, deprived of futures, hemmed in on all sides by racism, failed by their own leaders and representatives and unwilling to stand by as, first fascists and then police officers, invaded their streets."[87]

Most internal minority-majority strife in the United Kingdom is the result of these types of incidents. However, international altercations pitting Western governments against Muslim-majority states and transnational Islamic organizations have also reverberated in the British domestic context in the years since the Rushdie affair and 1991 Persian Gulf War. Following the bombing of military sites in Iraq by American and British warplanes in December 1998, for example, Muslim advocacy groups responded with public protests in London, Bradford and Leeds. One Islamic organization—the fundamentalist *Al Muhajroun*, which is based in London—issued a statement stressing that the "reaction of Muslims will be that this has been an attack on them and this is a declaration of war."[88] Similar demonstrations followed the American bombing of a pharmaceutical factory in Khartoum, Sudan, in retaliation for the Sudanese government's alleged complicity in the terrorist bombing of the United States

Embassies in Nairobi, Kenya, and Dar-es-Salaam, Tanzania, in August 1998, and were even more prevalent during the run-up to and conduct of the 2003 Second Gulf War.

The broader international security implications of such episodes include the potential for the recruitment of British Muslims by transnational terrorist organizations such as Al Qaeda. For example, although the hijackers responsible for the 11 September 2001 attacks on the World Trade Center and the Pentagon had Middle Eastern origins, linkages have since emerged between Al Qaeda and the United Kingdom's Islamic communities. In one case, a British-born Muslim—Ahmad Omar Saeed Sheikh—was convicted and sentenced to death in Pakistan for planning the kidnapping and murder of Wall Street Journal reporter Daniel Pearl in January 2002 in Karachi. Pearl was abducted while working on a story about Jamaican-Englishman Richard Reid, a convert to Islam whose attempt to blow up an American Airlines jet over the Atlantic in December 2001 was foiled.[89]

Additionally, the longstanding dispute between India and Pakistan vis-à-vis control over Kashmir has had a significant impact in Muslim communities in Britain. The recruitment of young Muslims from Pakistani enclaves in northern England to fight against Indian forces in Kashmir by a variety of radical groups, for instance, prompted the British government to establish the Terrorism Act 2000.[90] The measure, which came into force in February 2000, was designed to give the police greater legal latitude in tackling organizations that sponsor terrorist activities through recruitment and fundraising in the United Kingdom. Specifically, the new law makes it "illegal to raise funds for known terrorist groups and, crucially, to invite someone to receive terrorist training even though that training may take place abroad." Even stiffer legislation was put forth in the aftermath of the events of 11 September 2001, most notably a November 2001 provision allowing British authorities to detain suspected foreign terrorists without trial indefinitely. Though deemed necessary by the Blair government in order to assist the Bush administration in its war on terror, the measures could also prove counterproductive vis-à-vis the integration of Muslims domestically.[91]

Still, notwithstanding these developments, the impact of Muslim communities on British foreign policy has been marginal, particularly when compared with the French case. The proximity of North Africa to France and close political relationships Paris has forged with successive military-backed regimes in Algeria are sources of considerable domestic instability, most notably in the form of increased potential for terrorist attacks in large metropolitan areas. In the United Kingdom, on the other hand, the distance of the Indian subcontinent from London and the lack of a colonial relationship as turbulent as that between France and Algeria has mitigated the impact of that legacy on British foreign policy. The United Kingdom's integrative dilemmas vis-à-vis Muslim communities are considerably more focused on domestic-level factors.

Ultimately, determinations of the success or failure of the integration process will hinge on the roles played by second, third and fourth generation Muslims in British society over the long term. In order to encourage progress, government officials must engage rather than dictate to emerging generations of leaders of Muslim communities, most importantly at the local level but also regionally and nationally. On an encouraging note, two relatively recent initiatives are indicative of positive progress in this respect. First, British Prime Minister Tony Blair's decision to issue a first-ever governmental message to Muslims at the start of the Islamic holy month of Ramadan in January 1999.[92] Second, the Labour Party's pledge in its pre-June 2001 Parliamentary election manifesto to redress the under-representation of ethnic minority candidates on national party lists.[93] In conjunction with Blair's message, Derek Fatchett—a minister in the British Foreign Office—wrote an article in the *Muslim News* defining in general terms the means by which to improve relations between the government and Muslim communities in the United Kingdom. The article was instructive in its call for understanding that cuts in two directions. As Fatchett asserts, "[w]e need to show the people of the West that Islam is not about extremism or the terrorists who abuse its name. [But the] education needs to be in both directions. Just as we need to shatter the Western stereotypes of Islam, so we need to fight the suspicions in the Muslim world of the West and its motives."[94]

Measurement of Integrative Progress

The integration of Muslim communities into British society is a long-term project, with progress in the short term best measured on a gradual basis in a given context, whether at the local, regional or national level. While British governments in office over the past two decades have generally focused on integrative approaches applicable at the national level, the majority of the implications arising from the exclusion of Muslims are played out locally. As a result, it is logical to apply the general model proposed in the French case study to the contemporary United Kingdom in order to determine where Muslim communities stand in comparison to the majority in given municipalities in that context.

In terms of demographics, the concentration of Muslim communities in the poorest districts in the London, Bradford, Manchester, Glasgow and Birmingham metropolitan areas are indicative of the marginalization of Muslims. Interfaith and interethnic interactions in these contexts are often of a confrontational nature resulting from innate fear, mistrust and bitterness on both sides. As Abdul Gulzar, a youth worker for the Bradford Council, contends, "today's youngsters in places like Bradford have no direction in their lives, [but] you cannot force people to integrate. I think integration is important, but not in the [multicultural] way it is being put forward at the moment."[95]

Economically, unemployment rates among Muslims living in urban areas are triple, if not quadruple, the national average. Such inequality fuels feelings of disillusionment if not desperation within Islamic communities, particularly among second and third generation South Asians who believe the British government has not afforded them reasonable opportunities to prosper. While increases in ownership of private businesses by Muslims are indicative of economic progress, most Muslims with jobs remain confined to the unskilled labor sector of the economy and thus continue to have considerably lower income levels than is true of the national majority. The gradual incorporation of British-born generations of Muslims into the skilled labor sectors of the economy, on the other hand, is likely to facilitate their broader integration into the societal mainstream.

In the social context, one general indicator of the extent of minority integration is the receptivity of government institutions to Muslim demands. Perhaps the most notable such petition forwarded over the past decade was for British officials to make an effort to accurately count the number of Muslims residing in the United Kingdom. To the government's credit on this issue, it conceded to Muslim wishes by including a question on religious affiliation—albeit one that requests an answer on a voluntary rather than compulsory basis—in the 2001 national census.[96] Once the proportion of Muslims in the population is consistently gauged in a statistically reliable fashion, the government will have the requisite data figures to make reasonably credible decisions vis-à-vis levels of political representation and in public sector employment.

While the amendment of the census process in the favor of Muslim communities bodes well for the future, current levels of minority representation in public sector jobs remain markedly low. A June 1999 report commissioned by the Lord Chancellors Department in London, for example, noted that ethnic minorities made up 3.5 percent of the national population but accounted for just 1.7 percent of appointments and 1.75 percent of senior managerial positions in the British civil service at that juncture.[97] Similarly, a January 2000 Home Office report found that minority recruitment totals were declining in nine of 43 police forces and stagnant in seven others.[98] One positive result of these studies was former Home Secretary Jack Straw's demand that the London Metropolitan police force increase its number of ethnic minority officers from 4.1 percent at present to 25 percent by 2009.[99]

The Home Office also addressed the concerns of Muslims in particular in the commissioning of a Derby University report that recommended extending the 1976 Race Relations Act to cover religious minorities. Its findings were based in part on a questionnaire sent to 1,830 religious organizations and faith groups across the United Kingdom. According to Paul Weller, who headed the Derby research team that produced the report, "[b]ecause of the nature, frequency and seriousness of discrimination and unfair treatment on the basis of religion, numbers of individuals can feel at least a measure of exclusion in important areas of social life."[100]

A decision whether to act on the report's recommendations will fall to the Labour government elected in June 2001. Although the results of the election boosted the political standing of Muslims marginally, there is considerable room for improvement in the future. In terms of national and supranational representation, Britain's Islamic communities in Britain have three representatives at present—Sarwar and Mahmood in the House of Common and Conservative Bashir Khanbhai in the European Parliament. Khanbhai, who stood in the United

Kingdom's Eastern Region, was elected as the first-ever British Muslim EMP in June 1999.[101] Further increases in representation are most likely to occur as a result of an increased focus on those districts with the highest concentrations of registered Muslim voters, which include Birmingham Sparkbrook and Small Heath (27,808), Bradford West (21,746), Birmingham Ladywood (15,184) and Bradford North (10,302).[102]

While the political progress South Asians have made over the past two decades serves as a valid reason for optimism, it is also best viewed as a point of departure. In order to achieve the full integration of Muslims into British society in the future, considerable gains are necessary in each of the four major issue areas—those related to demographics, economics, social interaction and politics—featured in the integrative model proposed and discussed here. The model is useful primarily as a means to measure that progress, with movement toward or away from a confluence of minority and majority characteristics viewed as success and failure, respectively. Granted, long-term integration necessarily entails interactive policy formulation, coordination and implementation at the local, regional and national levels. However, given the prevalence of South Asian Muslims in particular localities and the resultant higher degree of interaction among Pakistani and Bangladeshi communities and government officials in those contexts as opposed to the limited dispersion of Muslims regionally and nationally in the United Kingdom, a local-level approach is more desirable in the short term.

Conclusions

This chapter had six fundamental objectives. First, to explain the development of Islamic communities in Britain. Second, to examine the characteristics of those communities to determine their societal standings. Third, to compare and contrast the identities of minority Muslim communities with that of the United Kingdom generally in order to discern what elements of those identities cause the greatest societal divisions. Fourth, to describe the British integration process, placing emphasis on its strengths and weaknesses as relates to Muslims. Fifth, to discuss the implications of that process. Sixth, to apply the model presented in the French case study to the United Kingdom.

The establishment of Islamic communities in the United Kingdom unfolded in three stages. First, Muslims migrated predominantly from South Asia through a combination of privately-sponsored guest worker programs designed to utilize foreign unskilled labor to rebuild the British economy in the 1950s and 1960s and personal initiative to escape economic hardship and political instability in India and Pakistan. Second, although the United Kingdom attempted to stem immigration flows through a variety of legal initiatives from the late 1940s to the late 1960s, the pioneer migrants—whether employed or not—remained, and their communities acquired a more culturally South Asian and religiously Muslim character via the large-scale reunification of family members. Third, Muslim communities grew in the urban districts in many of Britain's major metropolitan areas through the emergence of younger generations of Pakistanis and Bangladeshis who possess both South Asian and British cultural characteristics.

Unfortunately, Muslims are largely excluded from the benefits that accompany acceptance by the societal majority. Their communities are clustered predominantly in urban districts on the peripheries of large cities, where jobs are scarce and prosperity all but nonexistent. The relegation of Muslims to these environs is partly attributable to a clash of identities that is based as much on misperception as reality. The inaccurate societal perception of Islam as a radical religion whose adherents are fundamentalists wholly at odds with modern Western civilization has consistently fostered deep divisions between the majority and Muslim minorities in the United Kingdom. While legitimate political and religious differences exist on both sides, there is still potential for the development of a middle ground, within which Muslims could practice the five essential pillars of Islam without undermining the authority of the British state and its public institutions.

Although the equitable integration of Muslims into British society is necessarily a long-term project, it is by no means unattainable. To date, British governments—those of the past three decades in particular—have focused principally on multiculturalism as an integrative strategy. However, this model has proven largely ineffective, especially with respect to second and third generation Muslims, who were born in the United Kingdom, possess citizenship and yet feel alienated in a large part because of their economic travails and social and political marginalization. In short, the promotion of the coexistence of multiple cultures in British society has not facilitated the development of the type of hybrid Anglo-Islamic identity necessary to fully integrate current and future generations of Muslims.

While it is possible to apportion blame on both sides of the social equation, it is more constructive to discuss the potential for cooperation. Muslims are and will remain permanent members of British society. Interaction with the majority is inevitable, most notably so at the local level, where the amelioration of Anglo-Muslim relations is most necessary. Interaction, whether pursued at the individual, local, regional or national levels, often results in differences of opinion. In order to mitigate if not preclude instability within British society, both Muslims and Christians must work to overcome such differences en route to the construction of more conciliatory relationships. However, to co-exist peacefully if not cooperate fully, one side must accommodate the other. The extent to which each side is amenable to that course of action will determine the nature of the relationship between the two at a given point. In order to facilitate greater bilateral minority-majority congeniality in the United Kingdom, it is essential that the two sides bridge the middle ground in a manner that allows for the discussion if not comprehensive resolution of the concerns each expresses in the future.

The effective integration of Muslims into British society is an indispensable long-term objective largely because of the ongoing evolution of the state's demographics. As is true of states throughout Western Europe, the United Kingdom's white population is aging at a rate significantly greater than it is reproducing. The resultant decline in the "working-age" population (individuals between the ages of 15 and 64) of Europe generally and the United Kingdom specifically poses a significant threat to economic growth in those contexts this century. The best way to stem that decline, in turn, is through the use of foreign labor, which entails an increase in immigration. One estimate, for example, indicates that for Europe to satisfy the impending need for labor, it must attract 1.8 million newcomers annually through 2050.[103] As was true in the aftermath of the economic boom of the 1950s and 1960s, the United Kingdom is likely to require laborers from abroad in order to fuel economic growth from 2001-2050. Given the ethnic makeup of present British minority communities, many such migrants are likely to come from regions with high percentages of Muslim inhabitant, most notably South Asia and the Middle East. Their relegation to the margins of society is not likely to prove as politically feasible as was the case previously in light of the growing electoral strength of Islamic communities in the United Kingdom, particularly in municipal contexts. Demands for accommodation of cultural and religious needs of migrants will almost certainly increase and require the prompt attention of British politicians at the local, regional and national levels.

Ignorance of the implications of these demographic trends—while possible albeit not prudent in the short term—is not feasible over the long term. Integration is both a present and potential future problem in the United Kingdom, one that, if not redressed, possesses increasing potential to threaten British social and political stability, internal security and perhaps economic prosperity as well. The remedy is simple to state but will require a firm governmental commitment to achieve. It entails four related steps.

First, acknowledge the growing significance of the presence of Islam in the United Kingdom and do so in a positive rather than negative manner. The Blair government made progress with respect to this issue during its first term, most notably through the prime minister's personal interaction with Islamic communal leaders and increasing Home Office scrutiny of the exclusion of Muslims and other minority groups. Blair's issuance of official Ramadan greetings and attendance at a 2001 awards dinner sponsored by the *Muslim News*, Fatchett's article vis-à-vis minority-majority interfaith relations, and the inclusion of more Muslims than ever before on mainstream political party lists in the 2001 parliamentary election were all significant manifestations of this general trend. However, considerably more progress is necessary to ease Islamic communal concerns over the economic and social marginalization of Muslims living in low-income districts ringing large metropolitan areas such as London, Bradford and Manchester. Such marginalization is particularly destabilizing with respect to interactions between second and third generation Muslims and the police and members of the societal majority as evidenced by the spring and summer 2001 riots across northern England. In order to help reduce the likelihood of similar outbursts in the future, sustained Home Office engagement with Muslim communal representatives is critical. The constructive participation of members of minority groups and government officials is indispensable in this context; unilateral pronouncements and action plans will not suffice.

Second, work to ameliorate the exclusion of Islamic communities, placing an emphasis on the reduction of barriers between younger generations of Muslims and members of the societal majority. The participation of Muslims in their teens and 20s in the aforementioned rioting was hardly a coincidence. Similar to their counterparts in France, individuals in the second and third generations often feel a sense of alienation—both from their elders and society at large. Brawling with right-wing extremists and the police serves as a means to release those frustrations. Regrettably, it also reinforces the popular image of Muslims as violent extremists in the minds of members of the mainstream. In order to alter such perceptions, constructive minority-majority interaction is necessary at the local level, particularly in the cities where the rioting was most intense—Bradford, Oldham and Burnley. The achievement of progress in this issue area demands effort by individuals on each side of the socio-religious equation.

Third, gauge progress toward integration at the municipal level through the model proposed here. The indicators in the model are most immediately useful if applied locally. This is true of benchmarks ranging from decreases in unemployment and the resultant increases in income among Muslims in a particular urban district to the dispersion of those individuals across a given metropolitan area and subsequent increases in interaction with members of other ethnic and religious groups. The collection of data on these and the assortment of other benchmarks articulated previously is least elusive locally and thus easier to employ expeditiously to more fully integrate minorities at the micro than the macro level.

Fourth, once positive results are achieved locally, apply the model regionally and nationally. If Muslims and members of the British societal majority are able to overcome their ethnic and religious differences in one municipality, the potential for integrative progress at broader levels is likely to increase substantially. Elements of an effective program to integrate minorities in one district, for instance, may be transferable to another. Local and parliamentary representatives could work together to facilitate such transfers. In turn, as more and more Muslims of the second, third—and eventually fourth—generations begin to see improvements in their standards of living and perceived levels of acceptance by their neighbors, it is possible that they will become more receptive to proverbial olive branches offered by national leaders—both within and outside of the Labour government. Ultimately, through these means, the development of a more equitable and thus more socially and politically stable United Kingdom is an attainable long-term objective. Without the discussion and eventual implementation of these types of initiatives, on the other hand, the consequences of the exclusion of Muslims—manifested in violent outbursts such as the 2001 riots—will only grow more pronounced over time.

Notes

1.   Lewis, *Islamic Britain*, 1-2; LeBor, *A Heart Turned East*, 148-50.
2.   "Shades of Brown," *Economist* (31 May 2001); "Alone, Together," *Economist* (14 July 2001); "Findings on the Week and Troubles," *Muslim Council of Britain*, July 2001.
3.   Lewis, *Islamic Britain*, 159.
4.   LeBor, *A Heart Turned East*, 148.
5.   British Office for National Statistics, *Census 2001: Ethnicity and Religion*; General Register Office, Scotland, *Census 2001: Ethnicity and Religion*; "A Map of Muslim Britain," *Guardian* [London] (17 June 2002); "How Many British Muslims?," *Muslim Council of Britain* (2001).
6.   Rex, *Ethnic Minorities*, 220.
7.   Lewis, *Islamic Britain*, 11.
8.   Kettani, "Challenges to Organization of Muslim Communities," 29; Lewis, *Islamic Britain*, 11.
9.   D.A. Coleman, "International Migration: Demographic and Socioeconomic Consequences in the United Kingdom and Europe," *International Migration Review* 29 (1995): 156.
10. Thomas F. Pettigrew, "Reactions Toward the New Minorities of Western Europe," *Annual Review of Sociology* 24-1 (1998): 78.
11. Ceri Peach, "The Muslim Population of Great Britain," *Ethnic and Racial Studies* 13-1 (1990): 34.
12. Lewis, *Islamic Britain*, 17.
13. Colin Browne, *Black and White Britain: The Third PRI Survey* (London: Heineman, 1984), 24; Ibrahim El-Sohl, "Be True to your Culture: Gender Tensions Among Somali Muslims in Britain," *Immigrants and Minorities*, 12-1 (1994): 21-46.
14. Peach, "Muslim Population," 34-35.
15. Fred Halliday, *Arabs in Exile: Yemeni Migrants in Urban Britain* (London: I.B. Tauris, 1992).
16. Peach, "Muslim Population," 34-35; Lewis, *Islamic Britain*, 11; British Office for National Statistics, *Census 2001: Ethnicity and Religion*; General Register Office, Scotland, *Census 2001: Ethnicity and Religion*.
17. Lewis, *Islamic Britain*, 16-17.
18. Elinor Kelly, "Transcontinental Families—Gujarat and Lancashire: A Comparative Study," in *South Asians Overseas: Migration and Ethnicity*, ed. Colin Clarke, Ceri Peach and Steven Vertovec (Cambridge: Cambridge University Press, 1990), 253, 259.
19. Coleman, "The UK and International Migration: A Changing Balance," in *European Migration in the Late Twentieth Century: Historical Patterns, Actual Trends and Social Implications*, ed. Heinz Fossman and Rainier Münz (Laxenburg, Austria: International Institute for Applied Systems Analysis, 1994), 59-60.
20. Kepel, *Allah in the West*, 130.
21. Lewis, *Islamic Britain*, 8.
22. Charles Husband, "The Political Context of Muslim Communities' Participation in British Society," *see* Lewis and Schnapper (1994), 80.

23. *Islamaphobia: A Challenge for us all*; British Office for National Statistics, *Census 2001: Ethnicity and Religion*; General Register Office, Scotland, *Census 2001: Ethnicity and Religion*.

24. Ceri Peach, "South Asian and Caribbean Ethnic Minority Housing Choice in Britain," *Urban Studies* 35-4 (1998): 1,660.

25. *Estimates of Population*.

26. Lewis, *Islamic Britain*, 15; Muhammad Anwar, *Muslims in Britain: Census and Other Statistical Sources* (Birmingham, UK: Center for the Study of Christian-Muslim Relations, 1993), 4-7.

27. *Estimates of Population*.

28. British Office for National Statistics, *Census 2001: Ethnicity and Religion*; General Register Office, Scotland, *Census 2001: Ethnicity and Religion*.

29. British National Office of Statistics, *Health Survey for England* (London: British National Office of Statistics, 1999).

30. Lewis, *Islamic Britain*, 15.

31. Mark S. Brown, "Religion and Economic Activity in the South Asian Population," *Ethnic and Racial Studies* 23-4 (2000), 1,036; Roger Ballard, "The Pakistanis: Stability and Introspection" and John Eade, Tim Vamplew and Ceri Peach, "The Bangladeshis: The Encapsulated Community," in *Ethnicity in the 1991 Census: The Ethnic Population of Great Britain*, vol. 2, ed. Ceri Peach (London: HMSO, 1996), 121-61.

32. "Shades of Brown"; V.T. Robinson, "Boom and Gloom: The Success and Failure of South Asians in Britain," *see* Clarke, Peach and Vertovec (1990), 270; United Kingdom Action Committee on Islamic Affairs, *British Muslims and the General Election 1997* (London: United Kingdom Action Committee on Islamic Affairs, 1997); Davis, "Religion and Economic Activity," 1,045.

33. "Health Survey for England."

34. "Shades of Brown."

35. Lewis, *Islamic Britain*, 23; Ballard and Kalra, *Ethnic Dimensions of 1991 Census*, 32.

36. Davis, "Religion and Economic Activity," 1,055.

37. Pnina Werbner, "Islamic Radicalism and the Gulf War: Lay Preachers and Political Dissent Among British Pakistanis," *see* Lewis and Schnapper (1994), 98.

38. Muhammad Rafiq, *Asian Businesses in Bradford: Profile and Prospects* (Bradford, UK: City of Bradford Metropolitan Council, 1985), 4-8. Reference made in Lewis, *Islamic Britain*, 62-63.

39. Roland Gribben, "Measuring the Multicultural Revolution," *Daily Telegraph* [London] (21 August 2000).

40. Nielsen, *Muslims in Western Europe*, 45.

41. Parekh, "South Asians in Britain," 69.

42. *Health Survey for England*; Parekh, "South Asians in Britain," 69.

43. Peach, "Muslim Population," 36.

44. Camillia Fawzi El-Sohl, "Arab Communities in Britain: Cleavages and Commonalities," *Islam and Christian-Muslim Relations* 3-4 (1992): 250.

45. "Lessons from the Election," *Muslim News* (29 June 2001).

46. "Britain's first Muslim MP," *Daily Telegraph* (31 January 1998).
47. Auslan Cramb, "Suspended MP is Cleared of Bribing Rival at Election," *Daily Telegraph* (26 March 1999).
48. Hamed Chapman, "Relative Success for some Muslim Candidates," *Muslim News* (29 June 2001).
49. Quoted in Ahmed Versi, "Labour Race Record Attacked," *Muslim News* (23 June 1999).
50. LeBor, *A Heart Turned East*, 155.
51. Hamad Chapman and Ahmed Versi, "Over 200 Muslim Councillors," *Muslim News* (25 May 2001).
52. Vertovec, "Muslims, the State and the Public Sphere," *see* Nonneman, Niblock and Szajkowski (1996), 174.
53. "Religious Affairs Policy," *Common Sense* (July 2001).
54. Statham, "Political Mobilization by Minorities in Britain," 37-38.
55. Vertovec, "Muslims, State, Public Sphere,"175.
56. For a general description of the fundamentals of Islam, refer to the section on identity in the French case study.
57. Greenfeld, *Nationalism*, 53.
58. Joppke, *Immigration and Nation-State*, 103.
59. Ibid., 104-05.
60. Quoted in Lewis and Schnapper, *Muslims in Europe*, 80-81.
61. Quoted in LeBor, *A Heart Turned East*, 119.
62. Rex, *Ethnic Minorities*, 221.
63. Quoted in LeBor, *A Heart Turned East*, 138.
64. Ibid., 143.
65. Ibid., 151-52.
66. Lewis, *Islamic Britain*, 206-07.
67. Ibid., 206.
68. Joppke, *Immigration and Nation-State*, 100.
69. Ibid., 100-13.
70. Ibid., 106-13.
71. Ibid., 224.
72. Quoted in Michael Banton, *Promoting Racial Harmony* (Cambridge: Cambridge University Press, 1985), 71.
73. Ian A. Macdonald, *Race Relations: The New Law* (London: Butterworth, 1977), 517; Joppke, *Immigration and Nation-State*, 229.
74. Joppke, *Immigration and Nation-State*, 234.
75. Ibid., 236-48.
76. Lewis, *Islamic Britain*, 3.
77. Rex, *Ethnic Minorities*, 240.
78. Lewis, *Islamic Britain*, 154. Lewis notes that "[a]ny work which can be construed as insulting the prophet can be guaranteed to unite the most diverse groupings of Muslims in South Asia and throughout the South Asian diaspora."

79. Quoted in Annemarie Schimmel, *And Muhammad is His Messenger: The Veneration of the Prophet in Islamic Piety* (Chapel Hill: University of North Carolina Press, 1985), 4. Reference made in Lewis, *Islamic Britain*, 154.
80. Husband, "Muslim Communities' Participation in British Society," in Lewis and Schnapper, *Muslims in Europe*, 81.
81. Bradford Community Relations Council, *Annual Report 1988/89* (Bradford, UK: Bradford Community Relations Council, 1989), 6.
82. *Guardian* [London] (21 January 1991).
83. Lewis, *Islamic Britain*, 148-49.
84. Ibid., 149-53.
85. Thalhammer et. al, *Attitudes Towards Minority Groups*.
86. Ibid.
87. Arun Kundani, "From Oldham to Bradford: The Violence of the Violated," *Institute of Race Relations* (July 2001).
88. "Muslim Group Warns of 'Violent Backlash,' " *Daily Telegraph*, 18 December 1998.
89. Profile: Sheikh Omar Saeed," *BBC News*, www.bbcnews.co.uk (16 July 2002); "Islam's Young Radical Front," *BBC News*, www.bbcnews.co.uk (29 February 2002); "France to Assist Terror Suspect," *BBC News*, www.bbcnews.co.uk (12 December 2001).
90. Peter Foster and Maurice Weaver, "Young Britons Heed the Call to Arms for Holy War," *Daily Telegraph* (29 December 2000).
91. Forster and Ahmed Weaver, "Muslims Still Looking for Martyrs," *Daily Telegraph* (29 December 2000); Farewell, Londonistan?," *Economist* (2 February 2002); "And Throw Away the Key," *Economist* (17 November 2001).
92. "Fatchett's 'Id message for British Muslims," *Muslim News* (20 January 1999).
93. "Labour Manifesto to Address Ethnic Minority Under-Representation," *Muslim News* (14 May 2001).
94. "Fatchett's 'Id message for British Muslims."
95. Quoted in Mohammed Sajjad, "National Front Attacks Provoke Reaction from Bradford Muslims," *Muslim News* (27 July 2001).
96. Hamed Chapman, "Muslims Urged to Participate Fully in Census," *Muslim News* (3 February 2001); Philip Johnston, "Religion Enters Lists but Income is Still Taboo," *Daily Telegraph* (13 April 2001).
97. Ahmed Versi, "The Civil Service: Cold-Shouldering Non-Whites?," *Muslim News* (23 June 1999).
98. Fatema Hassan, "Institutional Racism Still Exists," *Muslim News* (31 March 2000).
99. A.J. McIlroy, "Met will Let Muslim WPcs Wear Traditional Headscarf," *Daily Telegraph* (23 April 2001).
100. Rachel Sylvester, "Call for Religious Discrimination Law," *Daily Telegraph* (24 February 2001).
101. Ahmed Versi, "First Muslim Elected in European Elections," *Muslim News* (25 June 1999).
102. "Top 100 Constituencies in Terms of Muslim Voting Potential," *Muslim Council of Britain* (May 2001).

Islam in Europe

103. Eberstadt, "Population Implosion," 42-50; Maurice Weaver and Philip Johnson, "Midlands communities will be mostly non-white in 15 years," *Daily Telegraph* (8 December 2000); Ambrose Evans-Pritchard, "EU 'will need immigrants' as working population falls," *Daily Telegraph* (11 January 2000).

Chapter 6

Islam in Europe: Past, Present and Future

Introduction

The first contact between Muslims and Christians within the present geographical confines of Western Europe came in April 711 in Xeres, a southern Spanish town just northwest of Gibraltar. As has often been the case in the history of Islamic-Christian relations, the encounter was confrontational rather than conciliatory in nature. Moorish Muslim combatants loyal to Caliph Yezid al-Wahid of the Umayyad dynasty of Damascus crossed the Strait of Gibraltar from North Africa and defeated the Spanish Christian army of Visigothic King Don Rodrigo on the banks of the Guadelete River. That victory marked the start of a period of Islamic occupation of the Iberian Peninsula that lasted nearly eight centuries. It also set in motion a process that contributed to the conception and subsequent evolution of the idea of a united Western Europe.[1]

Following the initial incursion, Ummayad forces rapidly expanded their imperial dominion across Spain and Portugal. By 718—less than 100 years after the death of the prophet Muhummad, who established Islam by way of a divine revelation in 610—Muslims controlled the entire Iberian Peninsula and were attempting to consolidate limited territorial gains in southern France. It was in the latter context that the Islamic incursion stopped and the development an entity now known—albeit not at that juncture—as Western European Christendom had its genesis. In October 732, Frankish ruler Charles Martel halted the advance of Muslim forces under the command of the Emir Abderaman at Poitiers in the province of Aquitaine. Twenty-seven years later, Martel's son, Pépin, defeated a Muslim army at Narbonne, sending the invaders south across the Pyrenees and ending the Islamic threat to French sovereignty.[2]

The military victories of Martel and his son provided the foundation for the construction of a Christian-oriented Western European sub-continental empire under the tutelage of the standard bearer of the family's third generation—the Carolingian Emperor Charlemagne. Born in 768 and crowned in 800, Charlemagne cast Christianity as the cornerstone of a consolidation process designed to unite a politically disparate array of kingdoms and principalities—whether by request, diplomatic persuasion or military coercion—under the Carolingian banner.[3] Partially, although by no means exclusively, a response to the Islamic challenge to Christianity on the continent, Charlemagne's regional dynasty is comparable at a general structural level to the integration project that has taken place in Europe over the past half-century, with supranational power centered in Aachen in the former case as opposed to Brussels in the latter.

Although the present European integration process is markedly more secular in nature—in theory, if not always in practice—and concentrates less power in the hands of individuals in comparison with multilateral institutions than was the case in Charlegmagne's era, the relationship between Islam and Christianity continues to affect the integration process in contemporary Western Europe generally and the roles the European Union (EU) plays in the domestic affairs of its member states specifically. In contrast to the Middle Ages, however, the construction of a common identity and consolidation of political authority across boundaries serve as possible means to help facilitate the inclusion of Muslim communities within, as opposed to force the expulsion of Islam, from the continent.

Consider the latest European Intergovernmental Conference (IGC), which was completed with the negotiation and signing of the Treaty of Nice in December 2000 and February 2001, respectively. In the context of the treaty is a 50-article Charter of Fundamental Rights that addresses issues including the treatment of minority groups, stipulating that all EU member states must "respect cultural, religious and linguistic diversity" and prohibiting all "discrimination based on any ground such as sex, race, color, ethnic or social origin, genetic features, language, religion or belief, political or any other opinion, membership of a national minority, property, birth, disability, age or sexual orientation."[4] Given the cited grounds of race, color, ethnic origin, religion and national minority status in particular, the treaty demonstrates the potential for the EU to contribute to the effective social integration of Muslims in Western Europe. Similarly, the charter's inclusion in the treaty—as well as in the context of a proposed European Constitution to be considered for approval and ratification by the EU's present and prospective future member states in 2004 and 2005—is illustrative of the significance of Islam in this region, which currently includes 12-15 million Muslim residents and is expected to house 23 million by 2013.[5]

While the domestic case studies presented previously have the potential to stand alone, they can also benefit from a further examination of the issue of Islam in Europe as it applies to the wider regional context. There are three fundamental reasons why. First, since the end of World War II, nation-states have steadily yielded elements of their economic, military and political sovereignty to an ever wider and more deeply integrated European community. The integration process has developed to such a degree that issues having an impact on one member state often affect other member states and the broader supranational institutions to which they all belong. Such issues include not just high profile projects like the launch of the Euro and the development of a European Security and Defense Identity but also to the domestic integration of minority groups. Second, the construction of collective supranational institutions required former Western European enemies to overcome centuries-old national differences. In the process, the definition of European identity changed for the better. It stands to reason that similar progress vis-à-vis the resolution of minority-majority ethnic and religious differences is possible through alterations in public perceptions pursued at the supranational level. Third, as was true of the national disagreements that culminated in two global wars emanating from the European continent over the first half of the twentieth century, the adversarial nature of Muslim-Christian communal relations in contemporary France, Germany and the United Kingdom has deep historical roots. As a result, it is necessary to touch upon the past as well as the present when discussing the standing of Islam in Europe.

With these observations providing an engaging point of departure, this chapter includes five related sections, each one of which features multiple parts. The sections unfold in the following manner:

Historical Overview

This section addresses the generally contentious nature of the relationship between Islam and Western European Christendom, both within and outside of the continent, in four parts. The first part discusses the initial appearance of Islam on the Iberian Peninsula, subsequent advance of Muslim armies into France, and Christian responses to the political and religious challenges posed by those incursions from the eighth to fifteenth centuries. It places an emphasis on the impact of Islam upon the construction of a common Western European identity. The second part examines Islamic-Christian relations in the Ottoman era, focusing on issues with long-term implications in European continental space—most notably the innate ethnic and religious divisions that continue to foster instability in the Balkans in the 2000s. The third part describes interactions among Western European powers and the Muslims residing in the regions of the developing world colonized by states such as France and the United Kingdom in the nineteenth and early- to mid-twentieth centuries. The fourth part touches on the return of Islam to the continent following the gradual post-World War II breakup of Western European colonial empires across the Greater Middle East. The third and fourth parts are brief given that many of the issues raised therein have already been discussed in greater detail in the domestic case studies.

Transformation of Western European Identity

This section addresses the reshaping of Western European identity over the latter half of the twentieth century—concurrent with, and to some extent related to, the growth of Muslim communities in its member states—in four parts. The first part sets the scene in post-World War II Europe, emphasizing the need for reconstruction within and reconciliation between former adversaries across the Western half of that region. The second part discusses the launch and subsequent deepening of the European integration process, focusing on the construction of institutions transcending borders as a means to ensure domestic political stability and economic prosperity. The third part touches on the perpetual challenges of intergovernmental cooperation on issues of domestic significance, particularly as pertains to the development of common EU social policies. The fourth part discusses the extent to which the end of the Cold War presented Western European leaders with a viable opportunity to concentrate on the preservation of social stability by developing supranational policies to help improve the domestic integration of minority groups.

Supranational Means to Domestic Integrative Ends

This section focuses on the role of the EU in fostering improvements in the social standing of communities of Muslims in its member states generally, and in the contexts of France, Germany and the United Kingdom specifically, in four parts. The first part discusses the fundamental strengths and weaknesses of supranational policymaking regarding the treatment of minorities—those possessing and lacking citizenship or legal residency alike—at the national level. The second and third parts examine the formulation and implementation of EU policies affecting Muslims residing in its member states vis-à-vis the issues of immigration and domestic integration, respectively. They each emphasize policies developed since the end of the Cold War. The fourth part compares and contrasts these policies in order to identify the elements of each likely to prove most useful in the future.

Finding a Place for Islam in Europe

This section addresses the potential for the development of a hybrid Euro-Islamic identity across borders in the twenty-first century in four parts. The first three parts describe Muslim, Western European national and EU perspectives, and proposals with respect to the potential for the successful completion of such an identity-building project. The fourth part draws on each of these approaches in presenting a formula to ensure greater cooperation among Muslims and Christians in Western Europe over both the short and long terms.

Conclusions

This section has two parts. The first part summarizes the key points of the four main sections of the chapter. The second part evaluates in general terms the present realities of, and related future prospects for, the relationship between Christianity and Islam in Western Europe.

Historical Overview

The first contacts between Muslims and Christians on the Iberian Peninsula were a byproduct of the concept of holy war (*jihad*), which was conceived by Muhammad as a means to spread the Islamic faith beyond the Saudi Arabian cities of Mecca and Medina during the seventh century. The allure of *jihad* was attributable both to mundane avarice and divine inspiration: territorial expansion in the mortal world and eternal rewards in the afterlife. Under the auspices of the *Koran*, which Muslims believe God revealed directly to Muhammad, those who died while carrying out *jihad* became martyrs and were thus automatically entitled to an afterlife of perpetual pleasures. As Paul Fregosi notes, for an adherent to the Islamic faith, "dying and killing can both be acts of great religiosity, either as a warrior of Allah . . . or as a martyr if he is killed. He is then assured an instant place in Paradise without having to wait, as lesser mortals have to do, until the Day of Judgement."[6]

With these worldly and otherworldly incentives to draw upon, Muhammad's descendents continued the pursuit of *jihad* in earnest after his death in 632, rapidly expanding the territory under Islamic control east as far as present-day India and Pakistan, north into the Byzantine Empire, and west into North Africa and, eventually, southwestern Europe. The Umayyad dynasty's initial encounters with Spaniards were preconditioned by Muslim notions of Christianity as the antithesis of Islam and Europeans as uncivilized barbarians, viewpoints originally cultivated during Muhammad's lifetime.[7] As Jane Smith explains, the "vast majority of the Muslims in the eastern part of the empire had little if any knowledge of the western regions of Christendom, as well as little interest in discovering anything about lands they considered bleak and remote, inhabited by peoples they thought to be little more than barbarians. They considered the Europeans' manners and habits to be loathsome, their level of culture exceedingly low and their religion superceded by Islam."[8]

These impressions of Western European Christendom did not change substantially when Umayyad armies first invaded Spain in 711. However, interactions with Spaniards were a practical necessity for the ensuing seven and one-half centuries, over the course of which Muslims occupied and governed wide swaths of the Iberian Peninsula. Two types of Islamic-Christian relationships prevailed in occupied Spain during this period—one positive and one negative—with each reflecting the philosophies of the Muslim leaders in charge. The first period was characterized by the caliphate of Córdoba's tolerance of its Christian subjects from the eighth to tenth centuries. The second period, on the other hand, reflected rising tensions between the Islamic and Christian worlds both within and outside of the Iberian Peninsula from the early eleventh century until the expulsion of Muslim forces from Grenada in 1492. It was generally concurrent with the conception and pursuit of the Christian version of *jihad*—the attack and occupation of the Middle Eastern Holy Land by Western Christian crusaders—in the High Middle Ages.[9]

Two distinct types of treatment of minority Christians were typical in these periods. Smith, for example, notes that under the reign of Córdoban emir Abd al-Rahman, "Christians generally were tolerated, protected and treated with charity," particularly those in the higher social classes.[10] The opposite was generally the case over the final four centuries of Muslim occupation. During this span, the traditional Islamic treatment of Christians as *dhimmis*, who were forced to acknowledge explicitly the superiority of Muslims in daily inter-faith interactions, was the rule rather than the exception. As Fregosi argues, the public standing of Christians governed by Muslims "in many ways resembled that of the Untouchables in Hindu society. They were the dregs, the people at the bottom of the pile."[11]

Islamic leaders designed and institutionalized myriad rules to reinforce the *dhimmi* system, including the following nine restrictions. First, Christians "could not carry a weapon or ride a horse, only a donkey." Second, they "were not allowed to wear shoes but had to walk barefoot." Third, a "Christian who claimed Jesus was divine was automatically executed." Fourth, and relatedly, a "Muslim who became a Christian or a Jew was also executed." Fifth, the "ringing of Church bells was forbidden." Sixth, "Christian religious processions were banned." Seventh, all non-Muslims "had to stand aside if a Muslim passed them in the street." Eighth, Christians "could not wear anything which had green in it, as that was the color of Islam. Nine, if a Muslim assaulted a non-Muslim the latter was "not allowed to fight back but [was] only permitted to ask [the] aggressor to stop hitting them."[12]

Yet, while the religious laws governing Christian behavior within Islamic territory may appear extreme, they were generally no worse than those that Christian rulers—most demonstrably Charlemagne—imposed on what they perceived as unbelievers in the context of Western Europe in the Middle Ages. Similar to early reactions of Muslims to Christianity, Western Europeans did not recognize Islam as a legitimate religion upon coming into contact with the Umayyads in Spain, Portugal and France.[13] As Richard Fletcher explains, the "idea of a 'new religion' was, strictly and literally speaking, unthinkable for the Christian intellectual of those times. . . . For them, there was one faith and that was the Christian faith."[14] As a result, Fletcher continues, Islam "was most plausibly interpreted . . . as a Christian heresy. Manifestly, it shared much with Christianity—monotheism, holy places like Jerusalem, veneration for patriarchs and prophets such as Abraham or Elijah. Yet Islam had perverted Christianity by offering a parody of holy scripture, by denying Incarnation and Resurrection and Trinity, by exalting its own pseudo-prophet, by declaring war on Christians and seizing their holiest places."[15]

Charlemagne's establishment of a Christian empire that controlled wide swaths of territory across the heartland of Western Europe in the eighth and ninth centuries was not exclusively attributable to the Muslim incursion in Spain. However, it was directly related to nascent Christian-Muslim rivalries on the continent in two ways. First, the emergence of the Carolingian dynasty as a regional power was sparked in part by Charles Martel's victory over the Umayyads at Poitiers in 732.[16] As Pierre Riché notes, "[b]y his military skill and political talent, Charles Martel had triumphed over a period of uncertainty. Europe had begun the eighth century moving toward a fragmented political order of autonomous princedoms under the local dukes. Charles Martel had arrested the process and assembled under a central power every region in the West."[17] The word Carolingian, Fletcher points out, "is derived from the Latin name, *Carolus*, of Pippin's father, Charles Martel, and it was later born by the family's most famous member, Pippin's son Charles, or Karl, known to history as Charles the Great, *Carolus Magnus*, Charlemagne."[18] Second, Charlemagne's emphasis on Christianity was indispensable to the maintenance of political cohesion despite the range of regional and local ethnic and familial loyalties within the empire over which he presided. As Peter Brown asserts, "[w]hat had once been a more open world, characterized by looser social and political structures and by far greater fluidity in its religious allegiances, found itself drawn into an ever-tighter system of religious control, fostered by men inspired by a new sense of order, and who enjoyed the protection of increasingly resourceful and self-confident Frankish kings."[19]

As was true of Muslim rulers in southern Europe—whether the Umayyads in Spain or their Ottoman contemporaries in the Balkans—Charlemagne restricted the rights of unbelievers (non-Christians rather than non-Muslims in the former contexts), but granted limited autonomy to local officials in order to administer the Carolingian dynasty effectively.[20] Brown, for instance, explains that "[f]aced by much resentment and non-cooperation, the best that Charles could do was to communicate that, in a shaken world, the new imperial order founded at Aachen represented the only effective guarantee of social and religious stability; and that those who joined in would be allowed to thrive at the expense of those who did not."[21] In contrast to the centralized bureaucracies through which the Romans and Byzantines maintained cohesion in their empires, the Carolingians employed a diversified system more suitable to the regionalized societies Charlemagne and his advisors governed.[22] As Brown notes, "[skilled] and enthusiastic scribes and educators were drawn to Charles' court, were formed there and then sent out to churches and monasteries that were the nodal points of an extensive large network of religious centers. The provinces of the east Roman Empire always lived under the shadow of Constantinople. They were never covered in the same way by an empire-wide network of centers of culture, each with roughly similar resources in every region, as was Charlemagne's Europe."[23] Ultimately, these regional administrators had two fundamental tasks to accomplish, which Fletcher describes as follows. First, "to bring the faith to pagan peoples newly brought under Frankish rule." Second, "to fortify the faith of peoples already nominally Christian, such as the King's Frankish subjects."[24]

Charlemagne's reliance on the allure of Christianity to consolidate Carolingian power was comparable to similar uses of that faith by other Western European leaders—of both the political and religious variety—to mobilize the requisite support to conduct large-scale military operations against Muslim adversaries within and beyond continental space during the Middle Ages. Notable examples included the re-conquest of the Iberian Peninsula and the Crusades, segments of which unfolded concurrently over the first half of the second millennium in the confines of Muslim controlled Spain and across a wide swath of the Middle East, respectively.[25]

The Crusades, a series of military campaigns designed to recover the Middle Eastern Holy Lands in which Christianity was born, spanned just under 200 years from the late eleventh to late thirteenth centuries. These campaigns had their genesis in a call to arms issued by Pope Urban II in November 1095 in response to a request from Byzantine Emperor Alexius Comnenus for assistance in an ongoing struggle against Muslim forces occupying holy sites, such as the Jesus Christ's places of birth (Bethlehem) and resurrection (Jerusalem).[26] Issued in the French town of Clermont, Urban's plea drew a diverse array of Christian recruits from across Western Europe, one demonstrative of the influence of religion— particularly among the lower classes—at this historical juncture.[27] As W.B. Bartlett contends, many "of the poorer sections of society were quickly gripped by the idea of the Crusade. Their zeal was fueled by itinerant preachers . . . who took Urban's message to heart and built on it, engendering an outpouring of religious fervor in the process."[28]

While a lack of formal military training and the presence of an unsustainable number of non-combatants (women, children and the elderly) in their ranks doomed the first Crusaders to failure in 1097, subsequent waves led by charismatic leaders, such as brothers Godfrey and Baldwin of Bouillon, succeeded in capturing Antioch in 1098 and Jerusalem in 1099.[29] Comparable to inter-faith military conflicts in the contexts of Islamic incursions into European territory, battles pitting Christians against Muslim defenders in the Middle East were brutal affairs that—once complete—rarely featured merciful treatment of the vanquished by the victors. Consider, for instance, Barlett's description of the Christian triumph at Jerusalem:

> Thousands of apocalyptic warriors exploded into the Holy City in a horrific Bacchanalia of death and destruction. This was the ultimate logical conclusion of a spiritual policy that not only accepted war but encouraged it as an act of penance. Fueled by uncontrollable emotions, the massacre was of inhuman proportions. There was no room for Christ here. This was the God of the Old Testament, a cruel God without mercy.[30]

As has been true over much if not all of the history of Islamic-Christian relations, the carnage at Jerusalem in 1099 prompted a strident Muslim response. In this case, the Islamic counter-offensive culminated in the Egyptian warrior Saladin's re-conquest of the holy city in 1187 and foreshadowed the ultimate expulsion of the Crusaders from the region via their surrender of Acre in 1291.[31]

Similarly, concurrent with the pursuit of the Crusades, but several thousand miles to the west, a successful Christian challenge to Islamic imperialism was unfolding on the Iberian Peninsula. Between 1050 and 1250, a conglomerate of principalities in northern Spain regained Christian control of the landmass comprising present-day Spain and Portugal through a successful series of campaigns against the occupation forces of the Arabo-Berber Almohad. The Muslims retained only the enclave of Granada, the fall of which in 1492 removed from Western Europe an Islamic presence that was not to reappear there in any substantial form until the latter half of the twentieth century.[32]

From the late fifteenth to mid-twentieth centuries, contacts between the leaders and peoples of the states presently holding membership in the EU and their counterparts in the Islamic world were limited primarily to a pair of related military and geopolitical undertakings. First, the defense of European territory from the advances of the Ottoman Empire (most notably during the fourteenth, fifteenth and sixteenth centuries). Second, the expansion of Western European power into regions of the developing world populated predominantly by Muslims via the establishment of colonial empires by states such as Britain, France, Germany and the Netherlands in the eighteenth and nineteenth centuries. Both issues are particularly germane here in light of their implications in the context of the twentieth and early twenty-first centuries, whether through the North Atlantic Treaty Organization (NATO) intervention to stabilize the Balkans or inter-state relationships among EU member states and their former colonies.

Threats to Western European territory emanating from the expansion of the Ottoman Empire reached their height in the sixteenth century. After gaining a foothold in the Balkans by virtue of a victory over the Serbian dynasty at the Battle of Kosovo in 1389, the Ottomans pushed steadily northward. They occupied Romania in 1504, took Belgrade—capital of communist Yugoslavia during the Cold War and the Republic of Serbia since then—in 1520, and assumed control of Hungary in 1529. Sieges of Vienna, immediately following the Hungarian conquest and again in 1574, were turned aside by the Christian defenders of Austria, who fought under the banner of the Habsburg emperors of Spain.[33] Indeed, the contentious nature of the contemporary relationship between the EU and Turkey is in part a reflection of these centuries-old Christian-Ottoman confrontations. As Ira Lapidus argues, much "of Ottoman history was shaped by their extraordinary commitment to conquest in the name of Islam. The Ottoman wars gave them a reputation among Muslims as the greatest of Muslim states devoted to the jihad. In Europe, they left the reputation of the scourge of God and terror for centuries. The image of the ferocious Turks lives on today."[34]

The era of colonialism had an equally deep impact upon current Muslim-Christian relations, both within and outside Western Europe. In the contexts of the French and British colonial empires in North Africa and the Indian subcontinent, for example, Islam proved a useful medium to mount independence struggles that eventually resulted in the establishment of the states of Algeria, Morocco, Tunisia, India and Pakistan. As John Obert Voll notes, for "two centuries . . . the combination of a renewal mission, opposition to local non-Islamic customs, and defense against foreign rule provided a highly successful format for the efforts to create alternative, authentic Islamic communities and states. For a time these jihads were more effective than virtually all other alternatives in resisting European expansion."[35] Yet, while Islamic resistance movements contributed to eventual decolonization, the linkages established between states such as Britain and France and the developing world during the colonial period also sparked migratory flows through which Muslims returned to the continent as guest workers and eventually residents and citizens in Western Europe. Ultimately, as the leaders of victorious and vanquished states began to redefine the idea of Europe at the regional level in the aftermath of World War II, the domestic ethnic and religious demography of the societies they served was also about to undergo marked changes.

Transformation of Western European Identity

Throughout European history, leaders of nation-states have pursued two over-riding objectives, with partial if not full achievement of each generally required to obtain and then retain the support of the people over whom they govern. First, safeguard the territory constituting their state from external security threats. Second, ensure domestic stability through the achievement of economic prosperity, whether universally—or at a minimum—among those members of society (particularly the military and political elite) whose backing is indispensable to the maintenance of authority. These objectives are not mutually exclusive; rather, they require the formulation and implementation of interconnected policies to overcome obstacles with implications manifested at both the domestic and international levels.

Prior to the end of World War II, European leaders had used a variety of strategies in order to mitigate, if not preclude, external threats and domestic instabilities. Notably, one such strategy—the pursuit of regional unification—was repeated periodically over the centuries. The particulars of the means employed to achieve that end were myriad but most came within frameworks that focused exclusively on the unilateral pursuit of interests by the rulers of given states. As discussed at greater length previously, for example, Charlemagne established a regional Christian dynasty on the battlefield. Napoleon Bonaparte and Adolf Hitler also sought regional hegemony through military conquest, framing expansion in terms of French and German nationalism, respectively. The architects of the Concert of Europe (Austrian Claus von Metternich and Frenchman Charles de Talleyrand among others) employed balance-of-power diplomacy in crafting an inclusive post-Napoleonic Wars settlement at the Congress of Vienna in 1815. Chancellor Otto von Bismarck used a combination of military force and diplomacy to unify Germany in 1871, then pursued its interests through the development of a complex web of regional alliances over the ensuing two decades.

Notwithstanding the short-term gains achieved by the above leaders, states and empires, none succeeded in the preservation of long-term stability and prosperity, either domestically or at the Western European regional level. Instead, they cultivated legacies of militarism and diplomatic manipulation that culminated in continental and widespread global devastation through the conduct of World War I and World War II over the first half of the twentieth century. As a result, in the wake of World War II, a new generation of leaders faced the related challenges of reconstructing the states over which they presided and redefining the idea of

Europe in a manner that would avoid the mistakes of the past. Derek Urwin explains, for instance, that the "idea of unity resurfaced again, but this time as part of an argument that retention of the historical notion of the independent state as the foundation of political organization had been discredited and that it should be abandoned, to be substituted by a concerted effort at unifying state practices that in time might lead to a comprehensive continental political community."[36]

At the conclusion of World War II, Western European leaders faced two fundamental challenges, one immediate and the other of a more long-term nature. First, they had to rebuild the infrastructures of cities and towns within and the economies of states across the continent. Second, they had to develop a new systemic model governing inter-state behavior to replace the outdated balance-of-power framework that contributed to the outbreak and conduct of two global conflicts from 1914-45 and the alienation and subsequent appeasement of the continent's largest state during the inter-war years. These challenges were related in two ways. First, none of the states of Western Europe possessed the requisite physical resources and political will to overcome either hurdle unilaterally. Second, because of such shortcomings, they needed assistance from an outside power with an interest in cultivating political stability and economic prosperity across the region.[37]

Put bluntly, after World War II, two nascent hegemons controlled the continent's geopolitical future. At the heart of a physically destroyed, economically bankrupt and emotionally exhausted Europe in need of regional redefinition, the United States and Soviet Union occupied what remained of the once mighty but now prostrate German colossus. The former presided over the Western half with Britain and France; the latter was in charge of the Eastern half (aside from collective Allied administration of Berlin). Each side possessed fundamentally different political and economic systems, with Washington and Moscow married to the philosophies of liberal democracy and capitalism, and totalitarianism and communism, respectively. Ultimately, the transformation of Western European identity came in the context of and had a profound impact upon the development and subsequent conduct of a global Cold War pitting the United States against the Soviet Union over a period lasting more than four decades. As Walter Laqueur notes, the "old European balance of power was replaced by the global balance of power between America and Russia. Europe paid a terrible price for its disunity: the division into so many nation-states with conflicting intensity. The fate of the continent was now being decided in Moscow and Washington."[38]

In order to prevent Soviet advances beyond Moscow's control of the Eastern slab of Germany and the states of Central and Eastern Europe, the United States needed the support of a cohesive Western Europe. The creation of such an entity would entail economic, political and military cooperation and thus the willingness of Western Europeans to overcome bitter inter-state animosities, particularly with respect to the Germans. For their part, the Western Europeans required economic assistance for the reconstruction that would necessarily precede the process of reconciliation.[39] As Simon Serfaty argues, "[u]nity among the nation-states of

Europe was a precondition for economic reconstruction not from one but two world wars; reconstruction was also the precondition for political unity not only within each European nation-state but among all of them as well. Without reconstruction first, the states of Europe could be saved neither from themselves nor from each other. Reconciliation would come next."[40]

American support for Western European reconstruction, which was manifested in the provision of more than $12 billion in economic assistance through the Marshall Plan between 1948 and 1952, was part of a multi-step bargaining process between the United States and its allies across the Atlantic. First, the administration of American President Harry S. Truman proposed and the Western Europeans accepted the Marshall Plan in exchange for a pledge to administer the aid multilaterally as the first step in a long-term regional integration project. Second, the Western Europeans requested that the United States maintain a long-term military presence on the continent in order to mitigate if not eliminate any security threats posed by their Soviet adversaries and recently reformed but still innately distrusted German partners. Third, Washington complied by establishing NATO in April 1949, with the guarantee of collective defense serving as a proverbial security blanket under the cover of which the Western Europeans could deepen and widen the integration process in the future.[41]

These agreements were necessarily connected, each serving to reinforce transatlantic and inter- and intra-European linkages at the intergovernmental level and change popular perceptions of past foes domestically. Serfaty, for example, explains that postwar

> European policies were guided by complementary goals; to foster a peaceful community
> of democratic states on the continent and to build a strong security alliance with the
> United States. . . . Both sides of the Atlantic understood that neither goal could be
> achieved without the other. Europe's will to unite had to be credible before the United
> States would accept the European 'invitation' to make an unprecedented peacetime
> commitment to the continent.[42]

Similarly, Urwin points out that the fact that Western European governments

> were able to turn in the late 1940s to debate the question of integration more intensely
> was due in no small measure to the healthier political, economic and military situation
> which the United States had helped to provide. . . . In attempting to assist Western
> Europe out of its payments crisis and by its commitment to the defense of the continent,
> the United States made an important contribution towards European integration.[43]

The related transatlantic and Western European integration processes proved an effective response to reduce if not erase potential threats to the external security and domestic stability of states such as Britain, France, Italy, Belgium, the Netherlands and the nascent Federal Republic of Germany in the late 1940s and early 1950s. However, neither process proceeded as smoothly as the Western

Europeans and Americans would have liked, either during the first several years of their respective existences or over the ensuing decades. The underlying reason: after centuries of emphasis on the inviolability of the sovereignty of states, integration entailed the gradual sacrifice—albeit at a glacial pace—of national governmental authority to supranational institutions. Ultimately, this type of transformation required popular approval that was naturally easier to obtain when the perceived risks—marked drops in standards of living; external threats to domestic security—exceeded the costs of saying yes to a redefinition of the idea of Europe. As Laqueur asserts, "[t]here were from the beginning considerable strains and stresses in the new European community, but there was also a welcome fresh spirit, a much-needed dynamism and the first stirrings of a new European patriotism. Though frontiers remained, they seemed to shrink in importance; small placards were seen to be saying: 'Another border but still Europe.'"[44]

After the distribution of Marshall Plan aid sparked the start of economic recovery, Western European leaders took their initial step in the direction of eventual political unity by founding the European Coal and Steel Community (ECSC) in April 1951. It included six members—France, West Germany, Italy, Belgium, the Netherlands and Luxembourg—which would henceforth produce and administer the subsequent distribution of coal and steel collectively rather than unilaterally. Next, at the behest of the United States, they attempted to extend inter-European cooperation to the security field through the development of an independent European Defense Community (EDC)—one lacking, that is, military contributions and political control from Washington. Ultimately rejected by the French Parliament in August 1954, the EDC was stillborn in large part because of concerns over the rearmament of West Germany in an entity lacking an American security component (the Federal Republic was admitted instead to NATO in April 1955). Lastly, the Western Europeans relaunched the integration process by deepening economic cooperation through the establishment of the European Economic Community (EEC) via the Treaty of Rome in June 1950. This ensured that integration continued despite the failure of the EDC.[45]

These institutional developments—both positive and negative—were the product of an underlying safety mechanism that allows transitory delays in the deepening and widening of European institutions but precludes the derailment of the integration process and thus ensures that it continues to progress. Put simply, when integration slows because of shortcomings in a particular context— economic, military or political in general terms—it is relaunched in another. This proved true during Cold War years and remains so in the post-Cold War era. Serfaty, for instance, explains, that the

> process of European unity can most clearly be viewed, and, hence, be taken most seriously, from a multiyear perspective that escapes the day-to-day disappointments of incomplete agreements and unfulfilled promises. Considered at any one time, and examined in the light of any one issue, 'Europe' can be legitimately dismissed as a failure. . . . But seen in the light of what has already been achieved, the gloom of the

moment fades as it becomes all too clear that no setback on the path to unity has ever been final.[46]

Similarly, Stanley Hoffman stresses that although the "nation-state has survived as the center of political power and the focus of citizens' allegiance . . . [it] coexists with a European enterprise that has real but limited powers, and considerable resilience."[47]

Over the initial four and one-half decades that followed the conclusion of World War II, the transitory successes, failures and—ultimately—progress in the Western European integration process came against the backdrop of an ongoing confrontation between the United States and Soviet Union that had the potential, if only rarely the practical likelihood, to threaten the continent's very existence. In this atmosphere, the Western Europeans steadily deepened and widened their communal economic and political institutions but always did so while facing a Soviet threat that required American power and leadership to hold at bay. The end of the Cold War, by contrast, gave Western European leaders a window of opportunity to focus primarily if not fully on cooperation in pursuit of integration within rather than the preclusion of security threats from without. As Serfaty concludes, the "new global war and the new local conflicts that loom ahead are being waged not between states and over boundaries, but within each state and over whatever remains of its territorial sovereignty. . . . This, alas, is a farewell to the visions and leaders of yesteryear. Ambitions have take precedence over convictions, and the will to succeed now, at this time, has replaced the urge to build over time."[48]

Supranational Means to Domestic Integrative Ends

Jean Monnet, one of the men most responsible for the genesis and subsequent pursuit of the European integration process, once wrote, "I have never doubted that one day this process will lead us to the United States of Europe; but I see no point in trying to imagine today what political form it will take. ... No one can say."[49] The complexity of the process Monnet describes is based predominantly on changes occurring in two contexts: the continental system the EU's member states inhabit and the domestic societies over which they govern. Since the end of the Cold War, for example, Western European security concerns have shifted in emphasis from the menacing presence of the Soviet Union in the East to instability in the Balkan South and the dual threats of illegal migration across the EU's borders and social unrest fostered by the marginalization of minority communities within its member states. As Paul Graham Taylor argues, in "every period throughout the history of the state—long before the European Community, there were views specific to that period about what could be permitted by way of extending competencies to common institutions without jeopardizing sovereignty. The history of the European Union [illustrates] this point well."[50]

The above issues, all of which relate at least in part to the evolving relationship between Islam and Christianity in Europe, require management at both the national and supranational levels. This, in turn, entails consultation and—however challenging it often proves—cooperation among the leaders of Brussels-based institutions such as the European Commission and those of its member states. As Andrew Geddes notes, "Europeanization implies the establishment of supranational authority (laws, rules, institutions and new patterns of political activity), which EU member states have helped establish but which affect policy management in member states. The effect is that the national and European levels become entwined. Debates at EU level cannot be separated from discussion of developments at [the] national level."[51]

The initial—and most substantial—contributions of Muslims to the European integration process to date came as a result of the guest worker programs of the 1950s and 1960s. In short, immigrants provided much of the requisite unskilled labor to rebuild Western Europe from the ravages of World War II and—in so doing—helped lay the foundation for economic integration institutionalized through the establishment of the ECSC and EEC. Unfortunately, Western European viewpoints of migrant laborers as a transitory and disposable means to the end of reconstruction (as described in the French, German and British case studies) mitigated the credit guest workers received then—and to some extent—even now. According to Geddes, for instance,

> [m]igrants helped build and reconstruct European nation states. Just as surely as European integration rescued the nation state, then so too did migration, but the language of crisis and threat can disguise the contribution that has been made and will be made in the future by migration. . . . [E]ven though both immigration and European integration were central to the post-war reconstruction of the [Western] European nation state, it is European integration that tends to get the credit.[52]

As Geddes suggests, the suspension of guest worker programs across Western Europe in 1973-74 did not erase the connection between immigration in general and that of Muslims specifically in the context of the integration process. Instead, over the ensuing quarter century, Islamic communities across the continent have had impacts upon and in turn been affected by the deepening and widening of the Brussels-based entity known first as the EEC, next as the European Community (EC) and presently as the EU. This the case in two policy areas in particular. First, the interconnected regulation of immigration flows and handling of asylum requests through inter-governmental and supranational cooperation in order to guarantee the internal security of EU member states. Second, amelioration of the treatment of minorities through initiatives designed to achieve gradual confluence on issues associated with justice and home affairs.

The establishment of the EEC served as an institutional means to create a common Western European market for good and services. However, although fundamentally an economic initiative, it had spillover effects in the region's internal political and security arenas. By reducing trade barriers, the Rome Treaty boosted economic growth, raising the standard of living and thus helping to buttress the domestic political stability of the EEC's member states. Additionally, implicit in the sense of regional solidarity the treaty fostered was a desire to develop safeguards against external threats to domestic stability, aside from those of the military variety covered by the Atlantic Alliance.

Perhaps the greatest of such perceived threats have been those posed by immigration. Thus, as a first cooperative step designed to mitigate influxes of new migrants and keep tabs on immigrants already residing within EEC member states, Western European leaders established the Trevi group for inter-governmental political and judicial cooperation in 1975. While the Trevi group was concerned primarily with the prevention of acts of terrorism, wider EC cooperation on immigration policy increased markedly—in the economic, political and social spheres in particular—as a result of the negotiation of the Single European Act (SEA) in 1986.[53] As described by Geddes, the SEA mandated a reduction of barriers to the "free movement for people, services, goods and capital within a single market, which would see a progressive extension of the common market and within which internal frontiers between member states would be removed."[54]

In accordance with the SEA, the gradual reduction and eventual elimination of checkpoints along the internal borders of all EC member states—excluding the United Kingdom—was formalized through the Schengen Convention of June 1990. The negotiation, passage and implementation of the Schengen measure had related theoretical and practical implications at both the Western European supranational and national levels, particularly as relates to responsibility for immigration control. Theoretically, Schengen was a manifestation of the continuing surrender of the power of states—in this case control over territorial boundaries—to supranational institutions. Practically, it required the establishment of bodies such as the Ad Hoc Intergovernmental Working Group on Immigration (AHIWGI) in 1986, Rhodes group for coordination among EC member states on free movement in 1988, the Mutual Assistance Group (MAG) for customs controls in 1989 and European Police Office (EUROPOL) in 1999.[55]

The responsibilities of these entities were at conception and remain today somewhat ambiguous. As Geddes notes, the "low politics of economic interdependence could not be separated from the high politics of state sovereignty because the economics of the free market and free movement became more closely connected at EC level with the politics and policy of immigration, asylum and internal security."[56] Demonstrative of Geddes' point was a June 1989 report (the Palma Document), in which the Rhodes group informed EC heads of government that more than "80 initiatives or pieces of legislation were needed to achieve free movement of people within the EC" and that the "EC institutions had competence to act [on] no more than one-fifth of these points."[57]

More concentrated efforts to improve coordination among inter-governmental and supranational West European institutions came in the contexts of the negotiation and implementation of the 1992 Maastricht Treaty and 1997

Amsterdam Treaty. The former treaty—named after the Dutch city where it was negotiated in December 1991—dealt principally with the eventual establishment of a common currency, achievement of full political union and enlargement into Central and Eastern Europe, but it also featured a pillar on Justice and Home Affairs (JHA). The JHA pillar represented the institutional genesis of a gradual transition in immigration and asylum policy coordination—albeit at a rather subdued pace—from an exclusive emphasis on the threats posed by contemporary and future influxes of foreigners to one focusing on the integration of past migrants and their descendents within the domestic societies of Western Europe.[58]

However, the Maastricht Treaty also stipulated that minority integration would remain primarily under the purview of the member states themselves rather than that of the EU. Included in the JHA pillar, for example, was a provision establishing and then granting European citizenship to all nationals of EU member states. Under the auspices of the provision, all individuals who acquire European citizenship are entitled to four basic rights. First, they may move freely and reside in an EU member state of their choice. Second, they may vote, run for office or do both in municipal and European Parliamentary elections. Third, they have the right to diplomatic protection. Fourth, they may petition the European Parliament.[59] The measure was beneficial to those Muslims—most notably those of the younger generations—already possessing national citizenship in given member states. Yet, notwithstanding the potential for the attainment of such benefits by some, the criteria for eligibility for European citizenship was still decided at the domestic level and thus continued to vary across national borders (as articulated in the previous chapters).

Ultimately, the inclusion of the JHA pillar equated to a postponement of indefinite length—rather than outright rejection—of the development of a formal EU role vis-à-vis the mitigation of the exclusion of Muslims from the Western European societal mainstream. According to Geddes, this "did not necessarily occur because the member states were not prepared to countenance supranational action for migrant inclusion. Rather, it was a tangible manifestation of the difficulties associated with securing agreement on the content of such a policy, given the widely divergent policy paradigms in member states and the need for unanimity if an EU context were to be established."[60] Furthermore, as Alan Butt Philip argues, the very existence of the JHA pillar was evidence that "[d]espite widespread resistance to EC institutional involvement in immigration matters, national governments [were] finding the EC being drawn into the evolution of policy for legitimate and practical reasons. Many aspects of immigration have an interface with EC competencies which the renewed emphasis on free movement and other social rights in the wake of the single market program [had] made clear."[61]

The Amsterdam Treaty, which was negotiated in June 1997, built upon the progress made regarding EU involvement in domestic immigration and minority integration policies. In the former context, for example, it increased the European Commission's role by mandating the gradual shift of "controls on the external borders, asylum, immigration and judicial cooperation on civil matters" from the inter-governmentally oriented JHA pillar (Title VI) to the supranationally based community pillar (Title IV) of the Maastricht Treaty. This shift resulted in the creation under the auspices of Title IV of a collective area of "freedom, security and justice," which explicitly guaranteed protections to non-national minorities residing in EU member states.[62] Although the treaty stipulated that the European Commission was not to assume full control of immigration and asylum policies for five years, it created the potential for a gradual improvement in public standing for migrants and their descendants across Western European during that span. Granted, Geddes explains, a "big question is the extent to which the movement of immigration and asylum into the new Title IV creates scope for the institutionalization of a migration policy context and political and judicial effects that help open 'social and political space' for migrants at EU level."[63] Nonetheless, he continues, the "five-year time limit for most immigration and asylum issues is important because it provides a deadline, and therefore, an impetus for action."[64]

In addition to the reapportionment of control over immigration issues, the Amsterdam Treaty mandated adjustments in the JHA pillar itself that may prove beneficial to minority groups—whether citizens or non-citizens—throughout the region. One such adaptation was the addition to Title 6 of the Maastricht Treaty of a provision to "prevent and combat racism and xenophobia" within the domestic societies of EU member states. Means to achieve this end—as articulated in the provision—include closer cooperation among member state police forces, customs authorities and judicial branches as well as approximation where necessary to achieve cross-border cohesion on criminal matters.[65] Although the enforcement of Title 6 measures remains firmly under the control of national governments, the treaty enhanced Brussels' role in JHA affairs—and indirectly in the protection of minority rights—through the insertion of a new Article 13 which "confers upon the Council, acting unanimously upon a proposal from the Commission and after consulting with the European Parliament, the power to take appropriate action to combat discrimination based on sex, racial or ethnic origin, religion or belief, disability, age or sexual orientation."[66]

Along with the legal particulars of these supplements, the Amsterdam Treaty signified an increasing degree of coherence in supranational and intergovernmental policymaking in the EU as relates to the interconnected issues of immigration and minority integration. This philosophical shift was evident in the context of an October 1999 summit in Tampere, Finland, dealing predominantly with immigration and judicial affairs. During that summit, EU leaders negotiated and released a 10-point action plan that included measures to speed harmonization of policies on the control of the flow of legal and illegal migrants and refugees and subsequent treatment of those individuals.[67] On the latter point, the plan "devoted special attention to the need to ensure fair treatment of third-country nationals residing legally and permanently on the territory of member states through an integration policy aimed at granting them rights and obligations comparable to those of EU citizens."[68]

Immigration-related themes were also touched upon in the contexts of the December 2000 Nice Treaty and proposed European Constitution, both of which will ultimately require ratification by member-state legislatures. Although devoted primarily to overseeing structural developments such as the nascent European Security and Defense Initiative, the first wave of enlargement to the East and the voting structure in the European Council, the treaty also had implications for Muslim communities across Western Europe in two related issue areas. First, the establishment of a Charter on Fundamental Rights to apply to all inhabitants of EU member states, whether citizens or non-citizens. Second, the enhancement of the role of the European Economic and Social Committee (ESC) in cultivating more inclusive civil societies across the region.[69]

Regarding the former, the Charter is composed of six chapters, which relate to dignity, freedom, equality, solidarity, citizens' rights and justice. Three of these chapters—those on freedoms, equality and citizens' rights—feature articles with potential applications in the amelioration of the public standing of minorities. Article 10 in the chapter on freedoms, for example, guarantees freedom of thought, conscience and religion to include the right "either alone or in community with others and in public or in private, to manifest religion or belief, in worship, teaching, practice and observance."[70] This article is germane to the resolution of imbroglios over issues such as the wearing of headscarves by Muslim girls attending public schools and the construction of cathedral mosques in densely populated areas. Similarly, Article 14 ensures parents the right to "ensure the education and teaching of their children in conformity with their religious, philosophical and pedagogical convictions."[71]

In addition, Articles 21 and 22 of the chapter on equality ban any discrimination based on "sex, race, color, ethnic or social origin, genetic features, language, religion or belief, political or any other opinion, membership of a national minority, property, birth, disability, age or sexual orientation," and explicitly mandate respect for "cultural, religious and linguistic diversity" throughout the EU.[72] In a related manner, in terms of supranational recourse for national or non-national legal residents of EU member states who feel they have received unfair treatment, Articles 42-44 of the chapter on citizens' rights include the following guarantees. First, "access to European Parliament, Council and Commission documents." Second, the "right to refer to the Ombudsman of the Union cases of maladministration in the activities of the Community institutions or bodies, with the exception of the Court of Justice and Court of First Instance acting in their judicial roles." Third, the "right to petition the European Parliament."[73] Collectively, these measures serve as instruments to help more fully integrate Muslims into the fabric of Western European societies and thus move a step closer to the development of a more cohesive regional community. However, the realization of that goal remains a daunting challenge, one likely to require the formulation of a more diversified concept of European identity with inputs from minority Islamic communities as well as national governments and supranational institutions.

Finding a Place for Islam in Europe

The integration of Islamic communities in the context of a fully united Western Europe demands concerted efforts on behalf of Muslims and their predominantly Christian majority neighbors in EU member states. In order to develop a common identity that includes the ethnic, religious, political and social components indispensable to all of the region's inhabitants, governments and individuals must display a willingness to work together. Developing strategies for collective action, in turn, requires an initial review of the ways in which Muslim communities, domestic governments—most notably those in France, Germany and the United Kingdom—and the leaders of EU's supranational institutions view the role of Islam in contemporary Western Europe. To achieve this objective, a three-part discussion is necessary, one that addresses, in turn, viewpoints expressed at the Muslim communal, domestic governmental and supranational levels.

Among Muslims, whether at the global level generally or in the confines of Western Europe specifically, there are three philosophical approaches to the practice of Islam within states in which it is not the faith of the majority. First, either partial or absolute rejection of the norms of the societal majority through withdrawal into Islamic enclaves where contact with members of other faiths is limited if not nonexistent. Second, abandonment of the strict practice of Islam—at least as defined formally under the strictures of the *Koran* (as articulated in the section on identity in the French case study)—in favor of unconditional assimilation into the non-Muslim societal mainstream. Third, adaptation of Islam to the norms of a particular domestic context in ways that are beneficial to minority-majority interactions but do not undermine the practice of the five pillars of that faith.

The Muslim guest workers who helped rebuild Western Europe in the aftermath of World War II adopted the second line of reasoning. Anticipating a short-term stay on the continent—whether in France, Germany, the United Kingdom or elsewhere—they were satisfied with a low-profile religious presence. However, once reunited with their families in the 1970s and 1980s, they began a rapid transition to lifestyles reflective of the first philosophical stance, often in line with the teachings of Islamic scholars based in Middle Eastern, North African and South Asian states such as Saudi Arabia, Algeria and Pakistan. Each of these approaches mitigated the potential for the development of a nascent Euro-Islamic identity. As Yvonne Haddad notes in citing colleague Azzam al-Tamini's general philosophy on the issue, many of the greatest obstacles vis-à-vis Muslim-Christian interaction in Western European societies

> are the consequences of Muslim perceptions and behavior. Some Muslims erroneously seek to overcome these obstacles by melting into Western culture and abandoning some or all of their Islamic identity. Others insist on avoiding these obstacles by resorting to isolation and hiding in cocoons, which some feel could eventually form ghettos similar to those occupied by the Jewish communities in previous centuries.[74]

The third approach is the most useful, particularly when cultivated among and applied by younger generations of Muslims to minority-majority social interactions in the Western European states in which they have resided for the vast majority of their lives if not since birth. According to Sami Zemya, for example, the "visibility of Islam is carried by a generation of Muslims who were born in Europe or have been living here for a very long time. This is the utmost proof that Muslims feel at home in Europe. They are demanding the right to be full citizens of the European states but by defending the right to certain cultural distinctions. They are just trying to obtain the same thing as their generational counterparts: a good future."[75] Similarly, Tariq Ramadan, a Muslim of Egyptian descent raised in the United Kingdom, argues that the "participation of the young in the process is, without doubt, of great importance, and, armed with their experience and comprehension of the European environment from within, they ought to formulate appropriate questions so as to allow [Islamic scholars] to give more accurate responses. More than any other group, they should think through the different steps of an Islamic education which fits the overall situation."[76]

Zemya describes the debate over the place of Islam in twenty-first century Western Europe as one split between two broad scholarly approaches—traditional and genealogical-pluralist. The first takes "Islam as a research subject in order to find out in what way Islam is concordant with presumed guiding principles of European societal organization," most notably democracy, human rights and tolerance. The second treats Islam as "an integral part of European history" rather than a "foreign body" and thus examines "what role, place and significance Muslims have within Europe both today and in history."[77] After dismissing the first method as divisive in its portrayal of Islam as an opposing philosophy with which to contrast Western European norms, Zemya focuses on the second approach. He stresses that in order to develop more inclusive spaces for domestic interfaith and inter-ethnic interaction in the EU, "it is not only the Muslims who must change but also the Europeans. Within such a society, there would be no clear distinction between two groups each with their own set of values and practices but only one society based on conviviality and commonality."[78] Ultimately, he faults Western Europeans for the present absence of such an entity, arguing that most "do not understand that Islam is what people make of its everyday" and that there "are as many Islams as there are Muslims." Thus, it is what "Muslims themselves say [that] is important," as opposed to popular misperceptions of what Muslims think.[79]

While Ramadan addresses many of the same basic questions, he tackles them from within rather than without, suggesting ways in which Muslims can contribute to the perpetually evolving idea of Europe without undermining their own related identities and religious belief systems. He does so through the presentation and discussion of three interconnected concepts. First, the development of a broad definition of Muslim identity, one articulated largely but not exclusively in terms of adherence to the five pillars of Islam. Second, the practical application of the key elements of that definition to life in EU member states as a means to distinguish contexts in which Muslims may and may not fully practice their religion. Third, the identification of ways in which Muslims and individuals of other religious belief systems can work multilaterally as opposed to autonomously in the construction of a more inclusive and thus more stable and successful European community.

Ramadan broaches the subject of Muslim identity formation by offering a descriptive model that attributes belief, belonging and loyalty to distinctive religious and communal entities on three tiers of descending importance. The first tier entails acknowledgement of the existence of one God and a pledge of allegiance to that spiritual entity. As Ramadan explains, a "Muslim belongs first to God and this belonging influences and sheds light on every specific social sphere he deals with and in."[80] The second tier relates to loyalty to immediate and extended family. The third tier revolves around a sense of belonging to a broader community that is bound together by a belief in Islam that transcends collective ethnic, linguistic, national and racial differences.[81] While generally applicable to Islamic communities across Western Europe in theory, Ramadan's model requires conscious efforts by individual Muslims to function effectively in practice. As he puts it, as long as a "consistent number of Muslims do not reach an autonomous perception of their own identity in the West, it will be very difficult for them, if not impossible, simply to believe that they have something to give to the society they live in. They will hardly consider that they are able to have a positive impact on this society."[82]

In order to conceptualize such identities, Ramadan suggests, a review of the elements of Islamic practice Muslims may pursue without restrictions and those they have trouble maintaining under Western European legal and social norms is particularly useful. On the positive side, he cites the existence of five basic rights vis-à-vis adherence to Islam within EU member states. First, the right to practice the five pillars. Second, the right to the pursuit of knowledge—as denoted in the *Koran*—through unfettered access to public education. Third, the right to establish religious and political organizations as illustrated by the proliferation of such entities in Muslim communities in France, Germany and the United Kingdom over the past two decades. Fourth, the right to autonomous political representation at the local, regional, national and supranational levels across the continent. Fifth, the right to appeal to the law in all religious, legal and administrative matters.[83]

On the negative side, Ramadan points out two difficulties experienced by Muslims in Western Europe regarding overt practice of their religious beliefs, both of which are linked to social norms and perceptions rather than constitutional provisions. First, the fundamental challenges associated with the expression of spirituality—often shared by members of other faiths such as Christianity and Judaism—in the modern, secular-based Western world. According to Ramadan, "[h]ere, Muslims are not dealing with legislation, laws, or rules, the problem is elsewhere and it is both profound and sensitive. It relates to the fundamental question for Muslim communities living as minorities in Europe: namely how to maintain a spiritual life in a modern—understood as secular and industrialized—

society and, consequently, how to transmit the necessary knowledge which permits genuine freedom of choice."[84] Second, the negative popular image of Islam as a monolithic fundamentalist faith, which was discussed at length in the French, German and British case studies. This misperception is deepened by external influences, most notably the portrayal of some Muslims residing in Western Europe as potential terrorist threats by governments including those currently in charge in Algeria and Turkey. As Ramadan explains, the "political situation pertaining in some Islamic countries, the interests and sometimes these governments' manipulations shed a very negative light on Muslims living in Europe and keep alive a set of prejudices and biases against Islam and Muslims.[85]

Ultimately, Ramadan sets four goals that Muslims must accomplish in order "to succeed in the challenge of a coexistence which would not be *peace in separation* but *living together in participation.*" First, the enhancement of intracommunal Islamic dialogue, principally at the local but also at the national and supranational levels across the region. Second, the short-term mitigation and eventual elimination of financial and political dependence upon external entities—whether state, international or transnational in orientation—by Western European Muslims. Third, the development of more effective organizations to undertake Islamic communal action at the continental level generally and in the French, German and British contexts in particular. And fourth, the pursuit of greater political participation by Muslims in the related Western European local, regional, national and supranational electoral and governmental processes.[86] With these objectives in mind, Ramadan concludes that "[i]f being a Muslim is to act, then it is a duty and a responsibility to be active in Western societies. This Muslim participation is undoubtedly the most appropriate means of developing a better relationship between Muslims and the institutions around them."[87]

Comparable to Ramadan's approach are those stances taken by Haddad and Tamini vis-à-vis the shifting focus in interfaith dialogue in the West since the end of the Cold War. Haddad, for example, notes that the "theme of the 1970s and 1980s, founded on the conviction that the message of Islam is powerful and persuasive enough that all Westerners will see the light and covert to Islam, appears to be waning. What Muslims are seeing instead is actually an antipathy toward Islam on the part of Westerners."[88] As a result, Tamini argues—echoing some of Ramdan's assertions—that Muslims of variegated ethnic and national backgrounds must cooperate to improve the public standing of Islam in Western Europe. He suggests two ways in which to pursue that objective. First, active participation to assist government officials to solve social problems such as racism and the deterioration of morality in Western society. Second, spreading the message of Islam in manners that are comprehensible in the West.[89]

However, notwithstanding the potentially constructive nature of the strategies suggested by Ramadan and Tamini in theory, their effective implementation is a daunting challenge, particularly considering the disparate nature of integrative approaches employed by Western European governments to date. Consider the French, German and British frameworks for minority integration presented in the previous chapters. Governmental emphases on the assimilation of individuals and acknowledgement of the presence of distinctive non-Anglo ethnic communities in France and the United Kingdom, respectively, have left little if any room for genuine interfaith dialogue in the development of broader, more inclusive societal norms. Similarly, although the German approach incorporates elements of both the French and British integrative systems, it is designed more as a means to buttress societal cohesion than as one to help accommodate minority communal concerns.

Perhaps the best means to cultivate a gradual change in attitudes transcending these and other Western European domestic contexts is through the development of a broader regional definition of identity over the long term. Such a definition must include an acknowledgement that the idea of Europe has itself changed appreciably since the establishment of the EEC in 1957 and subsequent structural transitions to the EC and now the EU. In the aftermath of the Cold War, Western European leaders refined their vision of community to include former communist states to the East. But, regrettably, they have continued to maintain a decidedly less open-minded stance with respect to enlargement as manifested in Western European communal relations with Turkey, a Muslim majority state of 63 million people governed by a democratically elected but militarily controlled secular administration. Straddling Europe and Asia, Turkey serves as a geopolitical bridge between the East and the West and the North and the South.

While NATO extended membership to Turkey in 1952—primarily if not exclusively at the behest of the United States—the EU has been considerably less accommodating. Turkey first applied for membership to the EU in 1978; its application was subsequently tabled and not formally accepted until December 1999.[90] Given that the EU left Turkey out when it moved forward with its previous round of expansion in July 1997, the most recent developments are encouraging.[91] Specifically, although the formal recognition of Ankara's application contained three long-standing caveats associated with domestic politics and economics and Greek-Turkish relations, the pressure to admit the Turks is likely to increase as Central and Eastern European states gain admission over the next decade. As *The Economist* contends, the EU "is meant to be a liberal organization, based on rational, non-discriminatory principles. It cannot say (to Turkey): 'We won't let you in because you are mainly Muslims.' It has to apply objective criteria."[92]

The EU has traditionally offered two fundamental reasons for its reluctance to grant membership to Turkey. First, the Turkish government's ignorance of human rights standards, manifested in its violent repression of Kurdish dissidents is wholly unacceptable. Second, Turkey does not meet the EU's free-market economic or democratic political standards. Additionally, EU member Greece has indicated it will not consider Turkey fit for membership until an agreement is reached on the status of Cyprus, which was split into Greek and Turkish segments in 1974 and has been a point of contention between Athens and Ankara ever since.[93] Opinions such as those expressed recently by German Ulrike Guerot demonstrate the contentious nature of these issues. In dismissing repeated calls from Washington for increased Western European open-mindedness toward

Turkey, Guerot argues that the "Americans have no conception of what EU membership entails. Yes, there is a security aspect; but if you want the EU to be a strong partner, you cannot have Turkey inside the EU."[94] Whether or not the EU will eventually extend a membership offer to Turkey remains an open question. However, it is clear that this is not likely to occur in the short term. Instead, Turkish accession is a long-term goal the achievement of which could help to redefine the idea of Europe at both the domestic member-state and wider regional levels.

Conclusions

This chapter's purpose was to examine the issue of Islam in Europe from a regional perspective that builds upon the observations presented in the case studies focusing on the French, German and British domestic contexts. It did so through the presentation and discussion of four related themes. First, the historical roots of the often contentious nature of the modern relationship between Islam and Christianity on the continent. Second, the evolution of the idea of Europe over the ages, with emphases placed on the post-World War II, Cold War and post-Cold War eras. Third, the past, present and likely future roles of supranational institutions in ameliorating the integration of minorities generally and Muslims in particular into Western European domestic societies. Fourth, the potential for the development of a hybrid Euro-Islamic identity through the collective engagement of minority Muslim communities, domestic majorities in EU member states and supranational institutions in Brussels. The following conclusions serve a means to link these points with respect to their related short- and long-term domestic, international and supranational implications.

The development of the notion of a cohesive Western European community dates to the Middle Ages, with the conception of the idea attributable in part to the threat posed to the continent by the invasion and occupation of the Iberian Peninsula by Muslim forces under the control of the Umayyad caliphate in the eighth century. While responses manifested in phenomena such as the establishment of the Carolingian dynasty and the Crusades were not based exclusively on irreconcilable differences between Christianity and Islam, religion clearly played a significant contributory role. Over the ensuing centuries, the nature of Euro-Islamic relations grew more rather than less confrontational, first through the rise of the Ottoman Empire and later as a result of British and French colonization of large swaths of the Muslim world from North Africa to South Asia.

Connecting these distinctive historical periods was an innate need for Western Europeans to define themselves in contrast to others, whether at the national, regional or global levels. Devastating episodes such as World War I and World War II were among the consequences of the establishment and maintenance of a regional system defined in terms of threats posed by external actors rather than the potential to achieve collective prosperity through cooperation across national borders. The Cold War, on the other hand, demonstrated that cooperation—at both the Western European and transatlantic levels—was an effective means to guard against outside threats concurrent with the cultivation of political stability and economic prosperity through regional integration. Yet, when the Cold War ended and the Soviet threat thus disappeared, many Westerners (policy practitioners and scholars alike) foolishly set about manufacturing and then proliferating the notion of a new global opponent: a radical Islamic civilization guiding the actions of Muslims of various strains across the world.

Coupled with the innate historical rivalries discussed previously, the post-Cold War construction by influential Western policy makers and academics of such an adversary resulted in the further alienation of already marginalized Muslim communities throughout Western Europe. Ironically, these communities were then and are still composed predominantly of the children and grandchildren of the guest workers who literally helped to lay the foundation for the formative stages of integration process that unfolded during the 1950s and 1960s. Despite marked increases in the proportion of Muslims—citizens and non-citizens alike—residing in EC member states during the Cold War, remarkably little was done either domestically or supranationally to repay these laborers and their descendants for their assistance in the physical and economic reconstruction of Western Europe in the wake of World War II.

Fittingly, although perhaps somewhat unwittingly, Western European statesmen created an opportunity to redress this issue in the context of the interconnected deepening and widening processes articulated in the Maastricht Treaty. By mandating the eventual realization of economic and political union and enlargement to the East, the treaty added a degree of flexibility to the very definition of the idea of Europe. Furthermore, in taking these decisions, national leaders ceded a degree of their respective states' sovereignty over issues with domestic economic, political and security implications to supranational institutions in Brussels. Ultimately, in so doing, they acknowledged that norms—whether developed locally, nationally or regionally—are not set in stone; instead, answers to questions as to what constitutes Europe geographically, philosophically and demographically change over time. Given these general observations, it stands to reason that supranational refinement of the meaning of Europe has the potential to change popular thinking on the public standing of Muslims in Western European societies. While the integration of Islamic communities in particular EU member states is best pursued through interaction among municipal government officials and minority leaders, supranational reforms can help alter perceptions of Muslims at the national and local levels. Specifically, initiatives such as the creation and subsequent deepening of intergovernmental and supranational cooperation through the JHA pillar and proposed European Constitution are useful means to formalize positive changes in thinking on majority-minority relations, whether framed in class, ethnic, linguistic, racial or religious terms.

Similarly, by gradually changing popular perceptions of the concept of an evolving community of European states to reflect the continent's religious diversity—mostly Catholic and Protestant in the West, Muslim in the South (especially if Turkey is included) and Orthodox in the East—the EU can help create opportunities for more constructive interfaith interaction within the domestic societies of its member states. As suggested by Ramadan, Muslims, for their part, must take advantage of this type of atmosphere to participate to a greater extent than is now the case in the enhancement of social stability and economic growth in the Western European states in which they reside. Rather than bemoan the non-Islamic nature of Western society, Muslims should acknowledge that the practice of the five pillars is not difficult to achieve in that context and go about their daily pursuits accordingly.

Put simply, the development and maintenance of political stability and economic prosperity in multiethnic and multi-religious societies requires cooperation among members of the majority and the minority. The sustenance of the resultant relationships entails periodic accommodations by one side to the other contingent upon circumstances at a given time or over a particular subject. Ultimately, in order to function effectively in any region, such cooperation must occur at a variety of levels, ranging from the municipal to the supranational. With respect to the issue of Islam in Europe, this is best achieved through a popular change of attitude initiated at the supranational level and then applied to the integration of Muslims locally, a formula that—while potentially effective—facilitates progress that is best measured over the long term as opposed to the short term.

The failure to achieve such progress has the potential to complicate if not directly stall the ongoing European integration process in four ways. First, by mistreating Muslims, whether at the local, regional or national level, member state governments may break supranational as opposed to domestic laws. By stepping in, as dictated under EU statutes, Brussels-based bodies are likely to alienate national governments. This, in turn, is likely to render leaders of the latter more reluctant to surrender additional sovereignty in the future. Ultimately, these developments could slow the integration process. Second, the marginalization of Muslims may cause European Commission complaints over Turkey's mistreatment of its Kurds to appear somewhat hypocritical in the context of the debate over the timetable for Ankara's accession to the EU. Western European states must practice what they preach in terms of policing their own citizens' behavior with respect to the rights of ethnic and religious minority groups. Third, perceptions of pervasive anti-Islamic sentiments in Western European societies generally could detract from the ability of EU member states to recruit ·workers from the Muslim world. Granted, that is not a threat at present. However, as decreasing birth rates drain the native-born labor pool across Western Europe over the balance of this century, demand for foreign-born workers is all but certain to increase dramatically. Unless that demand is met, economic growth will decline. Given the very nature of the European integration process since the end of World War II, such a decline will affect EU member states collectively. Fourth, the inability to equitably incorporate Muslims currently residing in Western Europe does not reflect well on the integrative prospects for additional minority groups the EU will take in as it enlarges to the East in the future.

European history is replete with examples of exclusion, whether of states from the continent's systemic structures or the marginalization of minority groups within given states or empires. Typically, the eventual consequences have been identical: intra- if not inter-state warfare and—in some cases—both. After enduring a collective 30 million deaths over the course of World War I and World War II, Europeans appeared to have learned a valuable lesson as to the need to conceive state- and institution-building strategies based on inclusion rather than exclusion. They applied that lesson well in establishing the EEC and gradually deepening and widening that institution over the ensuing 42 years. However, at present, all groups are not yet fully included. To date, the EU and its member states have yet to develop an effective means to integrate Muslim communities into their institutions and societies. Until these ends are achieved, the idea of a Europe whole and free will remain incomplete.

Notes

1.   Paul Fregosi, *Jihad in the West: Muslim Conquests from the 7ᵗʰ to the twenty-first Centuries* (New York: Prometheus Books, 1998), 91-96.
2.   Jane I. Smith, "Islam and Christendom: Historical, Cultural and Religious Interaction from the Seventh to the Fifteenth Centuries," *see* Esposito (1999), 314-16; Fregosi, *Jihad in the West*, 118-21.
3.   Peter Brown, *The Age of Western Christendom: Triumph and Diversity* (Oxford: Blackwell, 1996), 258, 279.
4.   European Information Service, *Charter of Fundamental Rights* (Brussels: European Commission, 2001).
5.   "Europe's Constitution: Your Darkest Fears Addressed, your Hardest Questions Answered," *Economist* (19 June 2003); Kettani, "Challenges to the Organization of Muslim Communities," 33-34; Ramadan, *To Be a European Muslim*, 120.
6.   Fregosi, *Jihad in the West*, 66.
7.   William Montgomery Watt, *A History of Islamic Spain* (Edinburgh, Scotland: Edinburgh University Press, 1965), 5-35.
8.   Smith, "Islam and Christendom," 329.
9.   Mark D. Meyerson, *The Muslims of Valencia in the Age of Fernando and Isabel: Between Coexistence and Crusade* (Berkeley: University of California Press, 1985), 1-9.
10. Smith, "Islam and Christendom," 320.
11. Fregosi, *Jihad in the West*, 107-08.
12. Ibid., 107.
13. Robert J. Burns, *Moors and Crusaders in Mediterranean Spain* (London: Variorum Reprints, 1978), 1-20.

14. Richard Fletcher, *The Barbarian Conversion: From Paganism to Christianity* (New York: Henry Holt and Company, 1997), 304.

15. Ibid., 304-05.

16. Louis Halphen, *Charlemagne and the Carolingian Empire* (New York: North Holland Publishing Company, 1977), 6-10; Allen Cabaniss, *Charlemagne* (New York: Twayne Publishers, 1972), 15-29.

17. Pierre Riché, *The Carolingians: A Family Who Forged Europe*, trans. Michael Idomic Allen (Philadelphia: University of Pennsylvania Press, 1993), 50.

18. Fletcher, *Barbarian Conversion*, 193.

19. Brown, *Age of Western Christendom*, 257.

20. Friedrich Heer, *Charlemagne and his World* (London: Weidenfeld and Nicolson, 1975), 9-29.

21. Brown, *Age of Western Christendom*, 279.

22. Rosamond McKittenck, *The Frankish Kingdoms under the Carolingians, 751-987* (New York: Longman, 1983), 102.

23. Brown, *Age of Western Christendom*, 281-82.

24. Fletcher, *Barbarian Conversion*, 194.

25. Watt, *History of Islamic Spain*, 112-62; Meyerson, *Muslims of Valencia*, 61-98.

26. Antony Bridge, *The Crusades* (New York: Granada, 1980), 17-28; Terry Jones, *Crusades* (New York: Facts on File, 1995), 19-22.

27. W.B. Bartlett, *God Wills It! An Illustrated History of the Crusades* (Gloucestershire, UK: Sutton, 1999), 26-27.

28. Ibid., 30.

29. Jean Richard, *The Crusades* (New York: Cambridge University Press, 1999), 1-124; Fletcher, *Barbarian Conversion*, 316-17.

30. Bartlett, *God Wills It*, 80.

31. Henry Treece, *The Crusades* (London: Souvenir Press, 1978), 257-82; Jones, *Crusades*, 81-162; Richard, *Crusades*, 442-73.

32. Watt, *History of Islamic Spain*, 112-62; Meyerson, *Muslims of Valencia*, 61-98.

33. Stanford Jay Shaw, *History of the Ottoman Empire and Modern Turkey* (New York: Cambridge University Press, 1976), 1-167; Halil Inalcik, *The Ottoman Empire: The Classical Age, 1300-1600* (London: Weidenfeld and Nicolson, 1973), 9-54.

34. Ira M. Lapidus, "Sultanates and Gunpowder Empires: The Middle East," *see* Esposito (1999), 374.

35. John Obert Voll, "Foundations for Renewal and Reform," *see* Esposito (1999), 543.

36. Derek W. Urwin, *The Community of Europe: A History of European Integration Since 1945* (New York: Longman, 1991), 7.

37. William Wallace, *The Transformation of Western Europe* (New York: Council on Foreign Relations Press, 1990), 35-45; Joan Hoff and Richard K. Vedder, eds., *The European Union: From Jean Monnet to the Euro* (Athens: Ohio University Press, 2000), 57-78.

38. Walter Laqueur, *Europe in Our Time: A History, 1945-1992* (New York: Penguin, 1992), 21.

39. Wallace, *Transformation of Western Europe*, 28-34.

40. Simon Serfaty, *Stay the Course: European Unity and Atlantic Solidarity* (Westport, Conn.: Praeger, 1997), 53.
41. Paul Graham Taylor, *The European Union in the 1990s* (New York: Oxford University Press, 1996), 8-57; Dusan Sjdjanski, *The Federal Future of Europe: From the European Community to the European Union* (Ann Arbor: University of Michigan Press, 2000), 7-25.
42. Serfaty, *Stay the Course*, 52.
43. Urwin, *Community of Europe*, 27.
44. Laqueur, *Europe in Our Time*, 122.
45. A.H. Robertson, *European Institutions: Cooperation, Integration, Unification* (London: Stevens and Sons, 1959), 1-117; Wallace, *Transformation of Western Europe*, 28-45.
46. Serfaty, *Taking Europe Seriously* (New York: St. Martin's Press, 1992), 59.
47. Stanley Hoffmann, *The European Sisyphus: Essays on Europe, 1964-1994* (Boulder, Col.: Westview Press, 1995), 67.
48. Simon Serfaty, *Memories of Europe's Future: Farewell to Yesteryear* (Washington, D.C.: Center for Strategic and International Studies Press, 1999), 6.
49. Jean Monnet, *Memoirs* (Garden City, N.Y.: Doubleday, 1978), 523-24. Reference made in Serfaty, *Taking Europe Seriously*, 157.
50. Taylor, *European Union in the 1990s*, 190.
51. Andrew Geddes, *Immigration and European Integration: Towards Fortress Europe?* (New York: St. Martin's Press, 2000), 15.
52. Ibid., 1, 17.
53. Robert O. Keohane and Stanley Hoffmann, *The New European Community: Decisionmaking and Institutional Change* (Boulder, Col.: Westview Press, 1991), 41-84.
54. Geddes, *Immigration and European Integration*, 67-68.
55. Alan Butt Philip, "European Union Immigration Policy: Phantom, Fantasy or Fact?," *West European Politics* 17-1 (1994): 171; European Information Service, *Area of Freedom, Justice and Security*, (Brussels: European Commission, 2000).
56. Geddes, *Immigration and European Integration*, 84.
57. House of Lords Select Committee on the European Communities, *Border Control of People* (London: HMSO, 1992), 55-64. Reference made in Butt Philip, "European Union Immigration Policy," 171.
58. Sjdjanski, *Federal Future of Europe*, 216-62.
59. Geddes, *Immigration and European Integration*, 102.
60. Ibid., 88.
61. Butt Philip, "European Union Immigration Policy," 179.
62. European Information Service, *The Amsterdam Treaty: A Comprehensive Guide* (Brussels: European Commission, 1997).
63. Geddes, *Immigration and European Integration*, 120.
64. Ibid., 121.
65. *Amsterdam Treaty: A Comprehensive Guide.*

66. Andrew Geddes, "The Representation of Migrants' 'Interests' in the European Union," *Journal of Ethnic and Migration Studies* 27-4 (1998): 698.

67. "EU: Tampere Summit," *Migration News* 6-10 (1999).

68. "Justice and Home Affairs: Commission Seeks to Ease Movement for Legal Immigrants," *European Report*, 17 March 2001.

69. "Europe's Constitution"; European Information Service, *Charter of Fundamental Rights*; European Economic and Social Committee of the European Union, "The European Economic and Social Committee: A Bridge between Europe and Civil Society," *European Economic and Social Committee* home page, www.esc.eu.int (June 2001).

70. *Charter of Fundamental Rights*.

71. Ibid.

72. Ibid.

73. Ibid.

74. Yvonne Yazback Haddad, "The Globalization of Islam: The Return of Muslims to the West," *see* Esposito (1999), 614.

75. Sami Zemya, "Is There a Place for Islam in Europe," *Center for Islam in Europe* (June 2001), 5.

76. Ramadan, *To Be a European Muslim*, 116.

77. Zemya, "Is There a Place for Islam in Europe," 1.

78. Ibid., 5.

79. Ibid., 4.

80. Ramadan, *To Be a European Muslim*, 155-56.

81. Ibid., 154-60.

82. Ibid., 181.

83. Ibid., 135-37.

84. Ibid., 138.

85. Ibid., 139.

86. Ibid., 219-24.

87. Ibid., 231-32.

88. Haddad, "Globalization of Islam," 627.

89. Ibid., 627.

90. Anne Swardson, "Six Nations Are Invited to Apply to Join EU," *Washington Post*, 10 December 1999. At a summit in Helsinki, Finland, the European Union (EU) invited Latvia, Lithuania, Bulgaria, Romania and Malta to begin accession talks. It also acknowledged Turkey as a formal applicant.

91. In July 1997, the EU invited the Czech Republic, Hungary, Poland, Estonia, Slovenia and Cyprus to begin accession talks.

92. "The Limits of Europe," *Economist*, 19 May 2001.

93. Swardson, "Six Nations Invited to Apply to Join EU."

94. Quoted in "Limits of Europe."

Chapter 7

Conclusions

Introduction

Put simply, the purpose of this book was to examine the effects of the development of Muslim communities on society and governance in Western Europe at both the domestic and supranational levels. The case studies of Islam in France, Germany, the United Kingdom and Western Europe served as a means to present and discuss the evidence relevant to those contexts in particular without dwelling on the broader connections that link them together. However, an evaluation of the similarities and differences in the Muslim communal, governmental and societal majority perspectives investigated in the case studies is necessary in order to develop a deeper understanding of the past, present and likely future impact of Islam upon the completion of a fully integrated Europe. This concluding chapter accomplishes that task through the presentation of five related sections, which unfold in the following manner:

Domestic Linkages—Muslim Communal Perspectives

This section distinguishes the similarities among and differences between Muslim communities in France, Germany and the United Kingdom in three issue areas. First, the genesis and subsequent growth of those communities over the past half-century. Second, the characteristics of those communities in the 1990s and 2000s. Third, identity formation in those communities generally and among the second and third generations specifically.

Domestic Linkages—Governmental and Societal Majority Perspectives

This section distinguishes the similarities among and differences between governmental and societal mainstream perspectives on interaction with and the integration of Muslims in France, Germany and the United Kingdom in two issue areas. First, the development of integration policies to equitably incorporate Muslims into mainstream society. Second, the implications of those policies.

Domestic-Supranational Linkages

This section distinguishes the similarities among and differences between domestic and supranational perspectives and policies vis-à-vis the issue of Islam in Europe in two parts. First, European perceptions of Muslims and the resultant implications with respect to the conduct of interethnic and interfaith relations—both at the inter- and intra-state levels. Second, the ways in which to utilize the institutions of the European Union (EU) to deal with the treatment of Muslims in the domestic societies of its member states.

Prospects for the Future

Taking into account the similarities among and differences between the Muslim and societal majority perspectives in the case studies, this section discusses the likely role Islam will play in the completion of the European integration project in two parts. First, an articulation of the positive and negative trends in Muslim-Christian relations in contemporary Western Europe. Second, a set of conclusions on the extent to which those positive trends have the potential to contribute to the development of a more inclusive, united Europe over the long term.

Significance of the Findings

This section has two parts. The first part restates each of the four theses put forth in the introduction and elaborates briefly on the extent to which the evidence uncovered in the course of researching the book and articulated in the subsequent chapters validates each thesis in turn. The second part explains incisively how the findings presented and discussed here contribute to the development of a deeper understanding of the issue of Islam in Europe.

Domestic Linkages—Muslim Communal Perspectives

The genesis of the development of Muslim communities in Western Europe was a primarily the product of the recruitment of guest workers to fill the demand for unskilled labor necessary for reconstruction in the aftermath of World War II. Each of the states under consideration here—France, Germany and the United Kingdom—relied at least to some extent on laborers with origins in the Islamic world to help fuel economic growth in the 1950s and 1960s. Whether under the auspices of state-sponsored recruitment programs (France and Germany) or private initiatives (the United Kingdom), most Muslims initially migrated to the continent with the intention of taking advantage of short-term economic opportunities in the developed world, then returning to their places of origin considerably wealthier.

Generally, such guest workers shared a common religious belief system, which gave credence to the five pillars of Islam. However, their ethnic backgrounds and interpretations of that faith differed—sometimes markedly; sometimes marginally—as did their previous relationships with and expectations of the host countries in which they accepted jobs. Waves of Muslim workers to France and the United Kingdom from the late 1940s to the early 1970s, for example, were composed predominantly of North Africans and South Asians, respectively. In each instance, the migrants left states that had recently gained their independence from former imperial powers, most notably Algeria, Morocco and Tunisia (from France), and India and Pakistan (from Britain). In the German case, on the other hand, influxes of workers came from Turkey, with the sender and host states thus lacking similar colonial linkages. Additionally, migrants with origins in Turkey were split between ethnic Turks and Kurds, with the former drawn to the Federal Republic almost exclusively by financial interests and the latter interested primarily in escaping government repression.

Most Muslims who migrated to Western Europe during the 1950s and 1960s expected to return home eventually rather than become permanent fixtures in their respective host societies. As a result, few believed interacting with members of the societal majority was indispensable to their long-term economic well being. Instead, most were content to remain in esoteric communities that were distinguished as much by language, ethnicity and nationality as by religion. Frenchmen, Germans and Britons, in turn, tolerated the presence of foreigners who presented little if any challenges to existing domestic norms. The practice of Islam by guest workers was largely confined to their hostels and had a considerably more secular appearance (laymen often served as imams at Friday services) than was true in their places of origin. This was generally the case throughout Western Europe. Subtle differences in religious interpretation between denominations of Muslims in France, Germany and the United Kingdom were inconsequential vis-à-vis their collective impact on those societies over the initial two decades of the post-World War II era.

However, the composition of Muslim communities changed in a manner not anticipated by either the guest workers or their French, German and British hosts in the aftermath of the October 1973 oil crisis. In short, when Western European economic growth first slowed and eventually stagnated in the 1970s, foreign laborers lost their jobs. Yet, instead of returning home to accept standards of living markedly lower than those that would result from prolonged unemployment in the West, they stayed put. Because former guest workers now lacked the resources to support their wives and children through remittances to states across the developing world, they focused on familial reunification in Western Europe. Overall, host governments were cooperative in this issue area, initially imposing only marginal restrictions on additions of wives and children to communities previously composed almost exclusively of male laborers.

Family reunifications in the 1970s fostered two subsequent developments that were comparable—albeit not identical—in French, British and German Muslim communities. First, Muslims began to place greater emphasis on the role of Islam in their daily lives than was previously the case. This resulted in the cultivation of a more publicly visible version of Islam with greater potential for rejection by Western European societies dominated by white, Christian majorities. Second, growth rates rose in Islamic communities, leading to pronounced increases in the proportions of Muslims in the populations of France, Germany and the United Kingdom over the last three decades of the twentieth century. By 1990, Muslims of various ethnic strains constituted the largest religious minority groups in each of those states.

Notwithstanding their diverse ancestral origins, Muslims living in the present confines of the EU share many common demographic, economic, socio-religious and political characteristics. Demographically, for instance, Muslims are concentrated in low-rent neighborhoods along the peripheries of major cities such as Paris, Marseilles, London and Berlin rather than more evenly distributed across a range of French, German and British geographic areas. While these types of settlement patterns are not uncommon among minorities groups in general, the relegation of Muslims to the fringes of society is somewhat more pronounced. In addition, these patterns have remained largely unchanged despite the development of second and third generations of Western European-born Muslims.

As a result of fertility rates among resident Muslims that exceed the national averages in France, Germany and the United Kingdom and continuing influxes of new migrants from the Greater Middle East and South Asia, Islamic communities are still expanding in those states. That growth has increased the sizes of Muslim neighborhoods without altering appreciably either their geographic distribution or collective capacity of their inhabitants to attain higher standards of living. Economically, families situated in the vast majority of these communities face two related hurdles. First, they earn considerably less money than members of the societal majority. Second, they raise larger families, which reduces further the relative value of their salaries.

On the whole, Muslims across Western Europe have higher unemployment and lower income levels than the national averages of the states in which they reside. In short, these trends are the result of their relegation either to the jobless rolls or the unskilled sector of a given economy. Such marginalization, in turn, is a product of educational—and at times—linguistic deficiencies, particularly among members of the first and second generations. Although such shortcomings are evident in Islamic communities throughout the region, there are differences as to the degree of economic hardship—both between particular countries, and ethnic and national groups within those domestic environs. Unemployment levels among Muslims, for example, are more pronounced in France and the United Kingdom (as high as four or fives times the national average) than is the case in Germany (usually no worse than double the national average). Similarly wide gaps in earnings exist between Muslims of varying ethnicities in Germany and the United Kingdom, with Iranians generally enjoying higher standards of living than Turks in the former context and Arabs better off than Pakistanis and Bangladeshis in the latter. Yet, in each of these cases, those facing the most adversity are in the ethnic groups of which the vast majority of the Islamic population is composed.

In terms of economic progress—both that achieved to date and prospects for future gains—among Western European Muslims, most improvements are associated with the establishment of businesses by individual entrepreneurs. More often than not, such businesses cater to the religious and cultural needs of Islamic communities as opposed to providing services desired by the societal mainstream. As a result, while useful in providing much-needed financial resources for their owners and employees, these enterprises have not helped to integrate Muslims into the wider French, German and British economies. In fact, their existence has led many Muslims—primarily but not exclusively those of the first generation—to believe that interaction with members of other ethnic and religious groups is unnecessary. Ultimately, this brand of self-imposed isolation serves to further marginalize Islamic communities to the detriment of Muslims and society at large.

Notwithstanding the success of businesses created to accommodate the religious requirements of Islam as mandated by the *Koran*—most notably the prohibition of the consumption of any meats other than those of the ritually slaughtered *halal* variety—Muslims of different ethnicities, denominations and age groups practice their beliefs in a variety of ways. This is the case not only in Western Europe but also in Muslim-majority regions of the world such as North Africa, the Middle East and Central Asia. With respect to the Western European context, for instance, second and third generation Muslims are often more lax in their adherence to even the most basic of the five pillars of Islam—daily prayers— than is true of their parents and grandparents. Some trends, on the other hand, transcend generations and ethnicities. Examples include maintaining the sunrise to sunset fast during the holy month of Ramadan and demands for the tolerance of Islamic practices (the wearing of head scarves by females in particular) in schools and other publicly funded institutions.

Those Muslims who attend services regularly in France, Germany and the United Kingdom most often do so in apartment-sized prayer rooms and converted warehouses because of the dearth of formal mosques in or near the communities in which they reside. While the number of cathedral mosques has risen over the past decade—most noticeably in the United Kingdom—the demand for facilities with the capacity for 1,000 or more worshippers remains unsatisfied and is likely to grow even more pronounced in light of the increasing proportion of Muslims in states throughout the EU. The willingness of local and national government officials to approve the construction of mosques with greater capacities in those contexts, in turn, is currently and will remain contingent upon the extent of the political power of Muslims—both individually and communally.

Islamic communities have had only marginal influence to date on the outcome of electoral campaigns for national and supranational bodies in Western Europe. There are, for example, just two Muslim MPs in the United Kingdom, one in Germany and none in France at present. However, acknowledgment of the significance of issues related to the presence of Islam in society have risen steadily at the local level in these states over the past two decades generally and in the past three municipal electoral cycles in France and Britain specifically. The lack of comparable progress in Germany is attributed to the stringency of citizenship—and thus voting—requirements applied to foreigners prior to the 2000 reform of the nationality law. As more Muslims acquire voting rights, Islamic influence—whether in terms of Turkish candidates on electoral lists or credence given to minority religious concerns in party platforms—is likely to grow during future *Länd* electoral campaigns.

In addition to inadequate representation in national parliaments and on local and regional councils, Islamic communities suffer from a lack of cooperation among Muslims with disparate ethnic, national and philosophical backgrounds. Such shortcomings are evident across the region, whether related to squabbles between Turks and Kurds in Germany, Algerian government supporters and detractors in France or Islamic fundamentalists and modernists in the United Kingdom to name but a few. In order to cultivate political identities useful in improving the economic and social standings of their communities, Muslim leaders must focus on issues germane to the residents of minority housing projects in cities like Marseilles, Berlin and Bradford. The influence of external state and non-state actors is more likely to exacerbate minority-majority and intra-minority ethnic and religious tensions than to boost the quality of life for Western European Muslims. Umbrella organizations such as the Central Council of Muslims of Germany and the Islamic Party of Britain have made some progress toward this end, but greater strides are necessary.

The eventual success or failure of inter-ethnic initiatives launched on behalf of Islamic communities in France, Germany and the United Kingdom will depend largely on the extent to which Muslims are able to develop common identities that mitigate ethnic differences and bridge generation gaps. Muslims throughout the EU share two principal characteristics with respect to the process of identity construction. First, there is a significant gap in connectivity to ancestral origins between members of the first generation and their children and grandchildren. This gap is manifested in differences in linguistic aptitude and preference (Arabic vs. French, Urdu vs. English or Turkish vs. German, for instance), choice of wardrobe (traditional vs. Western) and brand of religious practice (strict vs. sporadic adherence to the five pillars). Second, Muslims of the younger generations have more difficulty developing identities as they often feel caught between the cultures of their ancestors and the contemporary Western European societies in which they were born and have since experienced during their formative years.

On the whole, older Muslims have been content to focus exclusively on the cultural traditions of the countries from which they originally migrated rather than attempt to adapt to life in the West. In that sense, they bear some of the responsibility for their own isolation, particularly in the social interactive arena. The younger generations, on the other hand, face a markedly different dilemma. While Muslims in their teens and 20s have been educated in French, German and British schools and are thus considerably more adept at speaking European languages than their elders, they still feel excluded from the benefits of acceptance by the societal mainstream. Relegated to lives on the crime-ridden streets surrounding urban housing projects, young Muslims often have trouble identifying who they are. This undermines the potential for the creation of hybrid Euro-

Islamic identities that include ethnic and cultural as well as religious elements. Regrettably, instead of interacting with members of the white, Christian majority, Muslims of the most recent generations have grown increasingly more likely to turn inward. Ultimately, many have rejected Western European norms in favor of radical brands of Islam advocated by external state and non-state actors in North Africa, South Asia and the Middle East.

However, notwithstanding the discouraging nature of such trends, there is potential for progress over the long term. In short, present generations of Muslims and those to come have three available strategies to employ in defining and then expressing their identities. First, retreat into esoteric Islamic communities and limit, if not avoid altogether, interaction with the members of the national majority in the domestic contexts in which they are situated. Second, abandon Islam in favor of total assimilation into Western European societies. Third, strike a balance between these approaches by at least attempting to play active political and economic roles in France, Germany and the United Kingdom to the extent possible in accordance with the basic tenets of Islam.

The third approach is unquestionably the most constructive in that it will enable Muslims to try to alter misperceptions of Islam by remaining active in public life. Tariq Ramadan's contention that Muslims face no direct hurdles in adherence to the five pillars under French, German or British law is instructive in this respect in that it suggests that Muslims need not isolate themselves in order to remain true to their religious beliefs. Instead, by practicing those beliefs openly, they can demonstrate there is room not just for the peaceful coexistence of Islam and Christianity on the continent but also space for constructive daily engagement between believers of the two faiths.

Domestic Linkages—Governmental and Societal Majority Perspectives

Governments across Western Europe viewed the initial streams of Muslim guest workers in the 1950s and 1960s in strictly economic rather than ethnic, social or religious terms. Guest workers were a temporary means to fill the demand for unskilled labor necessary to boost postwar economic growth and—in the process— help nascent inter-state integration projects such as the European Coal and Steel Community and European Economic Community gather strength. As a result, French, German and British leaders did not perceive a need to develop policies to integrate Muslims into their societies. In short, they expected foreigners to leave once domestic labor supplies increased and thus generally did not consider the possibility that Islamic communities would become a permanent fixture on the continent.

Those expectations proved mythical when Muslims not only remained in the region despite losing their jobs in the aftermath of the 1973 oil crisis but also set about reunifying their families in French, German and British urban areas. National government policymakers in Paris, Bonn and London responded to these developments in an almost identical manner. First, they imposed measures—understandably different in terms of the legal particulars associated with their respective constitutions but sharing the same fundamental purposes—to stem the flow of immigrants across their borders. These measures were directed primarily toward migrants from the developing world and had, by design, a proportionally greater impact upon non-European peoples. Second, they sought to mitigate but not eliminate the ability of guest workers to move their families to the continent. Most policies dealing with the issue of family reunification were initially relatively liberal and thus largely ineffective in controlling the growth of Muslim communities, which rapidly acquired a more openly Islamic character than was the case during the guest worker period.

Over the balance of the 1970s and for much of the 1980s, most government legislation affecting Muslims in Western Europe was of a non-integrative nature. Instead of acknowledging the need to develop more inclusive societies, governments across the political spectrum sought first to reduce the potential for fresh influxes of migrants from the Islamic world and second to limit the civil rights granted to Muslims already residing in the environs of the European Community. French, German and British policymakers used a variety of means to pursue these objectives, ranging from the official abrogation of guest worker programs and increased policing of borders to the erection of legal hurdles to the acquisition of citizenship by foreign-born residents and their Western European-born children. The differences in such policies from one domestic context to another were related to legal means rather than end results. Because of the restrictive nature of the Federal Republic's blood-based nationality law, for instance, it was not difficult for either national or *Länd* officials to deny citizenship to Turks and their children. In France and the United Kingdom, on the other hand, existent citizenship laws were considerably more liberal. As a result, it was necessary for the governments of those states to amend laws in ways that made the acquisition of citizenship more difficult for individuals with ancestry in former colonies such as India, Pakistan, Algeria, Tunisia and Morocco.

Strategies formulated by governments in each of these issue areas were ineffective and ultimately served to threaten rather than ensure social stability for two related reasons. First, while migration flows into Western Europe generally and into France, Germany and the United Kingdom specifically slowed and eventually stagnated in the 1970s and 1980s, the proportion of Muslims in the French, German and British populations continued to grow during that period. This was primarily the result of the rapid growth of native-born second and third generations in Islamic communities. Second, the imposition of restrictions on citizenship for foreigners marginalized Muslims, fostering a sense of collective resentment with the potential to manifest itself in destabilizing eruptions of civil disorder in the municipalities where they lived.

By the end of the 1980s, Western European leaders began to recognize the need to give more credence to the development of methods to integrate rather than accept the permanent social exclusion of Muslims. While their methods in attempting to integrate minorities differ appreciably, the results have been similarly disappointing to date. Governmental emphasis on the assimilation of individuals and acknowledgement of the presence of distinctive non-Anglo ethnic communities in France and the United Kingdom, respectively, has left little if any room for genuine interfaith dialogue in the development of broader, more inclusive societal norms. Similarly, although the German approach incorporates elements of both the French and British integrative systems, it is designed more to promote societal cohesion than to help accommodate minority communal concerns.

In each of these cases, the inability to implement policies that enhance significantly the public standing of Muslims—whether measured on the basis of demographic, economic, socio-religious or political indicators—reflects an underlying distrust of Islam. Although religion—Christianity in particular—plays different roles in the British, German and French public spheres generally and in given regions and localities in their societies in particular, the perception of Islam as a threat still pervades the Western European consciousness. The Anglican Church, for instance, is an official state institution in the United Kingdom. Similarly, the German *Länd* of Bavaria endorses the mounting of Catholic crosses on the walls of classrooms in its schools. Even in France, where secularism itself has a pseudo-religious status, millions of students are educated in Catholic schools. Muslims in France, Germany and Britain, on the other hand, have struggled— albeit with some positive results—to gain government approval for the scattered construction of mosques and opening of Islamic academies. Put simply, such discrimination is the result of an innate but inaccurate characterization of all Muslims as Islamic fundamentalists. So long as this misperception persists, the integration of Muslims will remain a daunting challenge for states in Western Europe.

The marginalization of a given minority group has the potential to foster social and political instability in any domestic context. In the cases of France, Germany and the United Kingdom, the implications of the exclusion of Muslims are most pronounced in three issue areas—internal security, the dynamics of the domestic political system and the development and implementation of government policies. Irrespective of the apportionment of blame, the failure to fully integrate communities of Muslims into the mainstream societies of each of the above states has had and continues to have a marked impact upon minority-majority perceptions and interactions. This is openly evident in the stratification of the French, German and British societies along ethnic and religious lines, with European Christians enjoying substantially higher standards of living and sense of belonging than is true of Muslims of a range of ethnicities.

When one group of individuals—whether categorized ethnically, racially, religiously or through a combination of these terms—is, for whatever reason, denied the quality of life afforded to another, the potential for conflict between members of the two increases substantially. There are three fundamental ways in which such conflicts are manifested in contemporary Western Europe. First, above-average crime rates—most often of the violent rather than non-violent variety—in the urban districts in which Islamic communities are situated. Second, confrontations between younger generations of Muslims and the police that periodically escalate into large-scale riots emanating from but extending beyond minority neighborhoods in major metropolitan areas. Third, rising support for far-right political parties that portray minorities generally and Muslims specifically as threatening to the physical and economic security of members of the societal majority.

Regarding the first point, the French, German and British governments have responded in somewhat different ways to rising crime rates associated with minority-majority confrontations within and without Muslim enclaves ringing cities such as Paris, Marseilles, London, Bradford, Berlin and Duisberg. In the French case, for example, the national police have targeted Islamic communities by increased patrols as a means to prevent future terrorist attacks comparable to the 1995 subway bombings in Paris and Lyons rather than make daily life safer for Muslims. Encouragingly, over the past six years, there has not been any series of terrorist incidents in France similar in size and scope to the 1995 outbreak. However, overall crime rates in the *banlieues* have increased during that period.

While the British government has expressed and taken action on comparable concerns over the recruitment of discontented young South Asians by Islamic fundamentalist groups—most notably through passage of the 2000 and 2001 Terrorism Acts—it has also attempted to ease Muslim concerns vis-à-vis discrimination in police hiring practices. Similarly, German officials have had to address complaints of anti-Islamic bias concurrent with the appearance of media reports detailing marked rises in right-wing violence against foreigners over the past decade. Such publicity demands a more pronounced government response in the Federal Republic than is the case with respect to the targeting of foreigners by extremists in Britain and France—primarily because of Germany's repression of minorities during the National Socialist era. Yet, attacks on Turks have not decreased substantially since the September 2000 publication of a list describing 100 deaths attributed to members of right-wing groups from 1990-99. Nor have tensions between Muslims and the police fallen in the United Kingdom as evidenced by the 2001 riots in Bradford, Burnley and Oldham.

The intensity of the riots across northern England generally and in Bradford in particular was in part the result of Muslim perceptions of an inadequate response by police after members of the British National Front (BNF) harassed Pakistani youths. The same concerns had prompted smaller outbursts of violence by younger generations of Muslims in that region in 1995 and 1998. While support for the far-right political parties is marginal at the national level, fringe groups such as the BNF have attracted significant followings among individuals living in working-class white neighborhoods situated near Pakistani and Bangladeshi enclaves in the Greater Manchester, West Yorkshire and West Midlands metropolitan areas. Regrettably, this indicates that confrontation is at present a more likely short-term trend than cooperative engagement regarding ethnic and faith interactions in those districts in which members of the minority and majority most often come into contact.

While the existence of far-right political parties is a source of minority-majority conflict in France, Germany and the United Kingdom, one of these movements—the French National Front (FN)—has exhibited considerably more electoral influence than any of the others over the past 20 years. Granted, neo-Nazi parties have attracted much media attention in the Federal Republic because of Germany's dark history. The British National Front bears at least some of the responsibility for the outbreak of the recent riots in northern England, which were the worst of their kind in Western Europe in two decades. But the far right has not attracted substantial national support in either case. By contrast, the FN consistently received 15 percent of the vote in municipal, regional and national elections throughout the 1990s. While those numbers have decreased since the party split into two wings in December 1999, the far right remains a potent force in French politics.

There are equally pronounced differences in the extent of the impact of Islam on the conduct of foreign policy by the French as opposed to the German and British governments. Increases in the number of Muslims residing in France have affected development and implementation of foreign policy in Paris and to a greater degree than is the case with respect to similar demographic changes in Germany and the United Kingdom in the 1980s and 1990s. The Chirac government's refusal to support US-led military operations to remove Iraqi President Saddam Hussein's regime from power in 2003, for instance, was partially attributable to the potential backlash such action would trigger in France's Islamic communities. The same is true of French concerns over Washington's perceived favoritism toward Israel in the context of the perpetually troubled Arab-Israeli peace process.

Domestic-Supranational Linkages

Perceptions of Islam as a non-Western civilizational entity permeate conscious and subconscious thought processes at the domestic and supranational levels of governance in contemporary Western Europe. Individuals leading political parties, governments and institutions across the region, whether in national or supranational capitals or regional and municipal jurisdictions, share a common history with respect to Islam in at least two respects. First, the development of a collective European identity grew at least in part out of the need to meet the challenge to continental sovereignty posed by Islam—originally by the Umayyads in Spain and later by the Ottomans in the Balkans. Second, the vast majority of Western Europeans possess Christian roots. Although manifested in differing biblical interpretations and degrees of practice, an underlying belief in Christianity is a fundamental element in the identities of the vast majority of Western Europeans.

Each of these factors has an impact—albeit often of a more subconscious than conscious variety—upon the handling of issues related to Muslim-Christian relations in and beyond the continent. Impressions of Islam as a foreign rather than indigenous faith pervade decision-making processes at all levels of government within EU borders. The way in which such sentiments are expressed, on the other hand, differs from the supranational to the national, regional and local levels. Supranationally, for example, Western European officials have demonstrated their discomfort with Islam in the context of the EU's tenuous relationship with Turkey over the past quarter of a century. The EU tabled Ankara's initial bid for membership in that institution in 1974. Even since acknowledging Turkey's status as a candidate just over four years ago, the EU has continued to emphasize that that state still has considerable hurdles to overcome in the issue areas of economics and human rights before it can begin accession negotiations. By contrast, domestic prejudice against Islam is evidenced in a lack of micro-level accommodations made to Muslims by governments of given cities and regions. Although they lack the power to deny EU membership to a state from the Islamic state such as Turkey, municipal officials do possess the authority to deny permission for the construction of cathedral mosques or the provision of *halal* meats and separate-sex gym classes in public schools.

In short, these differences are related to the scope and focus of the evolving relationship between Christianity and Islam in Western Europe. Although the EU's bureaucracy is composed of officials born and raised in its member states— many of whom have previously served in the governments of those states—their tasks and approaches change once they matriculate to Brussels-based institutions. It is the EU's job to manage interactions between the region as a whole and states situated within the Islamic world. Thus, the European Council of Ministers and Commission—and not individual member state governments—oversee negotiations on Turkey's membership bid. By contrast, domestic governments (national, regional and local)—and not the EU's institutions—develop and implement most of the policies associated with the integration of Muslims into Western European societies.

In order to measure the impact of Muslim communities on foreign policy linkages between the EU and its member states, two related sets of contextual observations are instructive. They relate to influences exerted by state and non-state actors from the Islamic world on the Muslims of Western Europe, and the distinctions between domestic governments and the EU in dealing with the implications of those influences, respectively. Regarding the first issue area, states and transnational organizations situated in the Greater Middle East have the potential to foster instability within the EU's borders by encouraging Muslims to reject Western societal norms. There are both non-violent and violent manifestations of initiatives planned and implemented by these actors. They range from the verbal condemnation of Western religious and social norms generally and American and British economic, political and military activities in the Islamic world specifically to the recruitment of young Muslims to carry out terrorist acts both within and outside of Western Europe.

With respect to the second issue area, national and supranational leaders and institutions are subject to different limitations in the policy tools at their disposal for use in minimizing the above threats to domestic security and social stability. Domestic governments across Western Europe, for example, must balance concerns over reactions to policies toward states in the Islamic world by societal majorities and Muslim communities, whether deemed too conciliatory by the former or unduly discriminatory by the latter. In so doing, they are understandably more likely to side with the majority than the minority. Additionally, differences in relationships with the United States foster inter-European rifts in the treatment of given regimes.

The EU, on the other hand, has greater potential to develop at least a general consensus on the conduct of relations with state and non-state actors in the Islamic world. This is the case in part because the EU is considerably more removed from, and thus less affected by, expressions of concern among the citizens of its member states over economic and political engagement with Muslim regimes than is true of the leaders of the governments of those states. To its credit, the EU has taken advantage of this opportunity by expressing an affinity for diplomatic interaction with rather than condemnation of states and regimes that the United States has branded politically unsavory at best and rogues at worst. Notable examples include the conduct of diplomatic relations with Iran and a willingness to apportion less blame to the Palestinian Authority than the Israeli government for the collapse of the Arab-Israeli peace process since 2000. Granted, the EU must still strike a reasonable balance between engagement with states in the Islamic world and the condemnation of the actions of transnational groups created solely for the sponsorship of terrorism. However, any openness it exhibits in the former issue area will help to enhance Western European credibility among Muslims residing in states across the region and in turn reduce the potential for domestic instability in those contexts.

Regrettably, a common problem often undermines foreign and domestic national-supranational policy linkages that would otherwise have greater potential to improve Muslim-Christian relations on the continent. Distinctions between areas of responsibility vis-à-vis the treatment of and interaction with Muslims by governments and citizens of member states in and beyond the borders of the EU have grown increasingly ambiguous over time. Consider the issue of immigration. Since the negotiation and implementation of the Schengen Accord, member state governments have displayed an increasing level of interest in developing comparable if not identical immigration policies. With the removal of internal border controls required by the Schengen process, the outer boundaries of the EU—most notably those of the member states along the southern and eastern peripheries of that entity—grew in significance as focal points to stem the flow of unwanted migrants. As a result, the involvement of regional bodies became more necessary in the coordination of immigration policy formulation and implementation in the EU.

However, opinions vary at the national and EU levels with respect to the means for coordination of immigration policies. Put simply, national and EU officials have advocated intergovernmentalism and supranationalism, respectively, as the best methods to achieve effective control over migration flows. The former gives credence to coordination among national governments to ensure that migration into one state does not eventually present threats to another, whether defined in terms of economics, politics or internal security. By design, it emphasizes the authority of national governments over EU institutions. The latter, on the other hand, concentrates authority at the supranational level, with decisions debated and taken by the leaders of Brussels-based institutions to serve the collective interests of the EU rather than those of particular member states.

While different in philosophical orientation, these approaches are designed to achieve the same basic end: mitigation if not preclusion of the penetration of EU borders by individuals deemed as outsiders. Described generally, groups from four geographic regions—Central, Eastern and Southeastern Europe and North Africa present a greater threat than any others in this regard because of the proximity of the states in which they reside to the outer boundaries of the EU. Furthermore, among these groups, migrants from the latter two regions—the majority of whom are Muslims—tend to receive the most scrutiny. Differences in the treatment of these groups, in turn, is largely a product of the present state of the enlargement of the EU, with the newest members—and implicitly most acceptable ethnic and religious additions to the regional integration project—coming from Eastern and Central Europe rather than the Balkans.

Although the EU's influence vis-à-vis the issue of Islam in Europe is primarily evident in the regulation of the external influx of migrants, it has also had a more subtle impact on the integration of Muslims within Western Europe in recent years. The EU's influence in the latter context is encapsulated in the application of supranational laws designed to protect all minority groups and to the plight of Muslims in particular in states such as France, Germany and the United Kingdom. By pursuing uniformity in the development of common legal and social norms through treaty negotiations at regular Intergovernmental Conferences (IGCs), the EU has increased the potential for improvements in the treatment of ethnic and religious minorities. Consider the Charter on Fundamental Rights included in the context of the Nice Treaty and proposed European Constitution, which contains provisions germane to Muslim causes in principle if not in explicit wording. By forbidding discrimination on the basis of religion or ethnicity, for instance, the charter provides a legal basis for Muslims to demand accommodations that allow for the adherence to basic Islamic precepts while attending or working in publicly-funded institutions.

However, the extent to which supranational measures applicable to Muslims will serve to help create more equitable societies is contingent upon the legitimacy of the EU itself as perceived and expressed by the citizens of its member states.

On that point, future prospects are positive. Although the popularity of the EU fluctuates periodically, public acceptance of the concept of an inclusive, integrated Europe as originally envisioned in the aftermath of World War II has grown slowly but consistently over the past half-century. The more inclusive the definition of Europe becomes, the greater the long-term potential to ameliorate public acceptance of minority groups. Granted, the present exclusion of Muslims from the economic and social benefits enjoyed by members of the societal majority across the region is discouraging. But integrative progress, whether pursued at the local, national or supranational level, requires patience above all else. Whereas the European integration project has been underway for 50 years, sustained efforts to include Muslims in the societies of EU member states remain in its formative stages. As the former project draws ever closer to completion, the changes in perceptions it entails can help to push the latter process forward more rapidly.

Prospects for the Future

Comparing and contrasting the similarities and differences in the evidence presented in each of the case studies serves as a useful means to determine both positive and negative trends in the integration of Muslims into the fabric of Western Europe at present. The most relevant of these trends are related to demography, economics, social stability, security and politics.

Demographically, Islamic communities remain concentrated in many of the same French, German and British urban enclaves in which the guest workers of the 1950s and 1960s settled. Despite exhibiting higher growth rates than either the societal majority or other minority groups and thus perpetually increasing their proportion in the populations of those states, Muslims are only marginally more widely dispersed geographically than was the case a half-century ago. Although generally negative, such marginalization has one positive benefit. As the number of Muslims continues to grow—a certainty given present birth rates and the likelihood of the development of new migration flows from the Islamic world to satisfy increases in demand for workers in the twenty-first century—their relegation to already-bursting housing projects on the peripheries of major cities will become increasingly impractical and unsustainable. Ultimately, municipal, regional and national governments will have to focus greater attention on the integration of Muslims to avoid widespread social disorder emanating from Islamic-majority neighborhoods and electoral districts.

The economic prospects of second and third generation Muslims in Western Europe are not promising. High unemployment rates and substandard income levels among those fortunate enough to acquire jobs have led to markedly below average standards of living in Islamic communities. While blame for these trends does not lie exclusively on the shoulders of either Muslims themselves or the municipally and nationally elected officials who govern the districts and states within which they live, changes are essential to mitigate minority-majority conflict over both the short and long terms. The limited success of entrepreneurs from both the older and younger generations in establishing businesses catering to the religious and cultural needs of their communities is a positive step. However, it is not likely to result in higher levels of incorporation of Muslims in the skilled sectors of the French, German and British economies. Educational proficiency among Muslims must improve in order to ensure positive progress toward the achievement of that objective. Such progress, in turn, will require sustained efforts on behalf of both teachers and students—above all at the local level, where multicultural interaction is most unavoidable.

The marginalization of Muslims is one of the clearest sources of societal instability in Western Europe. Individuals residing in Islamic communities— particularly those who were born and raised on the continent—usually lack the educational proficiency and economic prosperity exhibited by ethnic Europeans of the same age groups. As a result, they grow frustrated and eventually a sense of desperation sets in, one that compels many to rebel against the societal mainstream. Such rebelliousness is most often manifested in criminal behavior that eventually leads to confrontations with members of the majority, other minority groups and the police. Rising crime levels in the *banlieues* of France, targeting of Turks by right-wing extremists in Germany and the 2001 riots in the north of England are all symptomatic of rising instability.

The security challenges posed by increases in instability fostered by adversarial minority-majority relationships have both negative and positive implications with respect to the integration of Muslims in France, Germany and the United Kingdom. On the negative side, violent behavior by young Muslims in the 1990s has buttressed societal misperceptions of Islam as a monolithic religion practiced by foreign extremists rather than citizens of modern states. Large-scale riots indicate that the penchant for violence evident among members of the second and third generations is considerably more widespread than that attributable to isolated acts of terrorism. On the positive side, when substantial proportions of communities riot, it suggests to public officials that a profound problem does indeed exist and thus demands sustained attention. Over the past two decades, for example, successive French, German and British governments have gradually shifted their policies vis-à-vis the presence of Muslims in their societies from those associated with social integration as opposed to the elimination of influxes of migrants from the Islamic world.

Regarding the impact of Islam on Western European domestic politics, trends are generally encouraging. Domestically, Muslims have played a considerably more active role in French, German and British electoral politics over the last decade than was the case in the 1970s and 1980s. This is particularly evident at the municipal level, albeit to a lesser degree in Germany than in France or Britain given lower levels of citizenship among Muslims in the former state as opposed to the latter pair. Islamic communities have gained higher levels of political influence primarily through the election of Muslim councilors and resultant increases in legitimacy of minority religious and cultural issues in electoral campaigns by mainstream political parties. On the other hand, representative gains have occurred on a lesser scale at the national level, where the election of Muslim MPs remains a daunting challenge, even in the districts in which Islamic communities account for a significant proportion of the electorate.

Trends in each of these five issue areas illustrate two main points. First, many policies already in place have proven effective in ameliorating the standing of Muslims in Western European societies. Second, the development of additional innovative initiatives remains indispensable in order to move the minority integration process forward in the future. These points are best categorized broadly in terms of domestic and supranational level policies and initiatives rather than through the reiteration of the minutiae of specific country-by-country examples discussed in the previous chapters.

At the domestic level, two present philosophical trends in the development and implementation of policies that affect Muslims have been particularly constructive. First, the shift in emphasis on Islam as an issue associated with the domestic integration of minorities rather than the control of migration flows across EU borders. This shift indicates clear governmental recognition of the permanence of the presence of home grown Islamic communities in Western Europe generally and France, Germany and the United Kingdom specifically. Second, the increase in dialogue between government leaders and representatives from Muslim communities, which are manifested in forms ranging from the creation of interethnic and interfaith umbrella groups to address Islamic concerns to the deliverance of Ramadan greetings by national leaders such as British Prime Minister Tony Blair and French President Jacques Chirac.

It is also possible to deepen these types of engagement by placing greater emphasis on minority-majority engagement at the local level within given states and also perhaps across borders. This type of endeavor could unfold in the following manner. First, a particular locality develops a method to increase constructive interaction between members of the majority and ethnic and religious minorities, whether through publicly or privately sponsored initiatives. Second, when any such program proves successful, individuals living in the municipality in which it was developed pass the information along to other communities—both within and outside of the country. While initially limited in scope, this general process could eventually help to more deeply integrate Muslims into domestic societies throughout the EU and also establish stronger links between Western Europeans of all ethnic and religious persuasions.

At the supranational level, positive trends regarding the standing of Islam in Western Europe parallel the deepening of the integration process itself, albeit in a somewhat indirect manner. The EU is by design an inclusive institution within which former enemies have overcome past differences to the benefit of the region as a whole. Theoretically—if not always directly in practice—the gradual ceding of domestic control over the governance of citizens to the EU should lead to the cultivation of more inclusive Western European societies. Similar to the reconciliation between adversaries that was indispensable to the establishment of the European Economic Community through the Rome Treaties and subsequent deepening and widening of that institution, disparate ethnic and religious groups also have a welcome opportunity to settle their differences in the context of the EU.

By pressing for the adoption of inclusive legal and social norms, the EU is creating more and more room for Muslims to define themselves as Europeans without undermining their religious beliefs or ethnic heritage. They must take advantage of these chances rather than accede to relegation to the societal periphery manifested in entrenchment in esoteric enclaves. By acknowledging and protecting the rights of all minority groups ensconced in EU treaties, member state governments can ensure that progress continues in the pursuit of a Europe whole and free. However, if Western European leaders—particularly those in the most influential three states in the EU (namely France, Germany and the United Kingdom)—accept the continued economic and social marginalization of Muslims, they will undermine the very legitimacy of the idea of an inclusive Europe. To remain inclusive, the EU must extend the benefits of membership to all individuals living within its borders, irrespective of race, ethnicity or religion. This was true in the past, is the case at present and will remain so in the future.

Significance of the Findings

The introductory chapter of the book put forward four theses for evaluation. Fittingly, the following concluding section revisits and elaborates briefly on the validity of those theses in light of the evidence presented in the case studies.

• First, the growth of Islamic communities concurrent with the aging of the majority populations of France, Germany and the United Kingdom over the past half-century has created an as yet unmet need to fully integrate Muslims of variegated ethnic backgrounds within the societies of those states. That need is certain to grow more pronounced as the proportion of Muslims residing therein increases.

The evidence presented and discussed in the domestic case studies indicates that Muslims have indeed been excluded from many of the economic, social and political benefits afforded to members of the majority in each of the above states. The limited integrative progress that has been achieved is welcome but by no means sufficient. Statistical projections indicate that the share of Muslims in the Western European population is likely to increase through a combination of high Islamic communal fertility rates within and the recruitment of workers from without to satisfy twenty-first century labor needs. As a result, the development of more inclusive societies is indispensable to the maintenance of economic prosperity and social stability over the long term.

• Second, the failure to fully integrate Muslims within the societies of France,

Germany and the United Kingdom has the potential to foster social and political instability in those states over both the short and long terms.

Manifestations of interethnic and interfaith violence involving second and third generation Muslims fosters societal instability. Examples such as the 2001 riots in northern England, the 1995 spate of terrorist bombings in France and perpetual annual increases in right-wing attacks against Turks in Germany in the 1990s, are demonstrative of this point. Increases in these types of incidents could both further marginalize Islamic communities and threaten the ability of local, and perhaps regional and national, leaders to govern effectively in the future.

• Third, the construction of an effective framework to fully integrate Muslims within the French, German and British societies—and, ultimately, in the broader Western European context—over the long term will necessarily entail interactive policy formulation, coordination and implementation at the local, regional, national and supranational levels. However, given the prevalence of Islamic communities in particular localities and the resultant higher degree of interaction among Muslims and governmental authorities in those environs as opposed to the limited dispersion of Muslims regionally and nationally in France, Germany and the United Kingdom, a local-level approach is more desirable in the short term.

While French, German and British governments in office over the past two decades have generally focused on integrative initiatives applicable at the national level, most implications arising from the exclusion of Muslims are played out locally. Economic shortcomings, for example, foster a sense of frustration and desperation that eventually causes young Muslims to lash out at members of the societal majority and the police, or both, in the districts in which they live. Restoring order and reducing minority-majority barriers are tasks usually handled by local elected officials and minority communal leaders rather than parliamentary representatives, presidents, prime ministers and their respective institutional bureaucracies. Thus, it is logical to address the issue at the local level first, before attempting to implement a universal integrative framework applicable at either the regional, national or supranational level.

• Fourth, once the full integration of Muslim minorities—or at least positive progress toward the achievement of that objective—is realized within given municipalities in France, Germany or the United Kingdom, wider-ranging regional, national and supranational level projects are likely to prove more feasible in light of insights drawn from the local level.

The credible evaluation of this thesis requires long-term testing that is impractical at present. In short, the integration of Muslims into the French, German and British societies is work in progress, not a project upon which construction is complete—in particular districts let alone nationally. Theoretically, it stands to reason that improvements in standards of living and increases in constructive minority-majority interaction have the potential for expansion from one municipality to another and eventually to the regional and national levels. But the viability of such processes demands practical application and testing that has yet to occur.

To place the over-riding significance of the arguments presented here in the proper perspective, it is best to begin by reiterating the fundamental reasons for selecting and investigating the topic. There are three such reasons. First, the growing presence of Islam has had a considerable impact on the governance of societies across Western Europe generally and those of France, Germany and the United Kingdom in particular over the past half-century. Yet, it has been neglected by scholars in relation to the attention given to more high profile issues such as transatlantic cooperation, European integration, and national and supranational leadership. This book endeavors to fill at least part of that void in research and interpretation. Second, examining the integration of Muslims in the French, German and British societies also affords one an opportunity to gain a deeper understanding of related issue areas—most notably those associated with domestic economics and politics, and internal security. Third, the increasing relevance of Islam in each of the above national constructs has affected the wider EU deepening and widening processes. As a result, it is essential to address supranational as well as national trends and developments germane to the evolving relationship between Islam and Christianity within and beyond the continent.

In short, the domestic and Western European regional case studies explained in a reasonably comprehensive manner how Muslim communities have had an impact upon and been affected by governments, citizens and institutions across the region. The domestic case studies drew on past research and recent statistical data in order to provide credible descriptions of the similarities and differences in the characteristics of Muslims living in France, Germany and the United Kingdom and the roles they have played in those societies. The broader regional case study addressed the broader implications of the presence of Islam on the continent in terms of the evolution of the definition of European identity and the extent to which that definition will become inclusive enough to accommodate Muslims as well as Christians in the future. Articulating explicitly the many links between the case studies, in turn, allowed for the presentation of insights that would perhaps have otherwise been overlooked.

With respect to the domestic case studies, five such points are indispensable when considering the prospects for the place of Islam in Western Europe in the future. First, the vast majority of Muslims residing in contemporary France, Germany and the United Kingdom are excluded from the benefits of full acceptance by members of the societal mainstreams of those states. Second, in each case, the proportion of Muslims in the population are presently rising and projected to continue to do so in the future. Thus, the need to integrate Muslims will not disappear of its own accord. Third, as a result, government leaders must fully recognize and openly acknowledge the relevance of present integrative shortcomings and work to more equitably incorporate Muslims into the French, German and British societies and face that challenge with renewed vigor. Fourth, they must attack the problem locally first rather than regionally or nationally given that the implications of the marginalization of Muslims are most pronounced in the municipalities where Islamic communities are situated. Fifth, ignoring or downgrading the significance of these issues will only increase the potential for further social and political instability fostered by the exclusion of Muslims and is thus not a viable option.

At the supranational level, four related points are equally relevant. First, issues that affect the governance of any one EU member state also have an impact upon the institution as a whole. As a result, the integration of Muslim communities into domestic Western European societies has implications in the contexts of the wider European deepening and widening processes. Second, the EU can help both to more fully integrate Muslims in its member states and alter perceptions of Islam across the region by deepening current and establishing additional treaty measures protecting the rights of ethnic and religious minorities. Third, in order to buttress its own credibility among Muslims, leaders in Brussels must continue to work to overcome their differences with the Turkish government in order to facilitate Turkey's eventual accession to the EU. Fourth, through these means, the EU can enhance its legitimacy as an inclusive entity and—in the process—help to continue to extend the idea of Europe beyond its current confines. Ignorance of the significance of the present and likely future relevance of Islam on the continent, on the other hand, could stall if not derail completion of the European integration project.

Bibliography

Documents and Official Sources

Bernard, Philippe. *La part des immigrès dans la population françaises n'a pas augmenté depuis vingt ans*. Paris: L'Institute National de la Statistique et des Études Economique (INSEE), 1998.

Boëldieu, Julien, and Catherine Borrel. *La proportion d'immigrés est stable depuis 25 ans*. Paris: INSEE, 2000.

Bradford Community Relations Council. *Annual Report 1988/89*. Bradford, UK: Bradford Community Relations Council, 1989.

British Office for National Statistics. *Census 2001: Ethnicity and Religion*. London: British Office for National Statistics, 2002.

_____. *Health Survey for England*. London: British Office for National Statistics, 1999.

Central Islam Institute Archives. *Muslims in* Germany. Soesen, Germany: Central Institute Islam Archives, 2001.

European Economic and Social Committee of the European Union, "The European Economic and Social Committee: A Bridge between Europe and Civil Society."*European Economic and Social Committee* home page, www.esc.eu.int (June 2001).

European Information Service. *Charter of Fundamental Rights*. Brussels: European Commission, 2001.

_____. *Area of Freedom, Justice and Security*. Brussels: European Commission, 2000.

_____. *The Amsterdam Treaty: A Comprehensive Guide*. Brussels: European Commission, 1997.

General Register Office, Scotland. *Census 2001: Ethnicity and Religion*. Edinburgh: General Register Office, Scotland, 2002.

German Information Service. *Citizenship Reform and Germany's Foreign Residents*. Berlin: German Information Service, 2000.

_____. *Population in Germany will Decline by more than 10 Million from Present 82 Million by 2050*. Berlin: German Information Service, 2000.

German National Office of Statistics. *Naturalization of 186,700 Foreigners in 2000*. Berlin: German National Office of Statistics, 2001.

_____. *Foreign Population from a Choice of Islamic Countries in* Germany. Berlin: German National Office of Statistics, 2000.

_____. *Population of Turks in Germany between 1961-1992*. Berlin: German National Office of Statistics, 1996.

_____. *Distribution of Foreigners According to Age Groups and Selected Nationalities*. Berlin: German National Office of Statistics, 1992.

House of Lords Select Committee on the European Communities. *Border Control of People*. London: HMSO, 1992.

Muslim Council of Brtiain. "How Many British Muslims?" London: Muslim Council of Britain, 2001.

Thalhammer, Eva, Viasta Zucha, Edith Enzenhofer, Brigitte Salfinger and Gunther Ogris. *Attitudes Towards Minority Groups in the European Union*. Vienna: SORA, 2001.

Thave, Suzanne. *L'emploi des immigrés en 1999*. Paris: INSEE, 2000.

United Kingdom Action Committee on Islamic Affairs, *British Muslims and the General Election 1997*. London: United Kingdom Action Committee on Islamic Affairs, 1997.

Newspapers and Serials

BBC News (Available Online). 12 December 2001-16 July 2002.
Daily Telegraph (London). 18 January 1998-23 April 2001.
Economist (London). 7 October 1995-5 July 2003.
Guardian (London). 21 January 1991-17 June 2002.
Le Monde (Paris). 6 March 2001-23 April 2002.
Muslim News (Available Online). 20 January 1999-27 July 2001.
Time International. 25 January 1999-30 April 2001.
Washington Post. 9 January 2000-25 November 2000.

Monographs

Angenendt, Steffen, ed. *Asylum and Migration Policies in the European Union*. Berlin: Research Institute for the German Society for Foreign Affairs, 1999.

Anwar, Muhammad. *Muslims in Britain: Census and Other Statistical Sources*. Birmingham, UK: Center for the Study of Christian-Muslim Relations, 1993.

Ayuh, Nazih N. *Political Islam: Religion and Politics in the Third World*. New York: Routledge, 1991.

Banton, Michael. *Promoting Racial Harmony*. Cambridge: Cambridge University Press, 1985.

Barrett, David B., ed. *World Christian Encyclopedia: A Comparative Study of Churches and Religions in the Modern* World. New York: Oxford University Press, 1992.

Bartlett, W.B. *God Wills It! An Illustrated History of the Crusades*. Gloucestershire, UK: Sutton, 1999.

Bataille, Philippe. *Le Racisme au Travail*. Paris: Le Découverte, 1987.

Baubock, Rainer, ed. *From Aliens to Citizens: Redefining the Status of Immigrants in Europe*. Vienna: European Centre Vienna, 1994.

Bernard, Philippe. *L'immigration*. Paris: Le Monde Poche, 1993.

Borjas, George. *Friends or Strangers: The Impact of Immigration on the U.S. Economy*. New York: Basic Books, 1990.

Bridge, Antony. *The Crusades*. New York: Granada, 1980.

Brown, Peter. *The Age of Western Christendom: Triumph and Diversity*. Oxford: Blackwell, 1996.

Browne, Colin. *Black and White Britain: The Third PRI Survey*. London: Heineman, 1984.

Brzezinski, Zbigniew. *Out of Control: Global Turmoil on the Eve of the Twenty-first Century*. New York: Touchstone Books, 1993.

Burns, Robert J. *Moors and Crusaders in Mediterranean* Spain. London: Variorum Reprints, 1978.

Cabaniss, Allen. *Charlemagne*. New York: Twayne Publishers, 1972.

Calhoun, Craig. *Critical Social Theory*. Oxford: Blackwell, 1995.

Carmon, Naomi, ed. *Immigration and Integration in Post-Industrial Societies: Theoretical Analysis and Policy-Related Research*. Warwick, UK: Centre for Research in Ethnic Relations, 1996.

Caron, François. *An Economic History of Modern France*. New York: Columbia University Press, 1979.

Clarke, Colin, Ceri Peach and Steven Vertovec, eds. *South Asians Overseas: Migration and Ethnicity*. Cambridge: Cambridge University Press, 1990.

Corbett, James. *Through French Windows: An Introduction to France in the Nineties*. Ann Arbor: University of Michigan Press, 1994.

Dejong, Gordon F., and Robert W. Gardner. *Migration Decision Making: Multidisciplinary Approaches to Microlevel Studies in Developed and Developing Countries*. New York: Pergamon Press, 1981.

Durkheim, Emile. *The Division of Labour in Society*. Glencoe, Il.: The Free Press, 1933.

Esposito, John L. *Islam: The Straight Path*. New York: Oxford University Press, 1998.

_____. *The Islamic Threat: Myth or Reality*. New York: Oxford University Press, 1995).

Esposito, John L., ed. *Oxford History of Islam*. New York: Oxford University Press, 1999.

Fletcher, Richard. *The Barbarian Conversion: From Paganism to Christianity*. New York: Henry Holt and Company, 1997.

Fossman, Heinz, and Rainier Münz, eds. *European Migration in the Late Twentieth Century: Historical Patterns, Actual Trends and Social Implications*. Laxenburg, Austria: International Institute for Applied Systems Analysis, 1994.

Fregosi, Paul. *Jihad in the West: Muslim Conquests from the 7th to the twenty-first Centuries*. New York: Prometheus Books, 1998.

Fukuyama, Francis. *The End of History and the Last Man*. New York: Avon Books, 1992.

Gang, Ira N., and Klaus F. Zimmerman. *Is Child Like Parent? Educational Attainment and Ethnic Origin*. Bonn, Germany: Institute for the Study of Labor, 1999.

Geddes, Andrew. *Immigration and European Integration: Towards Fortress Europe?* New York: St. Martin's Press, 2000.

Gellner, Ernest. *Reason and Culture: The Historic Role of Rationality and Rationalism*. Oxford: Blackwell, 1992.

Gourévitch, Jean-Paul. *La France africaine: Islam, intégration, insécurité: infos et intox*. Paris: Le Pré aux Clercs, 2000.

Greenfeld, Liah. *Nationalism: Five Roads to* Modernity. Cambridge: Harvard University Press, 1992.

Halliday, Fred. *Arabs in Exile: Yemeni Migrants in Urban Britain*. London: I.B. Tauris, 1992.

Halphen. Louis. *Charlemagne and the Carolingian Empire*. New York North Holland Publishing Company, 1977.

Heer, Friedrich. *Charlemagne and his World*. London: Weidenfeld and Nicolson, 1975.

Hoff, Joan, and Richard K. Vedder, eds. *The European Union: From Jean Monnet to the Euro*. Athens: Ohio University Press, 2000.

Hoffmann, Stanley. *The European Sisyphus: Essays on Europe, 1964-1994*. Boulder, Col.: Westview Press, 1995.

Horrocks, David, and Eva Kolinsky, eds. *Turkish Culture in German Society Today*. Providence, R.I.: Berghahn Books, 1996.

Hucko, Elmar, ed. *The Democratic Tradition: Four German* Constitutions. Oxford: Berg Publishers, 1989.

Hunter, Shireen T. *The Future of Islam and the West: Clash of Civilizations or Peaceful Coexistence?* Westport, Conn.: Praeger, 1998.

Huntington, Samuel P. *The Clash of Civilizations and the Remaking of World Order*. New York: Schocken Books, 1996.

Inalcik, Halil. *The Ottoman Empire: The Classical Age, 1300-1600*. London: Weidenfeld and Nicolson, 1973.

Jones, Terry. *Crusades*. New York: Facts on File, 1995.

Joppke, Christian. *Immigration and the Nation-State: The United States, Germany and Great Britain*. New York: Oxford University Press, 1999.

Keohane, Robert O., and Stanley Hoffmann. *The New European Community: Decisionmaking and Institutional Change*. Boulder, Col.: Westview Press, 1991.

Kepel, Gilles. *Allah in the West: Islamic Movements in America and Europe*, trans. Susan Milner. Stanford: Stanford University Press, 1997.

Kritz, Mary M., Elizabeth M. Petras, Charles B. Keely and Silvano M. Tomasi, eds. *Global Trends in Migration: Theory and Research on International Population Movements*. Staten Island, NY: Center for Migration Studies, 1981.

Laqueur, Walter. *Europe in Our Time: A History, 1945-1992*. New York: Penguin, 1992.

LeBor, Adam. *A Heart Turned East: Among the Muslims of Europe and America.* New York: St. Martin's Press, 1998.

Levitt, Cyril, Scott Davies and Neil McLaughin, eds. *Mistaken Identities: The Second Wave of Controversy over "Political Correctness."* New York: Peter Lang, 1999.

Lewis, Bernard. *Islam and the West.* New York: Oxford University Press, 1993.

_____. *The Multiple Identities of the Middle East.* New York: Schocken Books, 1998.

Lewis, Bernard, and Dominique Schnapper, eds. *Muslims in Europe.* New York: Pinter Publishers, 1994.

Lewis, Philip. *Islamic Britain: Religion, Politics and Identity Among British Muslims—Bradford in the 1990s.* London: I.B. Tauris, 1994.

Macdonald, Ian A. *Race Relations: The New Law.* London: Butterworth, 1977.

Malbet, A.N. *Migrations et Conditions Sanitaire.* Paris: L'Harmattan, 1995.

Mayer, Jochen, and Regina T. Riphahn. *Fertility Assimilation of Immigrants: Evidence from Count Data Models.* Bonn, Germany: Institute for the Study of Labor, 1999.

McKittenck, Rosamond. *The Frankish Kingdoms under the Carolingians, 751-987.* New York: Longman, 1983.

Meier-Braun, Karl-Heinz. *Integration oder Rückkehr.* Munich: Grünewald, 1988.

Meyerson, Mark D. *The Muslims of Valencia in the Age of Fernando and Isabel: Between Coexistence and Crusade.* Berkeley: University of California Press, 1985.

Modood, Tariq, and Pnina Werbner, eds. *The Politics of Multiculturalism in the New Europe: Racism, Identity and Community.* New York: Zed Books Ltd., 1997.

Monnet, Jean. *Memoirs.* Garden City, N.Y.: Doubleday, 1978.

Myrdal, Gunnar. *Rich Lands and Poor.* New York: Harper and Row, 1957.

Newhouse, John. *Europe Adrift: The Conflicting Demands of Unity ,Nationalism, Economic Security, Political Stability and Military Readiness Now Facing a Europe Seeking to Redefine Itself.* New York: Pantheon Books, 1997.

Nielsen, Jorgen S. *Muslims in Western Europe.* New York: Pinter Publishers, 1992.

Noiriel, Gerard. *The French Melting Pot: Immigration, Citizenship and National Identity,* trans. Geoffroy de Laforcade. Minneapolis: University of Minnesota Press, 1996.

Nonneman, Gerd, Tim Niblock and Bogdan Szajkowski, eds. *Muslim Communities in the New Europe.* Ithaca, NY: Ithaca Press, 1996.

Peach, Ceri, ed. *Ethnicity in the 1991 Census: The Ethnic Population of Great Britain,* vol. 2. London: HMSO, 1996.

Piore, Michael J. *Birds of Passage: Migrant Labor in Industrial Societies.* Cambridge: Cambridge University Press, 1979.

Pipes, Daniel. *In the Path of God: Islam and Political Power.* New York: Basic Books, 1983.

Portes, Alejandro, and Ruben Rumbaut. *Immigrant America: A Portrait,* 2nd Edition. Berkeley: University of California Press, 1996.

Portes, Alejandro, and John Walton. *Labor, Class and the International System*. New York: Academic Press, 1981.

Rabinow, Paul, and William M. Sullivan, eds. *Interpretive Social Science: A Second Look*. Berkeley: University of California Press, 1987.

Rafiq, Muhammad. *Asian Businesses in Bradford: Profile and Prospects*. Bradford, UK: City of Bradford Metropolitan Council, 1985.

Ramadan, Tariq. *To Be a European* Muslim. Leicester, UK: Islamic Foundation, 1999.

_____. *Muslims in France*. Leicester, UK: Islamic Foundation, 1999.

Richard, Jean. *The Crusades*. New York: Cambridge University Press, 1999.

Riché, Pierre. *The Carolingians: A Family Who Forged Europe*, trans. Michael Idomic Allen. Philadelphia: University of Pennsylvania Press, 1993.

Robertson, A.H. *European Institutions: Cooperation, Integration, Unification*. London: Stevens and Sons, 1959.

Roy, Olivier. *The Failure of Political Islam*. Cambridge: Harvard University Press, 1994.

Schimmel, Annemarie. *And Muhammad is His Messenger: The Veneration of the Prophet in Islamic Piety*. Chapel Hill: University of North Carolina Press, 1985.

Serfaty, Simon. *Memories of Europe's Future: Farewell to Yesteryear*. Washington, D.C.: Center for Strategic and International Studies Press, 1999.

_____. *Stay the Course: European Unity and Atlantic Solidarity*. Westport, CT: Praeger, 1997.

_____. *Taking Europe Seriously*. New York: St. Martin's Press, 1992.

Shadid, W.A.R., and P.S. Van Konigsveld, eds. *Muslims in the Margin: Political Responses to the Presence of Muslims in Western Europe*. Kampen, Netherlands: KOK Pharos Publishing House, 1996.

_____. *Political Participation and Identities of Muslims in Non-Muslim States*. Kampen, Netherlands: KOK Pharos Publishing House, 1996.

Shaw, Stanford Jay. *History of the Ottoman Empire and Modern Turkey*. New York: Cambridge University Press, 1976.

Silverman, Maxim. *Deconstructing the Nation: Immigration, Race and Citizenship in Modern France*. New York: Routledge, 1992.

Sjdjanski, Dusan. *The Federal Future of Europe: From the European Community to the European Union*. Ann Arbor: University of Michigan Press, 2000.

Sonn, Tamara, ed. *Islam and the Question of Minorities*. Atlanta: Scholars Press, 1996.

Soysal, Yasemine N. *Limits of Citizenship: Migrants and Postnational Membership in Europe*. Chicago: University of Chicago Press, 1994.

Stark, Oded, ed. *Research in Human Capital and Development: Migration, Human Capital and Development*, vol. 4. Greenwich, Conn.: JAI Press, 1986.

Stark, Oded. *The Migration of Labor*. Cambridge, UK: Blackwell, 1991.

Taylor, Paul Graham. *The European Union in the 1990s*. New York: Oxford University Press, 1996.

Islam in Europe

Tibi, Bassam. *The Challenge of Fundamentalism: Political Islam and the New World Disorder.* Berkeley: University of California Press, 1993.

Todaro, Michael P. *Internal Migration in Developing Countries.* Geneva: International Labor Office, 1976.

Treece, Henry. *The Crusades.* London: Souvenir Press, 1978.

Urwin, Derek W. *The Community of Europe: A History of European Integration Since 1945.* New York: Longman, 1991.

Vertovec, Steven, and Alisdair Rogers, eds. *Muslim European Youth: Reproducing Ethnicity, Religion, Culture.* Aldershot, UK: Ashgate Publishing Limited, 1998.

Vertovec, Steven, and Ceri Peach, eds. *Islam in Europe: The Politics of Religion and Community.* London: Macmillan, 1997.

Walker, R.B.J., ed. *Culture, Ideology and World Order.* Boulder, Co.: Westview Press, 1984.

Wallace, William. *The Transformation of Western Europe.* New York: Council on Foreign Relations Press, 1990.

Wallerstein, Immanuel. *The Modern World System: Capitalist Agriculture and the Origins of the European World Economy in the Sixteenth Century.* New York: Academic Press, 1974.

Watt, William Montgomery. *A History of Islamic Spain.* Edinburgh, Scotland: Edinburgh University Press, 1965.

Weiner, Myron, ed. *International Migration and Security.* Boulder, Co.: Westview Press, 1993.

Wihtol de Wenden, Catherine. *Citoyennete, Nationalite et Immigration.* Paris: Arcantere, 1987.

Wilcox, Walter F., ed. *International Migrations,* vol. 2. New York: Gordon and Breach Science Publishers, 1931.

Articles

Abdullah, Muhammad. "Der Islam will in Deutschland harnisch werden." *Die Brucke* 58-1 (1992).

"A Decade of Death." *Searchlight* (November 2000).

Ashley, Richard K. "The Geopolitics of Geopolitical Space: Toward a Critical Social Theory of International Politics." *Alternatives* 13-4 (1987).

Bafekr, Sigrid, and Johan Leman. "Highly-qualified Iranian Immigrants in Germany: The Roles of Ethnicity and Culture." *Journal of Ethnic and Migration Studies* 291 (1999).

Brown, Mark S. "Religion and Economic Activity in the South Asian Population." *Ethnic and Racial Studies* 23-4 (2000).

Butt Philip, Alan. "European Union Immigration Policy: Phantom, Fantasy or Fact?" *West European Politics* 17-1 (1994).

Caldwell, Christopher. "The Crescent and the Tricolor." *Atlantic Monthly* 287-11 (2000).

Cesari, Jocelyne. "Remarks on Political Participation of Muslims in Europe," *Muslims in Europe Post-9/11 Conference.* Oxford University (April 2003).

Coleman, D.A. "International Migration: Demographic and Socioeconomic Consequences in the United Kingdom and Europe." *International Migration Review* 29-1 (1995).

DeBula Baines, Cynrthia. "L'Affaire des Foulards: Discrimination and the Price of a Secular Public Education System." *Vanderbilt Journal of Transnational Law* 29-1 (1996).

Eberstadt, Nicholas. "The Population Implosion." *Foreign Policy* 123-2 (2001).

El-Sohl, Camillia Fawzi. "Arab Communities in Britain: Cleavages and Commonalities." *Islam and Christian-Muslim Relations* 3-4 (1992).

El-Sohl, Ibrahim. "Be True to your Culture: Gender Tensions Among Somali Muslims in Britain." *Immigrants and Minorities*, 12-1 (1994).

"EU: Tampere Summit." *Migration News* 6-10 (1999).

Fawcett, James T. "Networks, Linkages and Migration Systems." *International Migration Review* 23-2 (1989).

Festy, Patrick. "Les populations immigrès en France." *Population* 13-6 (1993).

Freeman, Gary P. "Immigration as a Source of Political Discontent and Frustration in Western Democracies." *Studies in Comparative International Development* 10-3 (1997).

Freeman, Gary P., and Nedim Ogelman. "Homeland Citizenship Policies and the Status of Third Country Nationals in the European Union." *Journal of Ethnic and Migration Studies* 24-3 (1998).

Geddes, Andrew. "The Representation of Migrants' 'Interests' in the European Union." *Journal of Ethnic and Migration Studies* 27-4 (1998).

Goldberg, Andreas. "The Status and Specific Problems of Elderly Foreigners in the Federal Republic of Germany." *Journal of Comparative Family Studies* 27-1 (1996).

Gurfinkiel, Michel. "Islam in France: Is the French Way of Life in Danger?" *Middle East Forum* (March 1997).

Hammer, Juliane, "Making Islam Part of Germany." *Islam Online*, www.islam_online.net (2000).

Hargreaves, Alex G. "The Beurgeoisie: Mediation or Mirage." *Journal of European Studies* 28-2 (1998).

Harris, J.R., and Michael P. Todaro. "Migration, Unemployment and Development: A Two-Sector Analysis." *American Economic Review* 60 (1970).

Hoffman, Mark. "Critical Theory and the Inter-Paradigm Debate." *Millennium Journal of International Studies* 16-2 (1987).

Hopf, Ted. "The Promise of Constructivism in International Relations Theory." *International Security* 23-2 (1998).

Kaplan, Robert D. "The Coming Anarchy." *Atlantic Monthly* 281-2 (1994).

Katz, Eliakim, and Oded Stark. "Labor Migration and Risk Aversion in Less Developed Countries." *Journal of Labor Economics* 4 (1986).

Klusmeyer, Douglas B. "Aliens, Immigrants and Citizens—the Politics of Inclusion in the Federal Republic of Germany." *Daedalus* 122-2 (1993).

Koopmans, Ruud. "Germany and its Immigrants: An Ambivalent Relationship," *Journal of Ethnic and Migration Studies* 28-3 (1999).

Kritz, Mary M., Lin Lean Lim and Hania Zlotnick, eds. *International Migration Systems: A Global Approach.* Oxford, UK: Clarendon Press, 1992.

Kundani, Arun. "From Oldham to Bradford: The Violence of the Violated." *Institute of Race Relations* (July 2001).

Kutschera, Chris. "Murky Business Behind the 'Halal' Label in France." *Middle East* 50-4 (1996).

"La population de la France en 2000." *Population et Societés* 31-3 (2001).

Lauby, Jennifer, and Oded Stark. "Individual Migration as a Family Strategy: Young Women in the Philippines." *Population Studies* 42 (1988).

Lewis, W. Arthur. "Economic Development with Unlimited Supplies of Labor." *Manchester School of Economic and Social Studies* 22 (1954).

Manco, Ural. "Turks in Europe: From a Garbled Image to the Complexity of Migrant Social Reality." *Center for Islam in Europe* (December 2000).

Massey, Douglas. "Social Structure, Household Strategies and the Cumulative Causation of Migration." *Population Index* 56 (1990).

Massey, Douglas, and Felipe Garcia Espana. "The Social Process of International Migration." *Science* 237 (1987).

Massey, Douglas, Joaquin Arango, Graeme Hugo, Ali Kouaouci, Adela Pellegrino and J. Edward Taylor. "Theories of International Migration: A Review and Appraisal." *Population and Development Review* 19-3 (1993).

Mearsheimer, John J. "Back to the Future: Instability in Europe after the Cold War." *International Security* 15-2 (1990).

Minorities at Risk Project. *Turks in Germany.* College Park, Md.: Minorities at Risk Project, Center for International Development and Conflict Management, 1999.

"New Data and Facts on the Islamic Associations in the Federal Republic of Germany." *Muslim Review* 10-2 (2000).

Onder, Zehra. "Muslim-Turkish Children in Germany: Sociocultural Problems." *Migration World Magazine* 24-11 (1996).

Peach, Ceri. "South Asian and Caribbean Ethnic Minority Housing Choice in Britain." *Urban Studies* 35-4 (1998).

_____. "The Muslim Population of Great Britain." *Ethnic and Racial Studies* 13-1 (1990).

Pettigrew, Thomas F. "Reactions Toward the New Minorities of Western Europe." *Annual Review of Sociology* 24-1 (1998).

Pratt Ewing, Katherine. "Legislating Religious Freedom: Muslim Challenges to the Relationship between 'Church' and 'State' in Germany and France." *Daedalus* 129-3 (2000).

Ranis, Gustav, and J.C.H. Fei. "A Theory of Economic Development." *American Economic Review* 51 (1961).

"Religious Affairs Policy." *Common Sense* (July 2001).

Schmidt, Christoph M. "Immigrant Performance in Germany: Labor Earnings of Ethnic German Migrants and Foreign Guest-Workers." *Quarterly Review of Economics and Finance* 37-1 (1997).

Siegfried, Andre. "La France et les problemes de l'immigration et de l'emigration." *Les Cahiers du Musee Social* 2-3 (1946).

Sjaastad, Larry A. "The Costs and Returns of Human Migration." *Journal of Political Economy* 70-5 (1962).

Stark, Oded. "Migration Decision Making: A Review Article." *Journal of Development Economics* 14 (1984).

Stark, Oded, and David Levhari. "On Migration and Risk in LDCs." *Economic Development and Cultural Change* 31 (1982).

Stark, Oded, J. Edward Taylor and Shlomo Yitzhaki. "Migration, Remittances and Inequality: A Sensitivity Analysis using the Extended Gini Index." *Journal of Development Economics* 28 (1988).

Taspinar, Omer. "Europe's Muslim Street." *Foreign Policy* 135-2 (2003).

Taylor, J. Edward. "Remittances and Inequality Reconsidered: Direct, Indirect and Intertemporal Effects." *Journal of Policy Modeling* 14 (1992).

Todaro, Michael P., and Lydia Maruszko. "Illegal Migration and U.S. Immigration Reform: A Conceptual Framework." *Population and Development Review* 13 (1987).

Top 100 Electoral Districts in Terms of Muslim Voting Potential." *Muslim Council of Britain* (May 2001).

"Verwaltungsgericht Berlin." *Islamic Federation of Berlin* (19 January 1997).

Waltz, Kenneth N. "The Emerging Structure of International Politics." *International Security* 18-3 (1993).

Wendt, Alexander. "Collective Identity Formation and the International State." *American Political Science Review* 88-2.

Wihtol de Wenden, Catherine. "Immigrants as Political Actors in France." *West European Politics* 17-1 (1994).

Zemya, Sami. "Is There a Place for Islam in Europe," *Center for Islam in Europe* (June 2001).

Index